D1196431

Published under the auspices of
THE CENTER FOR JAPANESE AND KOREAN STUDIES
University of California, Berkeley

THE FAILURE OF DEMOCRACY IN SOUTH KOREA

SUNGJOO HAN

The Failure of Democracy in South Korea

UNIVERSITY OF CALIFORNIA PRESS
Berkeley, Los Angeles, London

University of California Press
Berkeley and Los Angeles, California
University of California Press, Ltd.
London, England

ISBN: 0-520-02437-0
Library of Congress Catalog Card Number: 73-76100
Printed in the United States of America

TO MY MOTHER

CONTENTS

TABLES

PREFACE

During this past "modern" century in the history of Korea, successive generations of politically conscious Koreans have been preoccupied with different problems, each unique but closely related to the others.

Survival as a nation was the main concern in the late nineteenth and early twentieth centuries, when various powers competed for control of the Korean peninsula. *Independence* was the major aspiration of the Korean people during the Japanese rule, between 1910 and 1945. *Unification* was the preoccupation of those Koreans who found their land divided between the North and the South, following the Second World War. For those who witnessed and suffered from the abuses of Syngman Rhee's dictatorial rule and who helped bring about the eventual overthrow of the Rhee regime, *democracy* was the issue of primary concern. For the post-1961 generation, which has felt the apparent futility of liberal democracy in Korea, *economic development* has become the primary interest and goal.

As one who received his secondary and college education under the Rhee regime, and participated in the "April uprising," I find myself particularly interested in the question of whether liberal democracy is desirable, feasible, and practicable in Korea. Thus it is only fitting that my first book on Korean politics should be addressed to this subject.

The period of the Chang Myŏn government (1960–1961) presents an exceptionally fine opportunity to study the nature of the Korean polity, because of the relatively free atmosphere it offered to all forms of political activity and expression. The "hundred flowers" attempted their bloom and struggled among themselves during this time. By focusing on this period, and asking the reasons for the Chang government's failure to survive, I think we can gain a better understanding of the patterns of political behavior in Korea and their structural parameters. I hope that, despite my emotional attachment to the question of democracy in Korea, I have succeeded in approaching and handling the subject in an objective manner.

A dozen years have elapsed since the fall of the Chang Myŏn government. Three constitutional changes, three national referenda, and four presidential elections later, after rise and fall in the fortunes of numerous individuals and groups, the question of whether liberal democracy can and should be fought for in Korea remains very much alive. Those in power have learned new methods of managing, safeguarding, and exercising power; their opponents are struggling to find new and effective ways of playing their role.

In many ways, however, the basic elements which comprise Korean politics do not seem to have undergone a fundamental change. I believe that the nature of the problems involving Korean democracy has not changed very much, and that by examining the reasons for its failure twelve years ago we will have a better understanding of its problems today.

In writing this book I am much indebted to Prof. Robert A. Scalapino for his guidance and encouragement. I am also grateful to Prof. Maurice N. Richter, Jr., for his moral support, and to Profs. Chalmers A. Johnson, Michael C. Rogers, and Aaron Wildavsky, to whom I owe much intellectual debt. Prof. Chong-sik Lee gave me many helpful suggestions and made available to me much valuable material in his possession. My good friends and colleagues Steve Balch, Yong-mok Kim, Michael Rubner, Doh Chull Shin, John Starr, Michael Travis, and Se Hee Yoo took time to read parts or all of the manuscript and contributed to its improvement. I am also grateful to Mrs. Marjorie Hughes for her careful editing of this book.

I would like to express my gratitude to Prof. and Mrs. John T. Holden, formerly of the University of New Hampshire, for giving me courage, guidance, and support during the first two difficult years of my study in the United States. My deepest thanks are due to my mother, who made many sacrifices for her only son's study abroad. My wife Sungmii patiently bore the burden of revising and typing the manuscript while being a mother, wife, and teacher at the same time.

This study was made possible by the financial support of the Center for Japanese and Korean Studies, Berkeley, and the Research Foundation of the City University of New York. Needless to say, all facts and interpretations, with their possible errors and shortcomings, are my own responsibility.

S. H.

I

INTRODUCTION

On May 16, 1961, a coup d'état by a group of military officers in South Korea put to an end the nine-month-old government led by Prime Minister Chang Myŏn. It also meant the end of the Second Korean Republic, established in July 1960 after Syngman Rhee's ouster in the wake of student uprising three months earlier. The relative ease with which the coup was carried out was matched by the absence of any overt sign of resistance to the military takeover on the part of the Korean people. The end of Chang Myŏn's government marked the failure of an attempt to create and preserve a "democratic" government [1] in South Korea. The military coup only made decisive and explicit a failure that seemed apparent to many observers of and participants in the politics of the period. By May 1961 South Korea was experiencing serious political disorganization, as many sectors of Korean society lost confidence in their system of government and the leaders who ran it. The authority of the government was in serious jeopardy.[2]

The history of the Chang government illustrates an important problem that many newly developing nations face today: the inability to maintain constitutional and democratic political institutions. A

1. Edward Shils defines "political democracy" as "the regime of civilian rule through representative institutions and public liberties." See his "Political Development in the New States," *Comparative Studies in Society and History* 2: 4 (July 1960), 379. The idea of "democracy" will be further elaborated at the end of this chapter.

2. For a somewhat exaggerated version of the political, social and economic disruption during this period, see *Han'guk kunsa hyŏngmyŏngsa* [History of the Korean Military Revolution], I, Chap. 5, "The Corruption and Incompetence of the Democratic Party," pp. 150–170.

number of interpretations have been given to the events surrounding the 1961 military coup d'état. According to one view, held by Chang Myŏn himself and some of his political associates, there were really no serious failures in the government. They believe that the worst troubles were over by the time of the coup, and that the government failed to survive only because a handful of conspirators were successful in seizing power through naked force.[3] From another viewpoint, the constitution of the Second Republic, with its provisions for a weak executive branch in a parliamentary system, was primarily responsible for the downfall of the Chang government; the Second Republic needed a strong executive system which could cope with the social disorganization and rising popular demands following the fall of the Rhee government. This view's proponents contend that the chief executive should not have been at the mercy of selfish and unprincipled "party politicians" of the period.[4] In a third view, the inadequacy of Prime Minister Chang Myŏn's personal and political leadership was the main factor in his government's weakness. The great majority of political practitioners, as well as many impartial observers, felt that Chang was indecisive, inflexible, too honest, and often lacking in courage—and therefore, according to them, unfit to be a leader of the Korean people during the postrevolutionary period.[5]

Although these explanations cannot be considered wrong, their focus is narrowly directed to the Chang government itself and contributes little to our understanding of the larger picture concerning the nature of the South Korean polity.

A fourth view—which requires somewhat lengthier treatment, as it finds much support in contemporary social science theories—contends that Korean society was not ready for a democratic system of government: Korea lacked the proper pluralistic social base, governmental and administrative structure was too centralized, and the majority of the people lacked a democratic political culture, being incapable of making independent choices in political matters.[6]

3. See Chang Myŏn's own remarks in his memoirs, *Hanarŭi miri chukchi ankonŭn* [Except a Grain of Wheat Fall into the Ground and Die], pp. 61–91.

4. For example, Shin Sang-ch'o, "Sangno chŏngkwŏnŭi t'ansaenggwa tongyo" [The Creation and Toppling of a Slave Regime].

5. See various reminiscences by Chang's acquaintances in Chang Myŏn, *op. cit.;* also "Unsŏk Chang Myŏn," in *Chŏnggye yahwa* [Behind-the-Scenes Stories of Korean Politics], II, 333–358. W. D. Reeve, in his *The Republic of Korea,* p. 145, questioned whether "Chang was the right man at the helm at so difficult a time."

6. See, for example, Yun Ch'ŏn-ju, *Han'guk chŏngch'i ch'egye* [The Korean Political System], *passim.* The most outstanding treatment (and critique) of Korea's social and governmental centralization can be found in Gregory Henderson, *Korea: The Politics of the Vortex.*

Various scholars have attempted to link the process of social and economic development with political democracy. Many social scientists, such as Seymour Martin Lipset and James Coleman, have discovered statistical relationships between economic development and stable democracy.[7] Gabriel Almond and Bingham Powell propose that political "capabilities" (and, accordingly, the viability of a democratic political system) will increase with increased differentation of social structure and secularization of social norms.[8] Other social conditions of a viable democracy proposed by various scholars include social pluralism,[9] overlapping power relationships in a modern context,[10] congruence between the governmental authority pattern and the nongovernmental authority patterns of the society of which it is a part,[11] a democratic political culture among the general population,[12] and a "democratic consensus" among the political leaders.[13]

Another requirement of successful democracy is considered to be the adequate and balanced development of what some political scientists call the "political and administrative infrastructure."[14] Such infrastructure includes political parties, administrative apparatus, interest groups, the military, communications facilities, and educational institutions. Samuel P. Huntington persuasively argues that an inadequate or unbalanced institutionalization of political processes would bring about political decay rather than political development, and that political modernization—involving rationalization of authority, differentiation of social and governmental structure, and social mobilization—has to be accompanied by a corresponding "institutionalization of political organizations and procedures."[15] According to this view, while many aspects of modernization such as urbanization and higher literacy may be irreversible, political development is not; at the same time, the viability of political democracy also depends upon

7. Coleman, "Conclusion: The Political Systems of the Developing Area," in Almond and Coleman (eds), *The Politics of the Developing Areas,* pp. 532–576. See also Phillips Cutright, "National Political Development: Measurement and Analysis," and Lipset, "Some Social Requisites of Democracy"; this and other useful articles can be found in Cnudde and Neubauer, *Empirical Democratic Theory,* esp. Part Three.

8. Almond and Powell, *Comparative Politics, passim.*

9. For example, William Kornhauser, *The Politics of Mass Society.*

10. For example, Ralf Dahrendorf, *Class and Class Conflict in Industrial Society.*

11. Harry Eckstein, "A Theory of Stable Democracy," an appendix in *Division and Cohesion in Democracy: A Study of Norway,* p. 234.

12. Gabriel Almond and Sidney Verba, *The Civic Culture: Political Attitudes and Democracy in Five Nations.*

13. Herbert McCloskey, "Consensus and Ideology in American Politics."

14. Warren Ilchman and Norman Uphoff, *The Political Economy of Change,* Chap. 8.

15. Huntington, "Political Development and Political Decay."

the creation and institutionalization of sociopolitical infrastructure such as political parties and interest groups.

Although few would question the validity of the sociopolitical explanations mentioned above, it is difficult to apply them when it comes to specific countries and political systems. In addition to the fact that most of these theories are meaningful primarily within a cross-national comparative context, they do not adequately explain the relatively short-term changes and fluctuations within individual political systems.

It is clear that neither the immediate attributes of the Chang Myŏn government nor the broadly defined socioeconomic conditions are by themselves sufficient to identify the immediate difficulties of the Chang government and explain the failure of political democracy in Korea during the 1960–1961 period. The present study is an attempt to discover an explanation broad enough to take into consideration the nature of the larger society, yet specific enough to provide us with a focus in analysis of the interaction between the political regime and the society of which it is a part.

It is my contention in this study that one crucial factor in the collapse of the Chang government was the presence of acute ideological and social polarization. Such polarization, which was never conspicuous during the period of the Syngman Rhee government (1948–1960), became important because of the "free" political atmosphere it offered to all forms of political activity.

Of the various political and ideological cleavages which divided South Korea's political public into mutually antagonistic groups during the Chang period, two appear to have played an especially critical role in its survival and stability: the conflict between the "revolutionary" anti-Syngman Rhee forces and the "counterrevolutionary" pro-Rhee elements, and polarization between the more conservative and the more radical sectors of the society.

The Chang Myŏn government, which owed its creation to a loose coalition of intellectuals, newspaper editors, "liberal" students, and party politicians, was expected to satisfy the immediate aspirations of the anti-Rhee forces—namely, the "revolutionary" punishment of former pro-Rhee officials. The Chang government's commitment to due process and liberal democracy was largely responsibile for its initial failure to fulfill this expectation, thus decisively alienating many of its coalition partners. Subsequent punitive legislation of the National Assembly against former Rhee supporters in turn served to alienate former pro-Rhee elements, especially those in the bureaucracy, police, and military. As a result the Chang government not only lost the support of its electoral and intellectual constituencies, it also succeeded in neutralizing the effectiveness of its administrative and law-enforcement apparatus, particularly the latter.

The second ideological conflict, between the radicals and conservatives, proved to be a real obstacle to successful implementation of liberal democracy in South Korea. In the South Korean context, the general characteristics of a radical at the time of the Chang government were: (1) rejection of capitalism and the existing socioeconomic order, which he believed sanctified and perpetuated economic inequality; (2) antagonism toward the coercive apparatus of the state, including the police and the armed forces; (3) advocacy of national unification through peaceful means, and possibly through accommodation with the North Korean Communists; and (4) a negative attitude toward South Korea's heavy dependence on the United States and a general ambivalence toward the conflict between the Communist and non-Communist worlds. On the other hand, a conservative could be characterized by: (1) his belief in the imperative nature of anti-Communist struggle; (2) advocacy of reliance on the United States to protect the non-Communist nature of the South Korean polity; (3) rejection of the notion of class conflict; and (4) unreserved support for the anti-Communist camp in its struggle against the Communists.

The intense and often emotional antagonism between radical and anti-Communist groups was largely the result of their violent struggle during the immediate post-liberation period (1945–1947) and mutual slaughter during the Korean War (1950–1953). Throughout the period of the Syngman Rhee regime, conflict between the two groups never erupted openly because of the effective and ruthless suppression of radicals by the government, assisted by conservative groups such as the national police, the armed forces, and veterans' associations. Largely by design of the Rhee government and other conservative groups, and partly due to subversive activities of the North Korean Communist regime, most proponents of radical ideas were identified with Communists, and anything less than an unconditional anti-Communist stand led to persecution by the government. This strong anti-Communist stand was constantly justified by the ever-present threat of invasion or subversion from the North.

Given the threat from the North and the intense hostility between the two groups, mutual accommodation was difficult; the only course in South Korea seemed to be the complete suppression of one by the other. The notion of "orthodox" and "unorthodox" dissent discussed by Samuel P. Huntington and Zbigniew Brzezinski sheds much light on the political dilemma of liberal democracy in South Korea.[16] Ac-

16. Brzezinski and Huntington, *Political Power: USA/USSR,* pp. 104–121.

cording to these authors, orthodox dissent involves "efforts to improve the existing system in keeping with its underlying ideological values," while unorthodox dissent involves questioning the underlying ideological values themselves. One distinguishing characteristic of liberal democracy is that much "unorthodox dissent" is legal and tolerated; it becomes illegal only when it constitutes a "clear and present danger." However, when a society feels it cannot tolerate many areas of unorthodox dissent, liberal democracy becomes untenable. In a society like South Korea, which faces an immediate external threat and contains sharp internal division, all unorthodox dissent becomes socially dangerous, and any regime that attempts to tolerate such dissent would come under severe threat from either the opponents or supporters of the status quo.

It seems that acute ideological conflict among the political élite has an especially decisive effect on the politics of developing nations which lack other sociopolitical factors supporting political order in general and democracy in particular. In view of the fact that such a conflict is not a phenomenon unique to South Korea, this study, by offering an additional approach to the explanation of the feasibility of democracy, may have relevance to many other societies which have difficulty implementing liberal democracy. The study will examine the value orientations and power positions of the major sociopolitical sectors of South Korean society, including party politicians, the military, the police, the bureaucratic élite, student activists, and business leaders. A "sector analysis," as this approach might be called, is justified on the ground that in a partially mobilized society like South Korea, sociopolitical differentiations can be defined relatively easily; there are fewer social groupings of immediate political significance than in a more complex and differentiated society. By concentrating on these groups, I believe that we can find an effective way of explaining short-term and middle-range political changes in a developing country.

II

THE LEGACY OF THE FIRST REPUBLIC

The twelve-year period between 1948 and 1960 under President Syngman Rhee can be characterized by two closely related phenomena: the supremacy of state power over the rest of the society, and Rhee's personal dictatorship, supported by the national police.

Many factors contributed to the formidable power of the state and the police: the general proclivities of the great majority of the Korean people for obedience to the state and conformity with others; the absence of strong social organizations which could challenge the prerogatives of the state, represented by the police and the national bureaucracy; the highly centralized and well-disciplined nature of the police organization; and the existence of Communist threat from the North, as well as from within South Korea itself.

The absence of nationwide social organizations other than the police and the administrative bureaucracy greatly contributed to the supremacy of state power, and the prior existence of a well-organized police and bureaucratic apparatus presented a serious obstacle to the development of effective political parties in Korea. An analysis of the history of party politics in what is often referred to as Korea's First Republic (1948–1960) will support this assertion.

Until 1945, when Korea was liberated from its 35-year colonial rule by Japan, the Japanese governor-general exercised absolute power and authority over the Korean people, responsible only to his home government in Tokyo.[1] Major means of his rule consisted of imperial re-

1. A perceptive treatment of the political and administrative aspects of the Japanese occupation of Korea can be found in Pak Mun-ok, *Han'guk chŏngburon* [A Study of the Korean Government], pp. 159–292.

scripts, martial laws, declarations, and executive orders. Since these "laws" were issued without much consideration of their acceptability to the Korean people, the Japanese colonial administration required an effective and tightly organized police power. The number of policemen in Korea increased from 3,359 in 1906, four years before annexation by Japan, to 20,758 in 1923, four years after the outbreak of a nationwide anti-Japanese uprising in 1919. Police strength remained at that level until the outbreak of World War II.[2] As of 1939, approximately 40 percent (8,644 out of 23,268) of the police force consisted of Koreans, most of them at the lowest level.[3] During this period the Japanese police exercised far-reaching power over all aspects of life in Korea, including politics, the economy, cultural activities, and education.

The victory of the Allied Powers in World War II and Japan's consequent withdrawal from Korea did not weaken the state's power vis-à-vis the rest of the society. One important reason for this situation was that most of the Korean elements of the Japanese colonial administration—members of the police, bureaucracy, judiciary, and military—were given the opportunity to play an important role in the politics and administration of "liberated" Korea after 1945.

Following the Japanese surrender offer of August 10, 1945, the United States government decided "on the basis of military considerations" that the Japanese troops north of the 38th parallel in Korea should surrender to Soviet forces, and those south of this parallel to United States forces.[4] In accordance with the occupation plan, Gen. Douglas MacArthur, Supreme Commander for the Allied Powers in the Far East, selected Lt. Gen. John R. Hodge as Commander of the U.S. Army in Korea. As Hodge saw it, his tasks in Korea were to disarm the Japanese troops, maintain order, and "establish orderly government of Korea below the 38th parallel." [5]

Hodge's mission concerning the disarmament of the Japanese troops turned out to be a comparatively easy one, but the tasks of maintaining order and establishing an orderly government were difficult to accomplish, in part because of United States refusal to recognize the official status of an interim government which had been set up by the Koreans immediately after the Japanese surrender. This "government" was led by Yŏ Un-hyŏng, a leftist nationalist, who received considerable support from the intellectual sector, including the students and

2. *Han'guk kyŏngch'al chedosa* [A History of the Korean Police], p. 174.
3. *Ibid.*
4. U. S. Dept. of State, *The Record on Korean Unification, 1943–1960,* p. 4.
5. Hodge, "With the U. S. Army in Korea," p. 829.

school teachers, by virtue of his agrarian socialist philosophy and personal charisma.

Shortly before the Japanese surrender, Yŏ was approached by Abe Nobuyuki, the Japanese governor-general, about formation of an interim Korean government in order to protect the Japanese in Korea from reprisals. Yŏ accepted Abe's proposal, and when the surrender was announced on August 15 he established the Preparatory Committee for the Establishment of the Korean Government (*Kŏnguk Chunbi Wiwŏnhoe*), in collaboration with the Communists, on the basis of his underground organization which had been in operation since 1944. Yŏ enlisted the support of the socialists and progressive nationalists in an effort to organize a nationwide network for the task of creating a government.

Upon assuming the "power to maintain order" from the Japanese authorities, Yŏ organized "people's committees" throughout the country. These local organizations, which consisted primarily of college and high school students, school teachers, and electrical and railroad workers,[6] were largely successful in preventing widespread violence during the hiatus between the surrender of the Japanese on August 15 and the arrival of American troops in Korea on September 8.[7] The major significance of these people's committees was that, for the first time in modern Korean history, the power of the national bureaucracy and the police was effectively challenged and set aside by an alternative organizational effort.

On September 6 two days before the arrival of the American forces, Yŏ and his Communist allies established the Korean People's Republic (*Chosŏn Inmin Konghwaguk*), despite strong opposition from most of the prominent nationalists. In refusing to support the People's Republic, the conservative nationalists argued that its existence would impugn the legitimacy of the Korean Provisional Government which had been established in Shanghai in 1919.

However, on September 7, General MacArthur proclaimed that the Korean people had not yet had the chance to elect any individual or support any party through popular elections. Having denied the existence of an official Korean government, General Hodge and his staff were faced with the difficult problems of dealing with the power struggle among numerous political organizations, Communist intransigence and agitation, the hostility and suspicion of the moderate leftists who

6. See Yŏ's biography written by his brother, Yŏ Un-hong, *Mongyang Yŏ Unhyŏng*.

7. Han T'ae-su, *Han'guk chŏngdangsa* [A History of Korean Political Parties], pp. 25–30; see also Richard C. Allen, *Korea's Syngman Rhee: An Unauthorized Portrait*, pp. 73–75.

supported the People's Republic, and the general disorganization of society following the collapse of Japanese authority. These problems had to be met without the help of the people's committees led by Yŏ Un-hyŏng, since their legitimacy as an official arm of the government had been denied. General Hodge was therefore forced to turn to the bureaucratic and police organizations that had existed before the Japanese defeat.

Hodge's initial decision to retain the Japanese officials met strong popular indignation and opposition, and had to be rescinded. However, the Korean officials in the police and bureaucracy were nevertheless retained. As a result they were given an opportunity to protect themselves and support those who would defend them. The high-ranking officials and police officers who had collaborated with the Japanese had been quite concerned about the possible rise to power of the Communists or other leftists, as it would have meant the destruction of the existing social and authority structure, endangering their lives and their social positions. Fortunately for them, the American authorities in Korea chose to place primary emphasis on social order, and for that purpose they needed the services of those Koreans who had either willingly or unwillingly served the Japanese prior to 1945.

The Korean members of the Japanese colonial bureaucracy and police found a willing patron in the Korean Democratic Party (*Han'guk Minju-dang*), organized by conservative nationalist leaders who had been active in Korea during the Japanese occupation. Dr. Cho Pyŏng-ok, a leading member of the KDP, commanded the national police under the American Military Government between October 1945 and August 1948.[8] Cho was strongly anti-Japanese, but he was also uncompromisingly opposed to Communism. He concluded that the only way to prevent the Communists from taking over the southern half of Korea was through the creation of an effective police force. He was violently attacked by the Communists and criticized by liberal leftists as being partial to the reactionaries and Japanese collaborators. When intellectual and leftist leaders charged in August 1946 that his repressive measures were responsible for a mass revolt in the Taegu area, he justified his position in the following manner:

I am well aware of the accusation that the October riots were the result of a natural outbreak of the people protesting that I had hired many pro-Japanese police officers. However, I believe that we should distinguish be-

8. Cho Pyŏng-ok received his college education in the United States and obtained a Ph.D. in economics from Columbia University in 1925. He was one of the organizers and directors of the KDP. In 1960 he was the presidential candidate of the Democratic Party, the KDP's successor, only to die ten days before the election.

tween two types of "pro-Japanese" activities during the Japanese rule. There were on one hand those who were engaged in pro-Japanese activities because they supported the Japanese rule, and on the other those who simply held positions in the Japanese police in order to protect the livelihood of themselves and their families. A majority of these people cannot be considered as "pro-Japanese" police officers; instead, they were merely "pro-job" people. Many of these pro-job Koreans served as police officers, officials in the colonial administration, or members of the Japanese judiciary. Only a small minority of these individuals were Japanese collaborators in the real sense. Therefore, unless one had deliberately obstructed the nationalist movement for his personal promotion, I did not hesitate to appoint him to the national police force.[9]

As a result, most of the Koreans in the Japanese police force were brought into the Korean police force after 1945, and the Korean national police was marked by the dominance of former Japanese police officers throughout the Syngman Rhee administration. As late as 1960, those who had been with the Japanese police constituted about 70 percent of the highest-ranking officers (chiefs), 40 percent of the inspectors, and 15 percent of the lieutenants in the Korean national police force. Of the approximately 33,000 policemen throughout the nation, about 20 percent of the plainclothesmen and 10 percent of the uniformed policemen had served in the Japanese police.[10] It should be noted that Cho Pyŏng-ok's views concerning former officials of the Japanese colonial administration were shared by many of the leaders of the KDP. It was only natural that the police officers and members of the bureaucratic élite who had previously served the Japanese governor-general should regard the KDP with favor. This placed the KDP in a very advantageous position in the struggle for power during this period.

Many in the national police force also considered Dr. Syngman Rhee, who shared the KDP's view on former officials of the Japanese police and bureaucracy, as its most reliable protector. Like Cho, Rhee was uncompromisingly anti-Japanese, but he preferred cooperating with those Koreans who had worked for the Japanese to any kind of accommodation with the Communists. In fact, Rhee was the only one among the serious contenders for power at that time who was determined to eliminate the leftist elements completely, even at the cost of a permanent division of the country.

Rhee and the KDP received much help from the police sector in the November 1946 elections, which were held in order to establish an

9. Cho Pyŏng-ok, *Naŭi hoegorok* [My Memoirs], pp. 173–174.
10. *Tong-a Ilbo*, May 7, 1960, p. 1.

interim legislative assembly to work with the U.S. Army Military Government in Korea. These elections, in which the KDP captured 26 of the 45 seats, were marked by irregularities and meddling by the police, who were sympathetic to the conservative cause. Foreign observers noted that the elections were "undemocratic and superficial," heavily influenced by the police.[11]

Leaders of the KDP, although most had been anti-Japanese fighters themselves, accepted and defended high bureaucratic officials and police officers under the Japanese government in an attempt to counteract the organizers of the People's Republic and other leftist leaders. At the same time, lacking a leader with a popular national following, the KDP decided to ally itself with Syngman Rhee. But although he found its support useful on many occasions, Rhee never really trusted the KDP because of its compromising attitude toward the trusteeship plan of the big powers and the threat it posed to his own power.[12] Therefore, upon becoming president of the Korean Republic in August 1948, Rhee disassociated himself from the KDP and refused to give its leaders important government positions. Following his election by the National Assembly with KDP support, Rhee rejected the party's demand that he appoint Kim Sŏng-su, the KDP's leader, as prime minister. Cho Pyŏng-ok's desire to head the foreign ministry was also thwarted.[13] Rhee appointed only one leading member of the KDP to a position of any significance: Kim To-yŏn, a charter member of the party, became his first finance minister, and served Rhee for two and a half years in that position.[14]

With the assumption of the presidency of the new government, Syngman Rhee now came to command both the police and the national

11. George M. McCune, *Korea Today,* p. 76.

12. On December 21, 1945, the United States, the United Kingdom, and the Soviet Union reached an agreement, later concurred in by China, for the establishment of a provisional all-Korean government which would be under the trusteeship of the four powers for a period of up to five years. The agreement was met with strong disapproval and protest by Koreans of all affiliations. The Communists, the only exception, changed their position from initial opposition to support of the trusteeship provision, apparently on orders from Moscow. The KDP also opposed the announced trusteeship plan during the first Joint US–USSR Conference, held in early 1946, although not to a degree satisfactory to stalwarts like Syngman Rhee and Kim Ku. However, during the second session, in spring 1947, the KDP announced that it would sign a statement to uphold the Moscow agreement, ostensibly in order to become eligible for consultation by the Joint Commission. Syngman Rhee reportedly burst into tears when he was informed about the KDP's decision, exclaiming, "Now I can trust nobody. They are all betrayers!" See Pak Yong-man, *Kyŏngmudae pihwa* [Untold Stories of the Presidential Mansion], p. 45.

13. Cho Pyŏng-ok, *Naŭi hoegorok,* pp. 228–229.

14. Kim To-yŏn, *Naŭi insaeng paeksŏ* [A White Paper of My Life], pp. 195–197.

bureaucracy, the only organizations with nationwide effectiveness. They were present in all parts of the country, highly centralized, feared by the general population, and ready to serve a government which could effectively insulate them from political parties and public opinion. The police, with close links to village heads and local bureaucratic officials, constituted probably the "only strong, pervasive organization in Korean politics" throughout the Rhee administration.[15] Since both the provincial governors and the provincial police chiefs were placed under the command of the minister of internal affairs, who was a member of the president's cabinet, Rhee had extremely firm control of both the police and administrative organizations.

Until 1951, Syngman Rhee insisted that political parties were not desirable in Korea. When he returned from his thirty-year exile in the United States in October of 1945, Rhee found that his name had been presented to the public as head of both the Korean People's Republic led by Yŏ Un-hyŏng and the rival KDP. He refused to accept either of these figurehead positions. Instead he called for the creation of a national movement encompassing all political parties and social organizations ranging from the extreme left to the far right. The result was the formation of the National Society for the Rapid Realization of Independence.[16]

In effect, the Society was a loosely coordinated body of rightist parties and social organizations which responded to Rhee's call for a united effort to fight the trusteeship plan. Within a few months, major parties such as the KDP and the Korean Independence Party (*Han'guk Tongnip-tang*) led by Kim Ku, former head of the Korean Provisional Government, ceased to participate actively in the National Society, although a few individual members of these parties who personally supported Syngman Rhee stayed in it. The main action arm of the National Society was the Youth Association for the Rapid Realization of Independence, established on December 10, 1945, combining the nineteen existing youth and social organizations.[17] The Youth Association was organized on a national basis, and until 1948 was instrumental in mobilizing mass demonstrations against the trusteeship plan and in

15. Fifteen years later the Korean CIA was characterized in this manner by Robert A. Scalapino, following the 1961 military coup d'état. See his "Which Route for Korea?," p. 7.

16. For a detailed account of the formation of the National Society, see Yi Ki-ha, *Han'guk chŏngdang paltalsa* [A History of Political Parties in Korea], pp. 80–89.

17. A former aide to Syngman Rhee describes how he helped Rhee "abolish" the existing youth organizations, including the formidable National Youth Corps, in Pak Yong-man, *Kyŏngmudae pihwa,* pp. 84–89.

favor of immediate Korean independence. It later became a core group of the Korean Youth Corps (*Taehan Ch'ŏngnyŏn-dan*), established under the direction of Syngman Rhee on December 21, 1948. Neither the National Society nor its Youth Association, which operated under Syngman Rhee's command, developed into a political party. Both of them operated as Syngman Rhee's personal instruments which were well protected by the police and ready to act on Rhee's behalf. But they did not have a life of their own.

Syngman Rhee's lack of enthusiasm for building a political party is understandable if one realizes his aspiration to pose as leader of the whole nation rather than a group, his apprehension over the possibility that a powerful competitor might arise from under his wing, and the willingness of the bureaucracy, police, and intelligence personnel to serve him faithfully without a political party. Therefore, when the Korean National Party (*Taehan Kungmin-dang*) was formed on November 12, 1948, by Rhee's supporters in order to act as a government party, Rhee gave it only lukewarm support.[18] Like most other Korean political parties, the National Party was basically a parliamentary party lacking a nationwide grassroots organizational basis. However, the party had about 70 supporters in the National Assembly, out of a total membership of 198.

The Korean National Party's chief rival within the National Assembly was the KDP and, later, the Democratic Nationalist Party (*Minju Kungmin-dang*). The DNP was established on February 10, 1949, as the result of an alliance between the KDP and the supporters of National Assembly Speaker Shin Ik-hi, a former official of the Korean Provisional Government. With Shin's assumption of the leadership of the newly created DNP, Rhee's attitude toward the National Assembly became increasingly hostile. The DNP, by virtue of being a successor to the KDP, enjoyed a better organizational basis on the grassroots level than the Korean National Party. But its organizational basis was still of such a nature that the government could easily minimize its effectiveness.

The DNP was seriously weakened in the May 30th parliamentary elections when President Rhee let it be known that he was strongly against it. Rhee was especially unhappy with its attempt to bring about a parliamentary form of government through a constitutional amendment to curb the president's power. In his first nationwide speech tour as president, Rhee repeatedly stated that a parliamentary system of government would only bring about political chaos, and that the people should be aware that the DNP candidates were propos-

18. Han T'ae-su, *Han'guk chongdangsa,* pp. 243–244.

ing such a harmful scheme. After Rhee's visit, the atmosphere in terms of popular support for particular candidates and the police attitude toward them would change radically against the DNP.[19]

Important factors that contributed to the ascendence of police power were the intransigence of the Communists in South Korea and, later, the aggressiveness of the North Korean Communists. Before the South Korean government was established in 1948, the Communists, for reasons ranging from internal power struggle to mistrust of the American occupation, resorted to violent methods in South Korea. They were not successful in mobilizing popular support for their cause, but their violent tactics contributed much toward strengthening the relative power position of the rightist and police elements. There was a vicious circle in the relationship between the Communists and the American Military Government; riots incited by the Communists were firmly suppressed by the American authority through the Korean police force, the extralegal methods of the police in dealing with the leftists in turn bringing about more violent terrorism by the Communists.[20]

During this period, the national police were assisted by a youth organization known as the Country Protection Corps (*Hyangbo-dan*), under the direction of Police Chief Cho Pyŏng-ok, which was designed to assist the 25,000-man national police force in maintaining order against the saboteurs and opponents of the May 10th election in 1948. Within the Corps, "self-protection teams" were organized with "volunteers" in each police district.[21] Between March 20, when the registration of candidates for the National Assembly started, and May 10, the election day, the police reported that 348 government buildings were burned or destroyed, and 147 rightists—including candidates, campaigners, government officials, and their families—were killed, and 600 others wounded.[22]

In October 1948, slightly more than two months after President Rhee's inauguration, a South Korean Army regiment being dispatched to Chechu Island to quell a Communist-led revolt killed its commanding officers and attacked the government and police buildings in the Yŏsu and Sunch'ŏn area of southwestern Korea. During the uprising, in which some 2,000 persons, including many civilians, were killed,

19. Sŏ Pyŏng-jo, *Chukwŏnjaŭi chŭngŏn* [The Testimony of a Sovereign People: A History of Representative Government in Korea], p. 84.

20. See McCune, *Korea Today,* pp. 84–88. The Communists stepped up terrorism in all part of Asia following the Comintern's decision to call for an immediate revolution. On this point, see Scalapino, *The Japanese Communist Movement, 1920–1966,* Chaps. 2 and 3.

21. Cho Pyŏng-ok, *Naŭi hoegorok,* pp. 203–212.

22. *Ibid.,* p. 211.

only the police seemed demonstrably loyal to the government. Richard Allen has pointed out that civil liberties were in near-extinction following the Yŏsu rebellion, based on the "recognition" that the Communist threat had not yet been destroyed.[23] By early 1950 the police and their conservative patrons, who had experienced a brief period of crisis and uncertainty following the Japanese defeat in August 1945, seemed securely entrenched within the government, with Syngman Rhee as their powerful defender.

The outbreak of the Korean War in June 1950 brought Syngman Rhee new opportunities in his effort to maintain and consolidate his personal power. The nation was in a state of full mobilization under which many irresponsible acts of the government could be overlooked as wartime necessities. Many Koreans, as well as American officials, believed that Rhee's leadership was essential for success. However, during the two years of his rule Rhee had created much enmity among many politicians in the parliament—notably members of the DNP. In addition, numerous instances of corruption and misrule under the Rhee government, such as the National Defense Corps scandal and the Kŏch'ang massacre,[24] for which the war provided added impetus, turned many members of the National Assembly into opposition. Since under the constitution the president was to be elected by the National Assembly, this represented a serious problem for Syngman Rhee, whose first term was to expire in 1952.

Rhee's weak position within the National Assembly became quite evident when, on January 18, 1952, his proposal for the constitutional amendment providing for popular election of the president and

23. Allen, *Korea's Syngman Rhee,* p. 108.

24. The NDC scandal involved the death of some 90,000 men in the reserve force from starvation, illness, and freezing weather, while they were being evacuated from the central region to southeastern Korea. The government, in an attempt to prevent the Communists from enlisting South Korean men in the Communist army, forcibly rounded up all able-bodied men between the ages of 17 and 40 and marched them to the South, ill-equipped and underfed. The massive tragedy resulted from embezzlement by a few top military officers of funds allocated to support the Corps, consisting of some 200,000 men. The scandal was exposed in the National Assembly in March 1951 and resulted in the execution of five army officers.

The Kŏch'ang massacre involved the killing of some 200 villagers in mountainous south-central Korea by a South Korean Army division which had been assigned to the area to mop up Communist guerrilla forces planted by the North Korean Army during its retreat in the winter of 1950. When an investigation team of the National Assembly attempted to visit the area in April 1951, its members were fired upon by South Korean soldiers disguised as Communist guerrillas, and the investigation could not be carried out. Colonel Kim Chong-wŏn, who staged the fake skirmish, was later appointed director of the national police by Syngman Rhee.

vice-president, instead of their election by the Assembly, was defeated by the decisive vote of 19 to 183, with 1 abstention.[25] A few months later Rhee and his supporters proceeded to intimidate the Assembly with mass demonstrations and a martial law proclaimed ostensibly to check guerrilla activities near the provisional capital of Pusan. Following the proclamation of martial law, 47 assemblymen were arrested by the military police while en route to attend an Assembly session, and 9 of them were subsequently jailed on charges of participating in an international Communist conspiracy.

With many of the most active anti-Rhee assemblymen in jail or hiding to escape arrest, the National Assembly subsequently voted 61 to 0 to extend Rhee in office until the dispute on the constitutional amendment was resolved. The police then carried out an extensive search for missing assemblymen who were either boycotting the sessions or in hiding. Finally, on July 4, a total of 166 out of 183 assemblymen, including the ones previously jailed, were brought to the Assembly hall to obtain the quorum; the Assembly accepted the constitutional amendment requested by the President by a vote of 163 to 0, with 3 abstentions. A major victory for the administration was the provision for the election of the president and vice-president by direct popular vote.

During the months of his struggle to obtain a constitutional amendment, Rhee was well assisted by the Liberal Party (*Chayu-dang*), which he established in November 1951 as a government party. As noted above, Rhee first rejected the idea of leading a political party himself. However, shocked by the defeat of his supporters in the National Assembly elections in 1950, and in anticipation of a popular presidential election, Rhee hastily formed a political party of the administration to be headed by himself. Aware of the fact that he had only a weak and disunited group of supporters within the National Assembly, Rhee recalled Yi Pŏm-sŏk, former prime minister and defense minister, who was serving as his ambassador to the Nationalist Chinese Government in Taiwan, and entrusted him with the task of organizing the new party. In order to understand the nature of the newly organized party, it is necessary to examine closely the personal background of Yi Pŏm-sŏk, its chief organizer.

Before 1945, Yi Pŏm-sŏk was famous for his anti-Japanese military activities in Manchuria. In 1920, at the age of twenty-one, he was said to have led a 1,500-man force of the Northern Route Independence Army to a decisive victory over a regular Japanese brigade of some

25. Sŏ Pyŏng-jo, *Chukwŏnjaŭi chŭngŏn*, p. 125.

10,000 men.[26] Upon formation of the Liberation Army of the Korean Provisional Government in 1940, Yi was appointed its chief of staff. In this position he had a close relationship with the military and political leaders of the Nationalist Chinese government, including Chiang Kai-shek.

Yi returned to Korea on June 22, 1946, and within a few months he set about organizing the National Youth Corps (*Minjok Ch'ŏngnyŏn-dan*) on the basis of a "nation-first" and "state-first" slogan. For reasons not clearly understood even today, his National Youth Corps was generously supported by the American authorities with money and material.[27] Furthermore, the police could not obstruct its activities because of the American support it received. The National Youth Corps, often compared to Hitler's Jugend Brigade, attracted mostly "marginal men" such as former Communists who needed protection in a legitimate organization, rightist youths who resented struggle among the rightist organizations themselves, romanticists who were attracted to the Corps' ideological appeals, and others who were tired of the chaotic situation in Korean society. Some 20,000 young men initially responded to its call for membership in October 1946. The National Youth Corps was attacked by both leftist and rightist groups, but it expanded rapidly in organization and membership throughout the nation. At one point, Yi Pŏm-sŏk claimed that half of all Korean youths had been affected by Corps training.[28] Though this was an exaggerated claim, it indicates the extent of activities of the National Youth Corps.

Upon establishment of the Korean government, Yi was appointed prime minister and, simultaneously, minister of defense. He kept the prime ministership until April 1950, two months before the outbreak of the Korean War. The motivation behind Rhee's appointment of Yi to these important positions appears to have been quite complicated. Rhee's first nominee, Yi Yun-yŏng, a Christian and a nationalist from the North, had been denied the approval of the National Assembly because of opposition from the disappointed members of the KDP. It seemed to Rhee that Yi Pŏm-sŏk, because of his reputation as an anti-Japanese fighter, had a good chance of being approved by the Assembly; Yi's political clique within the National Assembly was not as formidable as the KDP (the National Youth Corps had six mem-

26. Much of the information concerning Yi Pŏm-sŏk and the National Youth Corps is from Yi Pŏm-sŏk, "Memoirs," in *Sasirŭi chŏnburŭl kisulhanda* [Collected Memoirs of Nine Political Leaders], pp. 53–84.

27. According to Yi himself, American support of his activities is attributable to his previous acquaintance with the American military officers and their concurrence with the aims of the Youth Corps (*ibid.*, p. 74).

28. *Ibid.*, p. 100.

bers in the National Assembly), and his military experience could be put to good use in confrontation with the threatening North Korean Communists. It is also by no means unthinkable that by placing Yi in his own cabinet, Rhee wished to prevent Yi's National Youth Corps from further growth and undesirable independent activities.

Within a few months Rhee established the Korean Youth Corps, with the aim of absorbing all existing youth organizations. When the National Youth Corps delayed joining the KYC, Rhee asked Yi to dissolve his youth organization or resign from his government positions.[29] The National Youth Corps joined the KYC on January 15, 1949. Despite its formal disbandment, however, members of the National Youth Corps remained loyal to Yi Pŏm-sŏk, and he kept in close touch with both the cadres and followers of the group. While Yi was serving as prime minister between 1948 and 1950, many of these individuals were placed in important positions in the military and the police. Thus, after September 1951, Yi Pŏm-sŏk and the remnants of his National Youth Corps were instrumental in the organization of Rhee's Liberal Party supporters. A parliamentary party also called the "Liberal Party" was formed simultaneously, but most of the assemblymen who joined it soon turned against Syngman Rhee in favor of Chang Myŏn, former ambassador to the U.N. and prime minister, briefly, in 1952. Many of them ultimately joined the opposition Democratic Party in 1955.[30]

In 1952 Yi Pŏm-sŏk served as Rhee's minister of internal affairs, and did everything he could to force passage of Rhee's constitutional amendment. However, as Richard Allen put it, Yi's success in "browbeating" the Assembly with mass demonstrations and intimidation by terrorists had also made a deep impression on Rhee. He now saw Yi as a man leading an organization that could not be left unchecked.[31] Therefore, when his Liberal Party nominated Syngman Rhee for the presidency and Yi Pŏm-sŏk for the vice-presidency, Rhee prevented the latter's election with the aid of his other cabinet officers and the national police force. The superiority of the police power over even the government party was dramatically demonstrated in this particular election. For the vice-presidential spot there were nine candidates, all but two of them supporting Syngman Rhee's candidacy for the presidency. Shortly before voting, President Rhee let it be known to Prime Minister Chang T'aek-sang, who had replaced Chang Myŏn in May, that he preferred to see the "most elderly" man among the vice-presi-

29. Pak Yong-man, *Kyŏngmudae pihwa*, p. 89.

30. For further details of the development of the Democratic Party, see Chapter Four of this book.

31. Allen, *Korea's Syngman Rhee*, p. 171.

dential candidates elected to the office. Chang T'aek-sang, whose personal rivalry with Yi Pŏm-sŏk was well known, made it his task to carry out the president's wishes.[32] Together with Minister of Internal Affairs Kim T'ae-sŏn, a faithful follower of Rhee and replacement for Yi Pŏm-sŏk, Chang conferred with the provincial governors and provincial and county police chiefs about the elections; subsequently the governors and police chiefs in turn held their own meetings with their subordinates.[33]

Rhee was elected in 1952 for his second four-year term as president by a vote of more than 5 million, compared with 80,000 for the runner-up, Cho Pong-am.[34] For the vice-presidency, Ham T'ae-yŏng, not well known but the oldest of the vice-presidential candidates, was easily elected, receiving almost 3 million votes—over 1 million more than Yi Pŏm-sŏk and about five times as many votes as Cho Pyŏng-ok, the opposition DNP candidate. The election results well vindicated a statement made by Prime Minister Chang T'aek-sang himself—that whatever might be said about it, there was no doubt that the police were the "number one organization in Korea." [35] What appeared to be a contest between the police-bureaucratic organization and a supposedly

32. Like Yi Pŏm-sŏk, Chang had a love-hate relationship with Rhee, although he was ready to serve Rhee whenever he was asked to. During the American Military Government, Chang, as the Seoul police chief, assisted Rhee in various ways, including the occasional provision of Rhee's living expenses (Pak Yong-man, *Kyŏngmudae pihwa,* p. 50). Following the establishment of the Korean government in August 1948, Chang became the first foreign minister. Chang had been designated minister of internal affairs by Syngman Rhee, but presumably Prime Minister Yi Pŏm-sŏk interfered and gave the position to Yun Ch'i-yŏng, Rhee's other faithful follower. In October 1952, Chang was forced to resign his post as prime minister when his meeting with a Japanese friend of his, a former mayor of Seoul, was exposed by a National Youth Corps-controlled newspaper and reported to Syngman Rhee.

Chang's political maneuvering is noted for its capricious and enigmatic qualities. In 1956 he joined Yi Pŏm-sŏk, his foremost political rival, to form the Republican Party, which disintegrated within a few weeks after its formation. In 1958 Chang headed the Liberal Party-sponsored Anti-Communist League in an attempt to turn it into his personal political organization. Shortly before the March 1960 elections, Chang withdrew his name as a presidential candidate, which resulted in the single candidacy of Rhee for the presidency. Chang charged that the police had seized his registration papers. However, the Democratic Party charged that Chang withdrew his name after the director of the national police promised compensation for his withdrawal.

33. Pak Yong-man, *Kyŏngmudae pihwa,* pp. 177–179. Pak was one of the few anti-National Youth Corps faction members in the leadership of the newly-created Liberal Party during this period.

34. Cho Pong-am ran again in 1956 and received more than 2 million votes. He was executed by the Rhee government in 1959 on charges of cooperating with North Korea to overthrow the South Korean government.

35. Sŏ Pyŏng-jo, *Chukwŏnjaŭi chŭngŏn,* p. 153.

pro-government party organization ended with a lopsided victory for the former.

It is clear that Rhee initially solicited the assistance of Yi Pŏm-sŏk and his "youth" organization in an attempt to fight his opponents in the National Assembly. They were also instrumental in electing many Rhee supporters to the provincial and city legislatures prior to the 1952 presidential election. Together with the military police that arrested the opposition assemblymen, Yi's group made a decisive contribution to Rhee's constitutional amendment. But the Liberal Party as such was never allowed to challenge the prerogatives of the police organization. Thus by late 1953, the National Youth Corps elements in the Liberal Party, including Yi Pŏm-sŏk, were all but removed, and a new party organization set up, with Yi Ki-bung as its leader. From this time on, the Liberal Party developed into a faithful instrument of Syngman Rhee, lacking a power base of its own. Now it could function only with the help of the police operating under the direction of the ministry of internal affairs.

At the time of its creation, in 1951, the Liberal Party had encompassed five so-called "core social organizations." They were the National Society (a continuing body of the National Society for the Rapid Realization of Independence), the Korean Youth Corps, the General League of the Korean Labor Unions, the General League of the Korean Farmers' Cooperatives, and the Korean Women's Association. These were all government-sponsored "official organizations" like the Korean Youth Corps. During the 1950s, no social organization could function effectively without giving unconditional support to Syngman Rhee and his Liberal Party. Most conspicuously "pro-government" were religious organizations (especially Christian and Buddhist), regional groups (such as North Korean refugees), and professional groups (art, athletic, and educational). The central political power penetrated deeply into these "voluntary" organizations, and the ubiquity of that political power prevented them from engaging in any independent activities.[36]

In order to prevent a resurgence of the National Youth Corps faction, the new leaders of the Liberal Party issued a "Guideline for the Purification of Party Organization." The party's local units were soon reorganized to correspond to electoral districts of the National Assembly. Until then they had been organized parallel with existing administrative units. The newly created party branches would cooperate closely with the local police for election of their own candidates to the National Assembly, chosen by the central party with the approval

36. See Shin Sang-ch'o, "Pressure Groups in Korea."

of the party president, Syngman Rhee.[37] This system worked well for Syngman Rhee and his subordinates.

In the National Assembly elections of May 1954, the Liberal Party gained a comfortable majority of 114 out of 203 seats, while the DNP elected only 15 members.[38] The Liberal Party was supported by the police and intelligence organizations such as the army counter-intelligence corps, which interfered extensively in candidate registration, voting, and ballot-counting processes. Those elected without party affiliation still constituted about one-third of the membership. One month after the opening of the third National Assembly, however, the number of Liberal Party assemblymen reached 137, one more than two-thirds of the total membership, or over twice the number of Liberal Party members in the previous National Assembly.

The emergence of a ruling party in the first half of the 1950s stimulated a "grand coalition" of the opposition factions, with the DNP as the core group. This resulted in the formation of the Democratic Party (*Minju-dang*) in September 1955. Such a coalition received much stimulation when the Liberal Party proposed and "passed" a constitutional amendment exempting Syngman Rhee from the two-term restriction on the presidency. The amendment received only 135 affirmative votes, one short of the required two-thirds majority. However, the Liberal Party's vice-speaker, presiding over the Assembly session, declared the passage of the bill. It was argued by the Liberals that 135 was the number one gets when the fractions are rounded off from two-thirds (135.333) of 203.

The opposition members then formed a "Committee to Defend the Constitution," which subsequently developed into the Democratic Party.[39] In forming this party, Rhee's opponents were of course

37. Nobody whose absolute loyalty to Syngman Rhee was even slightly doubted could be nominated by the party. On this point and other aspects of party organization, see Pak Yong-man, *Kyŏngmudae pihwa,* pp. 202–223.

38. The actual incidents of police interference in the 1954 elections are well described in Sŏ Pyŏng-jo, *Chukwŏngjaui chŭngon,* pp. 166–169. Sŏ was a reporter for various newspapers including *Han'guk Ilbo* and *Chosŏn Ilbo* during the period between 1948 and 1960. In the 1954 elections, the police and intelligence organizations concentrated on intimidating specific candidates such as Shin Ik-hi, Cho Pyŏng-ok, and Cho Pong-am. As a result, Cho Pong-am could not even register as a candidate. In a district not far from Seoul, one of Yi Ki-bung's close associates named Ch'oe In-gyu ran against Shin Ik-hi, then Speaker of the National Assembly and leader of the DNP. Ch'oe used the police to terrorize Shin's campaign workers and mobilized the voters for "practice voting," in which they were taught to vote for the Liberal candidate. Ch'oe lost the election to Speaker Shin. As minister of internal affairs in 1960, Ch'oe acted as the field general of the police force throughout the nation in unprecedentedly rigged elections. Ch'oe was executed by the military government in 1961.

39. This development will be further elaborated upon in Chapter Four.

strongly motivated by their desire to prepare for the forthcoming presidential election scheduled for 1956.

Thus one important development in South Korean politics during the period following the Korean War was the realignment of various politicians into two major opposing camps. Along with the development of two major parties, one can discern two other significant trends in postwar Korean politics. One was the increasing domination of the Liberal Party by "hard-liners" who urged more dependence on the police force for maintenance of their political power, at the expense of working for genuine popular support. The other trend, closely related, was increasing resentment by the public of the Liberal Party and the rule of the Syngman Rhee government.

Having secured the constitutional amendment in 1954, freeing him from the two-term restriction, Rhee received his party's unanimous nomination for a third-term candidacy.[40] The newly created Democratic Party launched an impressive campaign in the face of serious difficulties arising from Rhee's control of the police and financial resources. In major cities, rallies for the Democratic candidates were far larger than those for their Liberal counterparts. With the sudden death of the Democratic presidential nominee, Shin Ik-hi, just a few days before the election, Rhee was easily reelected, receiving 56 percent of the popular vote. Cho Pong-am ran second, with 24 percent of the votes cast. But in the vice-presidential race, the Democratic Party's Chang Myŏn won with 41.7 percent of the votes, over Yi Ki-bung's 39.6 percent.[41]

The 1956 elections suggested to the Liberal Party that the voters were turning against them and that no government intervention short of complete fabrication could have brought about the victory of its vice-presidential candidate. After Yi Ki-bung's defeat, members of the "anti-mainstream" faction within the Liberal Party attempted to reform the party so that it would have more appeal to the voters. But this required the resignation of its chairman, Yi Ki-bung, who was still trusted by Syngman Rhee. To politically conscious voters, Yi was the symbol of the irresponsible actions of the Liberal Party and the police. With him in command, the chances of the party's developing into a normal vote-getting organization were very small. Thus the only alternative open to the party was to employ even more repressive mea-

40. Syngman Rhee initially declared, as he had done in 1952, that he was not a candidate for the presidency. Just before the deadline for the registration of candidacy, Rhee accepted the "will of the people," who had been mobilized by the police and "official" mass organizations to beg him to continue in office, and permitted his name to be placed on the ballot.

41. Korean Government, *Taehanmin'guk sŏn'gŏsa* [History of Elections in Korea], pp. 477-479.

sures in future elections, and Rhee and the Liberal Party chose this course. Yi Ki-bung was retained as Speaker of the National Assembly after his defeat in the vice-presidential race.

In 1958 the Liberal Party lost more than 10 seats in the legislative elections despite massive police intervention in its favor, confirming that the party was in serious trouble. Therefore the party introduced a series of revisions to the already stringent security laws, in preparation for the 1960 presidential and vice-presidential elections. In this legislative struggle, opposition legislators were bodily carried out of the Assembly hall by some 300 guards, and detained in the basement, when they tried to conduct a sit-down strike against the bill. The Assembly guards had been especially recruited from the nation's police force for this occasion. The Liberals then rushed through 22 bills in a matter of a few hours.

Another major repressive measure was the closing down of a leading opposition daily, *Kyŏnghyang Shinmun,* on the grounds that it instigated a rebellion against the government. The newspaper was supporting the Democratic Party's Chang Myŏn, and there was no doubt that the government action was politically motivated.

As Rhee and Yi felt the need for suppression of the opposition, the "anti-mainstream" and "soft-line" Liberals were either purged or sidelined within the party, and the hard-liners placed in controlling positions. The most influential hard-liners during the later days of the Liberal Party included Chang Kyŏng-gŭn, Han Hi-sŏk, Yi Ik-hŭng, Im Ch'ŏl-ho and Kim Ŭi-jun in the National Assembly, and Ch'oi Ingyu and Hong Chin-gi in the Cabinet. A brief examination of their personal backgrounds will help us get a clear idea about the nature of the Liberal Party during those days.

Chang Kyŏng-gŭn served as a judge in the Japanese colonial judiciary before 1945. He was minister of internal affairs in 1957, the year in which hoodlums and thugs were allowed to terrorize the opposition leaders and their audience, while the police stood by. After June 1959, Chang was policy committee chairman of the Liberal Party. Han Hi-sŏk was a county magistrate during Japanese rule. After the Korean War, he served as vice-minister of internal affairs, vice-speaker of the National Assembly, and vice-chairman of the central committee of the Liberal Party. Han was among those few who masterminded government strategy for passage of the National Security Law in 1958, and the scheme for the fraudulent election of March 1960. Yi Ik-hŭng served as a police officer under the Japanese and worked in the Korean police force after the Liberation. In 1956, as minister of internal affairs, Yi conspired to assassinate Chang Myŏn, following

Chang's election to the vice-presidency. Im Ch'ŏl-ho served in the Japanese judiciary before 1945. He was chairman of the organizational department and vice-chairman of the central committee of the Liberal Party. Im was serving as vice-speaker of the Assembly at the time of the April uprising. Kim Ŭi-jun served in the Japanese judiciary as a prosecutor and judge. He was chairman of the propaganda committee of the Liberal Party; together with Chang and Han, he constituted the core of hard-liners in the party.

From the above description, some interesting observations can be made about the top echelon of the Liberal Party. All except one of the Liberal Party's leading hard-liners were trained as lawyers and served either as prosecutors or judges during Japanese rule. The only exception, Yi Ik-hŭng, was a policeman. They were all well-educated individuals with successful bureaucratic careers in their past. Most of them had close ties with the police organization by virtue of having been police officers or having served in the ministry of internal affairs. In short, they all seemed to hold what an opposition politician called the "pro-government syndrome." According to Ŏm Sang-sŏp, a Democratic assemblyman, such a person "cannot live except in the shadows of power for a number of reasons—political, psychological, etc." [42] These "power-dependent" people have no choice but to follow blindly whoever has power at the moment. At the same time, the only way they know of generating such power is by using an oppressive force; in Korea, the police provided such a force. Certainly members of the power-dependent élite had to compete among themselves for Syngman Rhee's favor, and whoever succeeded in this struggle could control the police for his own political purposes.

During the last four years of the Rhee administration, no policeman, high or low, could escape the pressure of the powerful members of the Liberal Party. The police chief in whose district the Liberal Party received proportionately less votes than in other districts was either fired or transferred to positions regarded as undesirable. It is significant that the political power of the influential members of the Liberal Party did not result from their personal popularity with the voters or their leadership ability, but from their ability to serve Syngman Rhee well. Syngman Rhee's power was attributable in part to his personal charisma, which however was rapidly deteriorating, and from his ability to manipulate coercive police force.[43]

42. Ŏm Sang-sŏp, *Kwŏllyŏkkwa chayu* [Power and Freedom], p. 265.

43. It is possible to argue that Rhee still enjoyed considerable "charisma" among the police officers of all ranks. However, the absolute loyalty of the police to the president was more the result of calculated judgment than of steadfast allegiance to Rhee.

Those who enjoyed political power under Rhee included, in addition to the leaders of the Liberal Party, his personal associates such as Kwak Yŏng-ju, his chief bodyguard; certain military officers such as Kim Ch'ang-yong, who headed the army counter-intelligence corps, and Wŏn Yong-dŏk, commander of the military police from 1953 through 1960; and a few opportunistic individuals like Shin To-hwan, who at the time of the April uprising headed the controversial Anti-Communist Youth Corps (*Pan'gong Ch'ŏngnyŏn-dan*), a collection of hoodlums supported by the Rhee regime in exchange for their terroristic attacks on its critics. This irresponsible power, based on coercive force, was heading toward a confrontation with the political public,[44] increasingly alienated from the Rhee government.

When the Korean government was established in 1948, belief in democratic values and practices was not widespread among the people at all levels of the society. However, increasingly large numbers began to demand "free and fair" elections, as the actual performance of the government became increasingly less democratic. The democratization of the public was largely the result of extensive democratic education and rapid urbanization following the Korean War. Since 1945, "education in democracy" has been taken very seriously in both the elementary and secondary schools. Extensive exposure of the urban and semi-urban population to the mass media was instrumental in convincing many Koreans of the virtues of democracy. The positive results of this democratic political education are seen in the fact that in many surveys young people have been found to be more "democratically oriented" than their elders.[45]

The process of urbanization was closely related with democratic socialization of the general public. In 1952, only 17.7 percent of the South Korean people lived in cities of 50,000 or more. This increased to 24.5 percent (5.3 million) by 1955, and 28 percent (7 million) by 1960.[46] This rapid urbanization can be attributed to expanded educa-

44. In his discussion of nationalism and social mobilization, Karl Deutsch distinguished between what he calls the "mobilized population," or "political public," and the "underlying population." Included in the category of "political public" are those who have been exposed to relatively intensive communication through economic, social, and technological development. (Deutsch, *Nationalism and Social Communication*, pp. 126–130). In the case of Korea, we might consider that the political public includes those living in cities and large towns who have had some kind of contact with the larger urban culture. The rest, the "underlying population," can be considered as generally coinciding with those people who maintain agriculture or fishing as their main occupation.

45. Yun Ch'ŏn-ju, *Han'guk chŏngch'i ch'egye* [The Korean Political System], pp. 189–248; see also Yong-ho Lee, "Democratic Political Culture in Korea," unpub. Ph.D. diss., Yale University, 1968.

46. *Haptong yŏn'gam* [The Haptong Annual], 1965, pp. 185–186.

tion, rapid increase in the number of "ex-military men" (approximately 200,000 a year), the influx of North Korean refugees during the Korean War, the destruction of demographic stability in the rural areas as a result of the war, and the general commercialization of the society.

The polarization of political forces into the pro-government Liberal Party and anti-government Democratic Party made it easier for voters to identify whom to vote for, and whom against, depending upon the level of their political consciousness. For the relatively mobilized population, the only easy and obvious way to uphold their newly acquired democratic values was to vote *against* the candidates and party of a government acting undemocratically, and *for* those opposing the government. According to Yun Ch'ŏn-ju, a political scientist who later became a member of the National Assembly, urbanization was clearly and positively related to the votes against Syngman Rhee and the Liberal Party. Yun showed that in the legislative elections of 1958, the Liberal Party elected only 13 assemblymen in cities of 50,000 people or more, while the Democratic Party elected 43 in these same cities. In the nation as a whole, the Liberal Party won a total of 126 seats, compared with 79 seats for the Democratic Party.[47] In the presidential election of 1956, Syngman Rhee received only 33.8 percent of the votes in Seoul, compared to 56 percent in the nation.[48]

The Liberal Party's weak showing in urban areas was largely due to its relative inability to perpetrate electoral frauds in the big cities. However, a more important factor was what Yun calls the "conformity votes" in the non-urban areas. With socialization and increased urbanization, however, the number of "conformity votes" decreased rapidly, which provoked the Liberal Party to use more "undemocratic" means.[49] As the Liberal Party employed increasingly repressive measures, its chances of winning popular votes in honestly held elections decreased correspondingly.

Between 1950 and 1960, Syngman Rhee's subordinates organized mass demonstrations on a number of issues in an effort to create support for Rhee and his government. There were mass meetings and parades opposing the proposed armistice agreement with the Communists, which left the country divided; demonstrations urging Syngman Rhee to run for reelection in 1952 and 1956; and mass meetings protesting the Japanese decision to repatriate Koreans living in Japan to North Korea. These mass mobilizations, officially organized and

47. *Taehanmin'guk sŏn'gŏsa*, p. 802.
48. *Ibid.*, p. 680.
49. Yun Ch'ŏn-ju, *Han'guk chŏngch'i ch'egye*, p. 242.

prompted, helped maintain and rejuvenate Rhee's popularity to a certain extent during the early fifties. However, by the second half of the decade, Rhee's personal appeal among the Korean people had disappeared, and his power had to be maintained almost solely by a coercive police force.[50]

The peak of election fraud was reached in March 1960, when practically all government employees were mobilized for the election of the Syngman Rhee ticket. While police meddling had been limited more or less to candidate registration, campaign activities, and balloting processes in the earlier elections, the ministry of internal affairs and the provincial police headquarters now became actual election centers, where the ballot counts were manipulated and fabricated.

In 1960 many Koreans were again disappointed by the death of Democratic Party candidate Cho Pyŏng-ok, Rhee's major opponent in the election campaign. Once more Rhee's reelection was assured in the absence of a serious opponent. With Rhee's age as a factor, the vice-presidential race became more important. Thus the real race was between the incumbent, Chang Myŏn, and Rhee's candidate Yi Kibung. In the election, opposition campaign workers were repeatedly arrested and beaten. Hoodlum members of the Anti-Communist Youth Corps were present in alternate voting booths on election day to see how the citizen cast his ballot. In many rural areas, three-man and nine-man "teams" were formed, with the "head" of each team, whose loyalty to the Liberal Party was unquestioned, ensuring that the other "team members" voted for the Liberal candidates. The police were openly in support of the Liberal candidates.

As it turned out, such efforts were not necessary, because the election results were completely fabricated by police headquarters and the ministry of internal affairs. On election day, Rhee received more than twice the necessary one-third of the votes. Yi Ki-bung was elected to the vice-presidency with some 8.4 million votes over Chang Myŏn, who received 1.8 million votes. The Democrats in the National Assembly charged that the election was "illegal, null and void." [51] Anti-government parades and demonstrations were launched in major cities

50. It should be noted, however, that the Korean people's respect for Rhee as a person remained high even after his resignation in 1960. A 1967 study of the political attitudes of Koreans residing in the United States shows that Syngman Rhee was still one of the most "respected" Korean leaders, with about 65 percent of the respondents indicating they either "revered" or "respected" Rhee. It is interesting to note, however, that Rhee was also one of the individuals about whom the respondents indicated most dislike (about 10 percent). See Robert A. Scalapino, Ki-shik Han, and Sungjoo Han, *The Political Attitudes of Korean Students and Academicians in the United States—1967*.

51. Kyŏng Cho Chung, *New Korea: New Land of the Morning Calm*, p. 49.

throughout the country before and after the election, to protest the frauds and irregularities.

With the near-complete alienation of the power structure from the public's political values, all that was needed for a major uprising was an incident that would intensify and articulate the common feeling of moral indignation. Early in April, as the nation began to rise against the rigged election, the people in Masan, a port city in southeastern Korea, discovered a sixteen-year-old boy's drowned body, shot, mutilated, and thrown into the bay. The boy had apparently been arrested by the Masan police while protesting the dishonest elections. Citizens and students poured into the streets and were fired on by the police during the riot.

During the weeks prior to April 19, high school students, mainly in provincial cities, sporadically demonstrated, protesting the illegal elections and the undemocratic and oppressive practices of the police and the Liberal Party. However, Rhee showed a lack of ability or willingness to comprehend the urgency of the situation. Concerning the Masan riots, Rhee stated on April 15 that it was his understanding that the incident had been "incited and engineered by Communist infiltrators." [52] Declaring that the crimes of those "thoughtless people" responsible for the Masan tragedy could not be "overlooked," Rhee warned against Communist propaganda and those "politically ambitious people who agitate and incite young people to riot." This statement by Rhee only confirmed his unwillingness to cease intimidation and coercion, further infuriating college and high school students.

On April 18, the demonstrating students of Korea University were attacked in Seoul by the police-protected hoodlums of the Anti-Communist Youth Corps.[53] Whatever legitimate authority Syngman Rhee's government claimed thus far was now completely lost in the minds of the students as well as the political public. The only thing that could have maintained Rhee's government was the use of powerful and brute force, and that alone. On April 19 such an attempt was made, and it was not until nearly 200 lives were taken and the army refused to shoot at the demonstrators that Rhee and his subordinates realized they had exhausted the coercive sources of power at their command.

On that day some 30,000 university and high school students poured onto the streets of Seoul, and thousands of them converged on

52. For the text of this speech, see Cho Hwa-yŏng (ed.), *Sawŏl hyŏngmyŏng t'ujaengsa* [A History of the Struggle in the April Revolution], pp. 63–65.

53. Korean Government, *Han'guk hyŏngmyŏng chaep'ansa* [History of the Korean Revolutionary Trials], I, 929–951.

Kyŏngmudae, the presidential mansion located in the northwestern part of the city. The police opened fire at the demonstrators, causing the students to riot. They were joined by hundreds of students throughout the nation in such major cities as Pusan, Kwangju, Inch'ŏn, Mokp'o, and Ch'ŏngju. In Seoul alone there were some 130 dead and over 1,000 wounded by nightfall. Shortly after the police began to shoot at the demonstrators, a state of martial law was declared in the major cities of Korea. Lt. Gen. Song Yo-ch'an, the army chief of staff, was assigned by Syngman Rhee to enforce martial law in the Seoul area.

After April 19, demonstrations and riots occurred every day, now joined by nonstudent elements; the army troops, however, merely stood by, guarding only against bloodshed and overt destruction of property. Events now moved quickly on the Korean political scene. Syngman Rhee ceased making reference to "Communist incitement" concerning anti-government demonstrations. On April 21, Rhee's Cabinet resigned, assuming blame for the revolutionary state of the country. The next day Rhee summoned two veteran politicians not holding government positions at the time: former prime minister Pyŏn Yŏng-t'ae and former mayor of Seoul Hŏ Chŏng. Rhee solicited their assistance in coping with the crisis situation. Both men had worked closely with Syngman Rhee, and Rhee had much trust in them. In their conference with Rhee, they refused to come into Rhee's Cabinet, stating that the situation was beyond their ability to control.[54]

Rhee was successful, however, in persuading Yi Ki-bung to withdraw from all political activities. Subsequently Chang Myŏn, the incumbent vice president, resigned from his office, urging Syngman Rhee to leave the presidency. Chang believed that Rhee would not leave his office so long as Chang, as vice-president, was to succeed to the presidency upon his resignation.[55] Instead of new elections, the demonstrators now demanded the outright resignation of Rhee himself.

President Rhee attempted to mollify the protesters by stating that he would sever all his ties with the Liberal Party and other social organizations. He also promised that government officials, including the police, would be kept from political interference in the future. Rhee then succeeded in persuading Hŏ Chŏng to accept the position of foreign minister, with the promise that Hŏ would be given "all powers of the government." [56] The chief significance of Hŏ's appointment as foreign minister was that in the absence of a vice-president he would

54. Hŏ Chŏng, "Memoirs," in *Sasirŭi chŏnburŭl kisulhanda*, p. 209.
55. Chang Myŏn, *Hanarŭi miri chukchi ankonŭn*, pp. 177–178.
56. Hŏ Chŏng, "Memoirs," p. 211.

become president, in the event that Rhee should decide to resign.

The demonstrators would not retreat once they had tasted the concessions and sensed Rhee's weakness. Many of them went on a rampage, destroying and burning the houses of the leaders of the Liberal Party and the Anti-Communist Youth Corps. A fresh wave of demonstrations was touched off on April 25, when some 300 faculty members of various universities marched through the streets of Seoul supporting their students' demand for the resignation of Syngman Rhee. Finally, on April 26, at the advice of his newly appointed foreign minister, Hŏ Chŏng, Commander of Martial Law Song Yo-ch'an, and United States Ambassador to Korea Walter P. McConaughy, Rhee announced his intention to leave the presidency. Rhee further promised that new elections would be held for both president and vice-president, and that the constitution would be changed from a presidential to a cabinet system of government.[57] Upon Rhee's resignation, Foreign Minister Hŏ Chŏng came to head the Korean government. The fall of the Rhee government meant the capitulation of police-maintained political power to the anti-police, anti-bureaucratic masses, spearheaded by the students. That the police force was the main backbone of the Liberal Party was clear by its overnight collapse following the paralyzation of the police after the April uprising.

Before we turn to an examination of the outcome of the April uprising, we should ask whether we can conceive of the situation in that period as "revolutionary." The concept of revolution has been understood in many different ways. Some scholars, mostly social scientists, interpret the term rather broadly. For example, Harry Eckstein defines it as "any attempt to alter state policy, rulers, or institutions by means deviating from previously shared social norms, 'warlike' in character, and involving the serious disruption of settled institutional patterns." [58] For some historians such as Crane Brinton and George Pettee, however, it represents major sociopolitical reorganization of the society, as in the French Revolution of 1789 or the Bolshevik Revolution of 1917.[59] A more specific interpretation has been given by Hannah Arendt, a political philosopher, to whom revolution means social and political changes resulting in the creation of a constitutional framework which would provide political freedom, defined in terms of citizen participation in the political process.[60]

57. The incoherent nature of this statement is characteristic of most of Rhee's public pronouncements. He was promising new elections and a constitutional amendment while leaving the office of the presidency.

58. Eckstein (ed.), *Internal War: Problems and Approaches,* p. 12.

59. Brinton, *The Anatomy of Revolution,* and Pettee, *The Process of Revolution.*

60. Arendt, *On Revolution.*

A common phenomenon in these differently conceived "revolutions" appears to be violent sociopolitical change resulting from or causing a change in the value system of the society. Thus Chalmers Johnson defines social stability in terms of harmony between the institutionalized power structure ("division of labor") and the social value structure ("ideological paradigm").[61] Johnson suggests that a potentially revolutionary situation can be said to exist when this harmony is broken.

The Korean situation in 1960 can be considered revolutionary in the sense that there was a clear breach on a major scale between the power structure of the Rhee government and the value system of the political public, especially the students. The April uprising was a revolutionary attempt by anti-government forces to destroy those forces which manipulated the police with the ultimate backing of Syngman Rhee. It is significant, however, that the demonstrating students and masses did not have an organized leadership of their own. Although leaders of the Democratic Party later claimed that they were largely responsible for touching off the protest movements, their actual leadership within the demonstrating masses was not present. Ironically, this absence of clearly definable leadership may have contributed to the early abdication of Syngman Rhee. However, it also had a lasting effect on the course that the "revolution" took after the fall of the Rhee regime.

The next chapter will examine the nature of major political forces at work, their attitude toward the April uprising, and their role in its aftermath.

61. Johnson, *Revolutionary Change, passim.*

III

PARTY POLITICIANS AND MILITARY OFFICERS

The April mass uprising erupted as a protest against the election irregularities committed by the Rhee regime, and resulted in its fall from power. Thus the uprising seemingly accomplished more than was initially intended. The accomplishment, however, was not in fact as impressive as it seemed on the surface. Little was done to make the political and administrative structures more compatible with the kind of democratic polity the protesters would have liked to create. Syngman Rhee and the Liberal Party had been heavily dependent upon the coercive force of the police in maintaining their power. In the immediate post-Rhee period, most of those who had supported his regime, including many high-ranking police officers and government officials, remained in their power positions. Furthermore, subsequent governments met with little success in creating and developing new political structures which would assist in the operation of a democratic government. They appeared neither interested in nor capable of bringing about fundamental changes in the socioeconomic and political structures of South Korea.

While the unorganized students and mass public provided the main energy in overthrowing the Syngman Rhee government, the outcome of the uprising was determined largely by the party politicians who had opposed Rhee and the high-ranking military officers who, despite their ostensibly nonpolitical stand, played a crucial role in the preservation of the existing socioeconomic structure.

PARTY POLITICIANS IN THE DEMOCRATIC PARTY

As shown in the preceding chapter, the conservative nationalists formed the Korean Democratic Party shortly after the Japanese defeat in 1945. This party became the main opposition political force during the Rhee period. Initially the KDP was established in response to the leftist-dominated Preparatory Committee for the Establishment of the Korean Government. The organizers of the KDP were mainly those Koreans who had opposed Japanese rule in Korea, but were not interested in any drastic change in the social structure. Among the eight original directors of the party, all but one had received education abroad—three in the United States, another three in Japan, and one in China.[1] Most of them were from the central and southern parts of Korea and had been engaged in educational or journalistic activities. Thus the leaders of the KDP represented a highly educated intellectual élite class whose opposition to Japanese rule was expressed in relatively moderate ways.

One significant fact about the leadership of the KDP was that a majority had close personal ties with Kim Sŏng-su, a wealthy educator from southwestern Korea who had brought together a wide circle of prominent men during the Japanese period by assisting them in their youth with funds and jobs, through various schools and enterprises under his control.[2] Song Chin-u, leader of the KDP during the period between September and December 1945, had been Kim's constant companion and adviser for some 30 years, since 1915, and had often publicly represented the schools and newspapers owned by Kim. It is possible to characterize the KDP as basically a group of close friends who shared a common life experience rather than any ideological commitment. This perhaps explains the fact that the bond among the members of this group proved more enduring than that of any other political group in South Korea.

Soon after its organization the KDP attracted a large number of property and land owners, former bureaucrats, and nonleftist poli-

1. Names of the directors can be found in Kim Chun-yŏn, *Han'guk Minjudang sosa* [A Brief History of the Korean Democratic Party], p. 15. Cho Pyŏng-ok's name was not included in the list of directors in Kim's book, probably because by the time Kim wrote the book Cho had withdrawn from the KDP to become director of the police department under the American Military Government. See also Cho Pyŏng-ok, *Naŭi hoegorok*, p. 145.

2. For a succinct discussion of the "Posŏng Group," see Henderson, *Korea: The Politics of the Vortex*, pp. 276–278. A brief account of Kim's life and his educational and political activities can be found in Paek Nam-ju, *Han'guk chŏnggye ch'irinjŏn* [Biographies of Seven Prominent Men in Korean Politics], pp. 63–68.

ticians of various kinds. At the same time General Hodge, Commander of the U.S. Military Government in Korea, and his staff accepted the party with favor because of its cooperative attitude toward the American occupation authority.[3] Many other factors—their educational background, administrative experience, and antileftist portfolio—also contributed to KDP members' being given many key positions in the American Military Government during the interim period. The KDP made good use of its close ties with the American authorities, and its relatively abundant financial resources greatly expanded and consolidated its organization and membership. By the end of 1947 the KDP claimed a membership of more than 865,000.[4] In the first National Assembly in 1948, the KDP had some 60 supporters, including 29 official members of the party.

However, the KDP group had a number of problems that would continue to plague them throughout the First Republic. In the first place, the absence of a leader with great stature and personal popularity among the general public forced them to look elsewhere for a man who could provide them with more charismatic and patriotic appeal. Two of its leaders, Song Chin-u and Chang Tŏk-su, who conceivably could have developed considerable personal following, were assassinated within a year of its organization. Another significant liability of the KDP was its stigma as a collection of former Japanese opportunists, wealthy landlords, and members of the bourgeoisie with reactionary views.[5] KDP's platform, which called for a basically free-enterprise system and land reform based on the principle of "reasonable compensation to the former landlords," seemed to substantiate such accusations. In addition, because of the involvement of many KDP members in the administration of the American Military Government, the KDP was blamed for many of the problems that existed before establishment of the Korean government. Conspicuous among such problems were the unchecked violence and terrorism of rightist groups, the apparent insulation of the American authorities from the Korean public, and their failure to carry out satisfactory social reforms.

When Rhee refused the KDP a share of power in his government, it sought to broaden its power base through alliances with other political forces, and as a result of such alliances the Democratic Nationalist Party was formed in 1949 and the Democratic Party in 1955. The KDP developed into a party of the parliament, persistently advocating

3. Cho Pyŏng-ok, *Naŭi hoegorok,* pp. 144–146.

4. Cited in Yi Ki-ha, *Han'guk chŏngdang paltalsa* [A History of Political Parties in Korea], p. 63.

5. A representative work of this kind is Ch'oe Hŭng-jo, *Minju kungmindangŭi naemak* [A Secret History of the Democratic Nationalist Party], *passim.*

a cabinet system of government. Since the constitution of the First Republic stipulated a presidential system of government,[6] changing the constitution was an important preoccupation of the KDP.

Members of the KDP (later the DNP) also showed traits of political behavior which can be considered quite "traditional."[7] They lacked systematic ideological themes to guide their action; many of them took pride in the fact that they had been born to the former *yangban*, or officialdom class;[8] and the main basis of their political activities remained the friendship circle of the so-called Posŏng group in the center, and personal and clan ties on the local level.[9]

Most of the KDP–DNP members held a heavily pro-American and America-dependent attitude, which could be attributed to their strong opposition to Communism as well as to many members' previous acquaintance with the United States through their earlier schooling. The legitimacy of their dependence upon the support of a Western power for South Korea's survival was sustained by the fact that Korea, unlike most other new states, had been colonized by a non-Western power. Many Korean nationalists looked upon the Western world as a liberator from their oppressive neighbor rather than as a colonialistic or imperialistic force.[10]

In the course of their long struggle against the Syngman Rhee regime, members of the KDP–DNP group also acquired what can be called the "opposition mentality," which made them highly suspicious of any political authority and unable to cooperate with the governing group except with a sense of shame and betrayal.[11] Such an attitude was analogous to what Edward Shils calls the "oppositional syndrome" found among the intellectuals of former colonies. Shils points out that

6. It is well known that Yu Chin-o, then chief consultant to the National Assembly in the drafting of the constitution in 1948, had originally proposed a cabinet system of government in his first draft. This was of course supported by the KDP. However, it was changed into a presidential system at the insistence of Syngman Rhee, who then expected to be elected president. For a good discussion of this particular point, see John Kie-chiang Oh, *Korea: Democracy on Trial*, pp. 12–14.

7. Members of the Democratic Party frequently cite Cho Pyŏng-ok's book, *Minjujuŭiwa na* [Democracy and I], as setting forth the ideological basis of the Democratic Party. However, this book deals primarily with the necessity of limiting political power, especially that of the president. It has little systematic treatment of any other aspects of government and society.

8. For example, Yun Po-sŏn, *Kugugŭi kasibatkil* [Thorny Road Toward National Salvation].

9. For the "traditional" characteristics of this group, see Henderson, *Korea: The Politics of the Vortex*, pp. 276–280.

10. Chong-sik Lee, *The Politics of Korean Nationalism*, pp. 277–278.

11. A similar phenomenon, the problem of the "perennial minority," has been ascribed to the Japanese Socialist Party by Robert A. Scalapino and Junnosuke Masumi, in their *Parties and Politics in Contemporary Japan*, p. 152.

they would refuse in principle to consider the problems of the government as real tasks needing resolution.[12] Such an attitude of the opposition politicians' group outlived the Rhee regime and continued to influence their behavior until after the establishment of the Chang Myŏn government in September 1960.

This group brought many of its conservative, pro-American, oppositional, and exclusivistic attitudes into the Democratic Party when it was created in 1955. The Democratic Party was formed as the result of a coalition between members of the DNP and former members of the Parliamentary Liberal Party who had been alienated from Syngman Rhee following the 1952 political crisis. They were also joined by individuals affiliated with the Young Korea Academy (*Hŭngsa-dan*) and the Chosŏn Democratic Party (*Chomin-dang*). The Hŭngsa-dan was organized by Korean residents in the United States under the leadership of An Ch'ang-ho (1878–1938) shortly after the annexation of Korea by Japan, in an effort to carry out educational and political activities in Korea. Membership consisted primarily of men from the P'yŏngan-do Province in northwestern Korea, and Syngman Rhee had a rather hostile attitude toward the solidarity of this group, although both Rhee and An had been active in the Independence Club (*Tongnip Hyŏphoe*) prior to Japanese annexation of Korea. Once Korea fell under Japanese domination, Rhee advocated direct political and diplomatic action for Koreans, while An was for long-term educative activities. An's supporters were mostly from the northwestern provinces, whereas most of Rhee's followers came from the central and southern provinces.[13]

The Chosŏn Democratic Party, formerly of Cho Man-sik in North Korea, consisted primarily of Christians from the P'yŏngan-do Province and had many members who simultaneously belonged to the Hŭngsa-dan. In response to the solidarity of the KDP–DNP group within the newly organized Democratic Party, this so-called P'yŏngan-do group allied itself with the members of the former Parliamentary Liberal Party, who were mostly from central and southern Korea. Most of the PLP members had had bureaucratic or judicial experience and had served the Syngman Rhee administration at one time or another. As a result of this alliance, what was subsequently known as the "new faction" of the Democratic Party was born, its members supporting the candidacy of Chang Myŏn for leadership of the new party; the KDP–DNP group came to be known as the "old faction."

It is difficult to firmly attribute any common characteristics to a

12. Shils, "The Intellectuals in the Political Development of the New States," in John H. Kautsky (ed.), *Political Change in Underdeveloped Countries*, p. 217.
13. From interview with Hŏ Chŏng by Chong-sik Lee, May 10, 1967.

Table III-1

SOCIAL BACKGROUND OF LEADING MEMBERS OF THE "OLD FACTION" OF THE DEMOCRATIC PARTY

Name	*Place of Birth*	*Year of Birth*	*Education*	*Career*
Kim U-p'yŏng	Chŏnnam (SW) *	1897 (58) †	Japan, U.S.	Journ. Bur. ‡
Yi Chŏng-nae	Chŏnnam (SW)	1898 (57)	Japan	Polit.
Cho Yŏng-gyu	Chŏnnam (SW)	1912 (43)	China	Polit.
Kim Chun-yŏn	Chŏnnam (SW)	1894 (61)	Japan, Germany	Polit.
Chŏng Chae-wan	Chŏnnam (SW)	1900 (55)	Japan	Bur.
So Sŏn-gyu	Chŏnbuk (SW)	1903 (52)	Japan	Bur.
Yi Wŏn-hong	Kyŏngnam (SE)	1903 (52)	unknown	Polit.
Kim To-yŏn	Seoul (CW)	1894 (61)	Japan, U.S.	Polit.
Son Kak-hyu	Ch'ungbuk (SC)	1896 (59)	China	Polit.
Pyŏn Kwang-ho	Chŏnbuk (SW)	1920 (35)	Japan	Polit.
Cho Han-baek	Chŏnbuk (SW)	1912 (43)	Korea	Polit.
Ku Ch'ŏl-hoe	Kyŏnggi (CW)	1915 (40)	Japan	Polit.
Chŏng Sŏng-t'ae	Chŏnnam (SW)	1915 (40)	Korea	Polit.
Ch'oe Ch'ŏn	Kyŏngnam (SE)	1900 (55)	unknown	Polit.
Yi Ch'un-gi	Chŏnbuk (SW)	1907 (48)	Korea	Bur.
Cho Pyŏng-ok	Ch'ungnam (SC)	1894 (61)	U.S.	Polit.
Yi Sang-don	Ch'ungnam (SC)	1912 (43)	Japan	Polit.
Yu Chin-san	Chŏnbuk (SW)	1905 (50)	Japan	Polit.
Yun Po-sŏn	Seoul (CW)	1897 (58)	Gt. Britain	Polit.
Sŏ Pŏm-sŏk	Seoul (CW)	1904 (51)	China	Polit.

* Region.

† Age as of 1955.

‡ Abbreviations stand for journalism, bureaucracy, and politics, indicating the initial occupation which gave the individual prominence.

group so diverse as the new faction of the Democratic Party. However, a comparison of the top leaders of the two factions (Tables 1 and 2) leads us to some interesting observations.[14] While all 20 top leaders of the old faction were born in the southern and central provinces, 8 (40

14. The names of each group's leaders are from Yi Ki-ha, *Han'guk chŏngdang paltalsa,* p. 307. I added to each group a few important names not included in Yi's lists. Cho Chae-ch'ŏn and Kim Sang-don are included in the old-faction group in Yi's list. However, since they changed their factional affiliation shortly after formation of the Democratic Party, their names have been added to the new-faction group.

percent) of the 20 new-faction leaders came from provinces north of the 38th parallel. Among the old-faction leaders, 11 (55 percent) had their political roots in the southwestern (Chŏlla-do) provinces. Among the new-faction members, 5 came from the northwestern (P'yŏngan-do) provinces. Thus, while the old faction was clearly dominated by men from the Chŏlla-do provinces, those from the P'yŏngan-do provinces constituted the largest single group in the new faction.

The average age of the old-faction leadership was fifty-one; there were 13 old-faction members who were fifty years of age or more, and only 1 under forty. For the new faction, the average age was forty-eight; there were 10 members fifty years or older, while 4 were under forty.

Table III-2

SOCIAL BACKGROUND OF LEADING MEMBERS OF THE "NEW FACTION" OF THE DEMOCRATIC PARTY

Name	*Place of Birth*	*Year of Birth*	*Education*	*Career*
Kim Yŏng-sŏn	Ch'ungnam (SC) *	1919 (36) †	Korea	Jud.‡
Chŏng Il-hyŏng	P'yŏngnam (NW)	1904 (51)	U.S.	Bur.
Song Wŏn-gyŏng	Ch'ungnam (SC)	1894 (61)	Japan	Journ.
Ch'oe Hŭi-sŏng	P'yŏngnam (NW)	1894 (61)	U.S.	Bur.
Yi Sŏk-ki	Ch'ungnam (SC)	1910 (45)	Korea	Jud.
Han Kŭn-jo	P'yŏngnam (NW)	1895 (60)	Japan	Jud.
Hyŏn Sŏk-ho	Kyŏngbuk (SE)	1907 (48)	Korea	Jud.
Hong Ik-p'yo	Kyŏnggi (CW)	1911 (44)	Korea	Polit.
Han T'ong-suk	Hambuk (NE)	1909 (56)	Korea	Bur.
Yi Ch'ŏl-sŭng	Chŏnbuk (SW)	1922 (33)	Korea	Polit.
O Wi-yŏng	Kyŏngnam (SE)	1902 (53)	Japan	Bank
Kim Chae-sun	P'yŏngnam (NW)	1923 (32)	Korea	Polit.
Ŏm Sang-sŏp	Chŏnnam (SW)	1908 (47)	Korea	Jud.
Kim Yong-sŏng	Seoul (CW)	1924 (31)	Korea	Journ.
Chang Myŏn	Seoul (CW)	1899 (56)	U.S.	Bur.
Kim Sŏn-t'ae	Chŏnnam (SW)	1912 (43)	Japan	Jud.
Cho Chae-ch'ŏn	Chŏnnam (SW)	1912 (43)	Japan	Jud.
Kim Sang-don	Hwanghae (NC)	1901 (54)	Japan	Polit.
Pak Sun'ch'ŏn	Kyŏngbuk (SE)	1898 (57)	Japan	Polit.
Chu Yo-han	P'yŏngnam (NW)	1900 (55)	China	Journ.

* Region.

† Age as of 1955.

‡ Abbreviations stand for judiciary, bureaucracy, journalism, and politics, indicating the initial occupation which made the individual important.

Thus, although the difference was not great, the new-faction leadership was definitely younger. The new faction had at least 9 members (45 percent) who had received their main education in Korea, while the old faction had only 3 such members.

One single factor that distinguished the new faction most clearly from the old faction was the career background of its members. While 16 (80 percent) members of the old faction had first distinguished themselves in politics, only 4 (20 percent) of the new faction had taken the same route to prominence; 12 (60 percent) of the new-faction members had been engaged in bureaucratic or administrative activities before their entry into politics, compared with only 3 (15 percent) of the old-faction members. A majority (7) of the new-faction members who had "bureaucratic" background had passed the higher civil service examination under Japanese rule and served in the Japanese judiciary. Most of the members of the new faction with bureaucratic background had worked also for the Syngman Rhee government for some time before their separation from Rhee.

A "typical" old-faction leader in 1955 would have been a man from one of the southwestern provinces in his early or middle fifties. He came from a reasonably well-to-do and well-educated family and had studied abroad, either in Japan or the United States. He had been engaged in some kind of anti-Japanese or other politically significant activities within Korea during the Japanese rule. He probably had a close personal tie with Kim Sŏng-su, through either Posŏng High School (now Korea University), the newspaper *Tonga Ilbo,* or one of the enterprises owned by Kim. After Shin Ik-hi's death in 1956, he supported Cho Pyŏng-ok for the leadership of the Democratic Party until Cho's death in March 1960.

A "typical" new-faction member in 1955 would have been between forty and fifty years old and born in either a northwestern or southeastern province. He had been educated in Japan and was active in the Japanese judiciary or other bureaucratic organizations. If he were one of the younger members he had received his education in Korea and served Syngman Rhee's administration as a bureaucrat or member of the Korean judiciary. Like the old-faction members, he would be strongly anti-Communist by virtue of either having been forced to flee from his home in the North by the Communists or having fought the leftists in the South as a prosecutor or leader of a rightist organization. His views were more practical and flexible than his old-faction counterpart's, and showed less traditional and conservative traits. He was as much "pro-American" as the old-faction member, but his attitude seemed less exclusivistic both in foreign and domestic politics.

At the same time, his commitment to a constitutional amendment for a cabinet system of government was not as firm as the old-faction man's. He supported Chang Myŏn, former Korean representative to the United Nations and prime minister under Syngman Rhee, for leadership of the new party.

On the local level, the most active supporters of the Democratic Party were those who had close personal and family ties with Democratic members of the national or provincial legislatures.[15] As a general rule, active supporters of the Democratic Party had no steady occupation other than their political activities. Many of them were deprived of job opportunities because of their affiliation with a party opposing the Syngman Rhee government. Many had some experience in public life, either as the head of a *ri* (village) or *tong* (city subward), and were quite interested in public affairs. Although their ultimate objective in political activities lay in obtaining some government position, this was a rather remote goal as long as Syngman Rhee and his Liberal regime were in power. They could still get some financial benefit from their party work by campaigning for his Democratic candidate during the campaign or working in the local party office during the off years.

In the late years of the Liberal regime, however, Democratic Party workers often had to provide their own expenses, and many of them were forced to sell or leave their farms for their political activities.[16] Their relationship with the Democratic candidates consisted primarily of clan ties, but other factors such as school and business contact were often important. As a rule, the candidate in a countryside district was expected to have strong clan ties in the locality and large private funds. During the early years of the First Republic, Kwak Sang-hun, vice-speaker of the National Assembly between 1954 and 1958, was denied nomination by the KDP because, according to Kwak, he "did not have any money." [17]

The leadership of the provincial party committee commonly fell to either of the two factions, depending upon whether the DNP or the old faction had built up a strong organization in that province.

In provinces like Kyŏngsang Nam-do in southeastern Korea or Kang-

15. My discussion of party politics on the local level is based upon interviews with former legislative members of the Democratic Party. They include Yi Ch'ŏl-sŭng from Chŏlla Puk-to, who was also deputy director of the party's organization department; Kim Yŏng-sŏn from Ch'ungch'ŏng Nam-do; and Kim Yŏng-sam from Kyŏngsang Nam-do.

16. Yi Ung-hŭi and Kim Chin-hyŏn, "Chŏngch'i chagŭm" [Political Funds: The Cost of Korean Democracy], p. 128.

17. "Kwak Sang-hun," in *Chŏnggye yahwa,* p. 51.

Table III-3
FACTIONAL AFFILIATION OF
PROVINCIAL CHAIRMEN OF THE DEMOCRATIC PARTY IN 1956 AND 1958

Province	*1956 Chairman*	*Faction*	*1958 Chairman*	*Faction*
Seoul	Chŏng Il-hyŏng	New	Kim Sang-don	New
Kyŏnggi	Hong Kil-sŏn	Old	Hong Kil-sŏn	Old
Ch'ungbuk	Shin Kak-hyu	Old	Shin Kak-hyu	Old
Ch'ungnam	Chin Yŏng-ha	Old	Kim Ki-hwan	Old
Kyŏngbuk	Yi Chae-yŏng	Old	Chu Pyŏng-hwan	New
Kyŏngnam	O Wi-yŏng	New	Kim Yong-jin	New
Chŏnbuk	Yun Che-sul	Old	Yun Che-sul	Old
Chŏnnam	Kim Yang-su	Old	Yang Pyŏng-il	Old
Kangwŏn	Pak Ch'ung-mo	New	Pak Ch'ung-mo	New
Cheju	Ko Tam-yŏng	Old	Ko Tam-yŏng	Old

wŏn-do in east central Korea, where the DNP had been relatively unorganized, party chairmanships went to the new faction.[18] The old faction was stronger in southwestern and central-western parts of Korea such as Chŏlla Nam-do and Kyŏnggi-do. Table III-3 shows the chairmen of the party committees in nine provinces and Seoul, and their respective faction affiliations, in 1956 and 1958.[19]

According to Table III-3, seven of the ten provincial chairmanships belonged to the old faction shortly after the formation of the Democratic Party; in 1958 the old faction controlled six provinces. Wherever new party branches were built, however, they usually fell to the new faction. In fact, the old faction gradually lost ground on the local level. This trend was attributable largely to the cliquish and conservative nature of the old faction. Another contributing factor was the election of Chang Myŏn, the leader of the new faction, as vice-president in 1956. He was considered to have a good prospect of succeeding Syngman Rhee, the aged president, and this helped induce many newcomers to join the new faction. In addition, members of the

18. According to O Wi-yŏng, who was chairman of the Kyŏngsang Nam-do provincial party committee between 1955 and 1958, party head Shin Ik-hi had pushed him for the provincial party chief position. Shin probably intended to curb the power of the KDP group by placing a few of the non-DNP members in key party positions.

19. The names of the provincial party chiefs are from *Kyŏnghyang Shinmun*, 1955–1958. Their factional affiliation is primarily based upon the list of faction members given on the eve of the split between the two factions into two separate parties, in August 1960 (*Kyŏnghyang Shinmun*, August 5, 1960, p. 1).

old faction found it difficult to keep up with the vigor and skill of their junior rivals in expanding their support. The new faction had placed special emphasis on the expansion of their organization on the local levels ever since the establishment of the party. Both the chairman and vice-chairman of the organization department of the party (Hyŏn Sŏk-ho and Yi Ch'ŏl-sŭng, respectively) were members of the new faction.

The rivalry between the new and old factions of the Democratic Party, which would seriously affect politics in the post-Rhee period, was best expressed in the personal relationship between Chang Myŏn and Cho Pyŏng-ok. Chang, a scholarly Catholic who was known to have had a relatively peaceful life even during Japanese rule, felt that Cho Pyŏng-ok, an indomitable, resolute, and rugged individual and a Protestant, was personally dominating and too free-wheeling, undisciplined, and often reckless.[20] On the other hand, Cho considered Chang politically inept, too cautious, indecisive, yet overly attached to political office. Chang's record during the Japanese rule was considered less than honorable, and his struggle against the Rhee regime as vice-president of the republic was too passive. While Cho was much involved in anti-Rhee activities in the National Assembly as the leader of the Democratic Party, Chang was relatively inactive, staying mostly in the vice-presidential residence during his four years in that office. As members of the five-man supreme council of the Democratic Party, Cho and Chang were primarily responsible for providing funds for party expenses.[21] Chang had more or less regular and organized sources from Catholic organizations and enterprises, while Cho's sources were generally unpredictable and often controversial. On many occasions, Cho was suspected by new-faction members of receiving illicit funds from Liberal sources.[22]

In the nominating convention of March 1956, Cho had given up his bid for the vice-presidential spot in favor of Chang Myŏn, in an effort to keep the newly created party together and with the understanding

20. In December 1948, shortly before recognition of the Republic of Korea government by the United Nations, both Cho and Chang were in Paris, respectively as President Rhee's special envoy and as Korea's chief delegate. When they went to see India's Nehru, whose support for the new Korean Republic was considered critical for its recognition by the United Nations, Cho criticized the Indian prime minister, saying that India had been indecisive and opportunistic. Chang felt that Cho had been too blunt and undiplomatic. Cho replied that it was necessary to force Nehru to make up his mind one way or the other. The next day India voted for recognition of the South Korean government. See Cho Pyŏng-ok, *Naŭi hoegorok*, pp. 254–256.

21. Kwak Sang-hun, "Memoirs," in *Sasirŭi chŏnburŭl kisulhanda*, pp. 255–256.

22. Yi Ung-hŭi and Kim Chin-hyŏn, "Political Funds," p. 128.

that he would have the next turn in 1960.[23] It was also implicitly understood that in case the Democratic Party won the election, and if a constitutional amendment were to be achieved, Cho would be given the position of prime minister under a new constitution.[24] There was no disagreement between the two factions about giving the presidential nomination to Shin Ik-hi.

In 1960, however, the old faction's proposal to agree beforehand on the nomination of Cho Pyŏng-ok for the presidency and Chang Myŏn for the vice-presidency was rejected by the new faction. Thus full-scale competition was waged between the two factions from the local levels in preparation for the nominating convention. In the course of the competition, violence erupted in the party conventions on the provincial and city levels, and animosity between the two factions became so serious that Cho Pyŏng-ok withdrew from the competition on October 9, 1959.[25] Cho shortly changed his mind about withdrawing from politics after a conference with Chang Myŏn, eventually winning the party's nomination for president on November 23, 1959, by 484 votes, three more than Chang Myŏn's 481 votes. Cho's victory in this competition was more a result of his personal popularity among the delegate members than the reflection of the strength of the old faction. Chang Myŏn, who received the vice-presidential nomination, then implied a threat that he would leave the Democratic Party unless he became chairman of the five-man supreme council of the party; he was subsequently elected to the position.

As a result of the division within the party, members of the two factions were often more preoccupied with the internal struggle than with their fight against the Liberal regime. Members of the old faction felt that the new faction was not interested in a basic change in the constitutional structure—that is, introduction of a cabinet system of government—but was merely using the party to elect Chang Myŏn as president and grab power. The new-faction members felt, in turn, that the old faction had neither political imagination nor support of the masses. They even suspected that some kind of underhanded deal was being contemplated between the old faction and the Liberal Party. Such suspicion sometimes erupted into charges by the new faction that old-faction members received help from the police in intra-party conflict, and political funds from the Liberal Party.[26] In many localities

23. Kwak Sang-hun, "Memoirs," p. 253; also, Cho Pyŏng-ok, *Naŭi hoegorok,* p. 376.

24. Kim To-yŏn, *Naŭi insaeng paeksŏ,* [A White Paper of My Life], p. 277.

25. *Han'guk Ilbo,* October 1, 1959–October 10, 1959.

26. Such a charge was made by members of the new faction in connection with much-publicized violence in a city party convention held in Pusan in September 1959. *Tong-a Ilbo,* September 25, 1959, p. 1.

the Liberal Party and the police tried to promote mutual suspicion between the two factions of the Democratic Party through bribing and blackmailing party workers. Closing down the newspaper *Kyŏnghyang Shinmun* in April 1959 was interpreted by many as a calculated move on the part of the Liberal Party to weaken the new faction in favor of the old faction of the Democratic Party.

Earlier in 1959, there was in fact a move between the Liberal Party and the Democratic old faction for a constitutional amendment aimed at bringing about a cabinet system of government. This move was the result of converging interest of these two otherwise disparate groups. Many members of the Liberal Party were concerned about the health and longevity of President Rhee and felt that political disaster that might follow Rhee's death could be avoided by adopting a parliamentary system, especially since the Liberal Party had a majority in the National Assembly. To the old-faction members of the Democratic Party, a cabinet system of government was something that they had long advocated, and they saw in it an opportunity to prevent Vice-President Chang Myŏn from assuming the presidency.[27] The Democratic new faction naturally rejected the proposal.

Late in 1959 the Liberal Party again tried to take advantage of the factional rivalry in the Democratic Party by proposing a constitutional amendment which would have eliminated split-party voting between the presidential and vice-presidential candidates. The old-faction leadership responded favorably to this proposal. This scheme was abandoned, again because of lack of enthusiasm on the part of Syngman Rhee and violent opposition by the new faction of the Democratic Party. Although both these moves failed to materialize, they contributed much to arouse the new faction's apprehension as to the motives of old-faction members. This three-way maneuver involving the Liberal Party and the two factions of the Democratic Party was to have a significant bearing on the development of events following the April uprising; the Liberal Party would again take advantage of the split within the Democratic Party.

Following the death of Cho Pyŏng-ok on February 24, and the presidential elections on March 15, 1960, the focus of the quarrel between the two factions centered around whether or not the Democratic members in the National Assembly and Vice President Chang Myŏn, whose term was to expire in August, should resign from their offices in protest against election irregularities. The old faction, lacking a leader who could run in a national election even if a new one was to be held, argued that they should resign immediately and try to bring about a whole new political framework. On the other hand, the new faction

27. Yi Ki-ha, *Han'guk chŏngdang paltalsa,* p. 370.

felt that it still had a stake in the system as long as Chang Myŏn remained vice-president and as long as the new faction had a majority of the Democratic membership in the National Assembly.[28]

It was obvious that the ability of the Democratic Party to mobilize the public for protest demonstrations was very much limited because of its factional split and its traditional and conservative nature. It had failed to establish close relationships with any major sectors of the society, especially the youth. Despite its failure to lead an organized mass protest movement, the Democratic Party nevertheless claimed the right to be the beneficiary of the April uprising which succeeded in ousting the Rhee regime. In order to explain how the Democratic Party, divided and stagnant as it was, succeeded in assuming power after Rhee's fall, it is necessary to analyze the nature of the Korean armed forces and their role in Korean politics.

MILITARY OFFICERS IN KOREAN POLITICS

The paralysis of the police force after the April uprising did not mean a complete absence of coercive power in South Korea. The Korean armed forces, with some 600,000 men, remained basically intact, and could have provided Rhee with the necessary force to suppress the anti-government demonstrators. It is also true, as Gen. Song Yo-ch'an, army chief of staff at the time of the April uprising, pointed out later, that nothing would have kept the soldiers who were brought into Seoul and other major South Korean cities, following the declaration of martial law on April 19, from opening fire at the demonstrators, had they been ordered to do so by their commanding officers.[29] Therefore it was of utmost significance that the military proved to be less than totally loyal to Syngman Rhee, and that General Song, who was given the power to enforce martial law, chose to keep his troops neutral between Rhee and the demonstrators during the crisis. There is little evidence to contradict General Song's later contention that he was personally responsible in large part for the army's neutral stand.[30]

However, General Song's conduct during this critical period requires explanation beyond his supposed sympathy with the demonstrators or

28. In the 1958 elections, 83 Democratic Party candidates were elected to the National Assembly. In an election for the minority leadership, O Wi-yŏng, a new-faction candidate, won with 39 votes, his old-faction opponent Kim Ŭi-t'aek getting 35 votes. Although it is difficult to argue that the line was drawn exactly along the factional split, the vote is indicative of the relative strength of the two factions within the Democratic Party in the National Assembly. The old faction was further weakened by the defection of 6 of its supporters to the Liberal Party at the end of 1959. *Haptong yŏn'gam, 1959*, p. 377, and *Haptong yŏn'gam*, 1961, pp. 125–126.

29. Song Yo-ch'an, "Memoirs," in *Sasirŭi chŏnburŭl kisulhanda,* p. 346.

30. *Ibid.*

his belief in the political neutrality of the military. What structural conditions prevented the Korean army from doing its best to save the Rhee regime? Furthermore, during an almost complete power vacuum following Rhee's resignation, what kept the army from taking power or at least strongly exerting itself in political affairs? An analysis of the main characteristics of the Korean military will help answer these questions, and also put in proper focus the role of the United States in the political crisis in South Korea in 1960.

The first pertinent characteristic of the Korean military was that most of its high-ranking officers had a generally pro-American attitude and were heavily dependent upon the moral and material support of American military officers in their public conduct. The establishment and growth of the pre-war Korean army can be attributed in large part to the efforts of American military officers then serving in Korea.[31] During the early days of the Korean constabulary, knowledge of the English language and close relations with the American officers were necessary ingredients for a successful military career. New recruits with some previous military experience in either the Japanese or Chinese armies were commissioned as officers upon completing an English language training course. Shortly after the outbreak of the Korean War, operational command of the Korean armed forces was placed under the American Commander of the U.N. Forces. Since then, the growth of the Korean armed forces had been closely supervised and scrupulously guided by the American advisers.

Most significant in this process was the enormous power that the American advisers had over personnel policy in the Korean armed forces. Maj. Robert K. Sawyer, a military historian and former member of the Korean Military Advisory Group, remarked: "Since KMAG lacked legal authority, it was important that key positions be occupied by Koreans who were receptive to American advice. Usually KMAG pressure served to eliminate the incompetent and inimical ROK officers." [32] The Korean Minister of Defense would ask the American advisers to report "uncooperative" ROK officers—an action, according to Sawyer, that "usually effected a quick improvement in the situation." [33]

Although the American advisers were ostensibly concerned primarily with the professional excellence of the Korean officers, their decisive voice on personnel matters tended to weed out elements recalcitrant or "uncooperative" to the Americans. Gregory Henderson has pointed

31. For a detailed account of this process, see Robert K. Sawyer, *Military Advisors in Korea: KMAG in Peace and War*, pp. 3–113.

32. *Ibid.*, p. 65.

33. *Ibid.*, pp. 60–61.

out that the Americans had their own favorites among Korean military officers, and "those without 'background' or education in the Korean sense sometimes got ahead through their patronage." [34] President Syngman Rhee personally had a deep trust in most of the American generals who served in Korea and always consulted them before appointing Korean generals to high military positions.[35] Therefore it was important for virtually all ambitious officers to be regarded by the American officers as reliable and friendly. Undoubtedly such a situation was received with a degree of hostility by those officers who were less than successful in dealing with the Americans, and consequently slower in being promoted than those better adjusted to the situation.[36] Because of the overwhelming and presumably indispensable nature of American support, Korean officers were mentally conditioned to depend upon the United States. In fact, recognition or commendation from American commanders was considered by most Korean military men the highest personal honor in their military career.[37]

Another relevant characteristic of the Korean military was the absence of a strong ideological orientation among most high-ranking officers. This is contrary to the theory of Morris Janowitz, who attributed strongly held ideology to military officers in new nations. According to Janowitz, there are four "ideological themes" commonly found among these officers: (1) a strong sense of nationalism and national identity, with pervasive overtones of xenophobia; (2) a strong "puritanical" outlook; (3) the acceptance of collective public enterprise as a basis for achieving social, political, and economic change; and (4) an "anti-politics" (i.e., professional) outlook.[38]

34. Henderson, *Korea: The Politics of the Vortex,* pp. 340–341.

35. In bargaining with the American officers, President Rhee often used his power to appoint Korean military officers to key positions. Before making appointments as the American advisers wanted him to, Rhee tried to extract promises, such as that the United States would help expand the Korean armed forces. Such "bargaining," of course, was done in the most subtle and diplomatic way by both the Korean president and the American military officers. However, Rhee seldom ignored the preferences of the Americans regarding military personnel matters. On this point, see Ko Chŏng-hun, *Pirok: kun* [The Military: An Unofficial Record], pp. 54–65.

36. Henderson thus pointed out: "The ability to speak English played an appreciable role. Maj. Gen. Park Chŏng-hi was one of the very few senior Korean officers known for paucity of English and lack of communication with his American advisors. Similarly, almost none of the 'young colonels' in the coup (of May 1961), unlike many of their colleagues, spoke English or communicated readily with Americans."

37. For example, see Lt. Gen. Song Yo-ch'an's account of his meetings with Gens. Douglas MacArthur and James van Fleet in his "Memoirs," in *Sasirŭi chŏnburŭl kisulhanda,* pp. 338–341.

38. Morris Janowitz, *The Military in the Political Development of New Nations,* pp. 63–67.

High-ranking Korean military officers failed to exhibit any of these ideological themes. The absence of a strong ideological commitment among Korean military men can be attributed to a number of factors related to their recruitment and training. The American military advisers who closely supervised the creation and growth of the Korean armed forces were consistently against any ideological education of the Korean officers, whose professional quality was their main concern. Their insistence on a non-ideological training was probably prompted by their own anti-political outlook. Instead of insulating the Korean military men from political pressures, however, it simply served to weaken their commitment to purposeful ideals.

An encounter in 1948 between Yi Pŏm-sŏk, prime minister and minister of defense, and the American military advisers, including Brig. Gen. William L. Roberts, chief American adviser to the Korean Constabulary, gives a good picture of the prevailing American attitude toward ideological education of Korean military officers.[39] Shortly after establishment of the Korean government in 1948, Minister of Defense Yi Pŏm-sŏk proposed a bureau of political education within the ministry of national defense, ostensibly to imbue the Korean troops with strong anti-Communist ideas. Roberts opposed Yi's proposal, stating that the creation of a political commissariat in the military would be unthinkable except in Hitlerian or Communist totalitarian systems; public information and education activities of the Korean troops should be undertaken by the individual military commanders and not by the ministry of national defense. According to Roberts, establishing a political education bureau, responsible only to the minister of defense, would amount to the creation of a separate apparatus with supervisory powers over the commanders of the various branches of the military. The reasons for American objection to a bureau of political education were threefold: the American officers' strong anti-ideological outlook, dictated by professional mores; [40] their apprehension concerning the true motives of the defense minister; [41] and their extraordinarily protective attitude toward the senior officers within the Korean Constabulary.[42]

39. The activities of these American officers in connection with the development of the Korean Army are described in detail in Sawyer, *Military Advisers in Korea, passim.* Ko Chŏng-hun's account was taken from his *Pirok: kun*, pp. 72–77.

40. Sawyer, *op. cit.;* Henderson, *op. cit.*, pp. 334–360; and Ko Chŏng-hun, *op. cit.*, pp. 119–120.

41. There were rumors, which of course reached the ears of the American advisors, that Yi was plotting a coup d'état against the Rhee government through his National Youth Corps (Ko Chŏng-hun, p. 77).

42. After renaming the Korean Constabulary the Korean Army in December 1948, President Rhee was also determined to appoint the first chief of staff from

The senior officers of the Korean Constabulary (later the Korean Army) consisted mainly of veterans of the Japanese Army. The highest positions were occupied by graduates of the Imperial Defense College in Tokyo; they included Army Chief of Staff Ch'ae Pyŏng-dŏk,[43] his successor Yi Hyŏng-gŭn, and Deputy Chief of Staff Chŏng Il-kwŏn.

The other major group consisted of graduates of the Manchurian Academy (Japanese), known as the "Manchurian officers." They included Administrative Deputy Chief of Staff Wŏn Yong-dŏk, Director of the Army Intelligence Bureau Paek Sŏn-yŏp, and Director of the Army Munitions Bureau Yang Kuk-chin.[44] Others with Japanese Army background included the "student officers," who had joined it during the Second World War as students,[45] and a few who had served as noncommissioned officers, including Superintendent of the Army Infantry School Song Yo-ch'an.[46]

Although there were some officers who had served with the Korean Liberation Army under Yi Pŏm-sŏk or with the Nationalist Chinese Army, most of them did not occupy important positions in the new Korean Army. Although they could claim to have been more "patriotic" than their Japanese-trained brethren, they were considered less acceptable to the American advisers from the professional point of view. Officers of the Tokyo and Manchurian groups, having served the Japanese, were hardly in a position to claim moral or ideological superiority over their more ideologically oriented colleagues. Their only preoccupation, understandably, was with fighting the Communists.

The top Korean military officers could hardly be characterized as strongly "nationalistic" or xenophobic. Neither did they accept "collective public enterprise as a basis for achieving social, political, and

---

among the officers of the existing Constabulary. This was of course very much in line with the wishes of the American advisers. Such a decision was significant because there were many other important figures with impressive military background who were not in the Constabulary.

43. General Ch'ae was killed during the early weeks of the Korean War under somewhat mysterious circumstances. He had been blamed for the disastrous defeat of the South Korean Army following outbreak of the war. He was also criticized for his cowardly actions, such as blowing up the Han River Bridge south of Seoul in the early morning of June 28, 1950, before the retreat from Seoul was complete.

44. Wŏn later became chief of the Joint Provost Marshal General Command which served Rhee as a political arm within the army, along with the Counter Intelligence Corps under Lt. Gen. Kim Ch'ang-yong. Paek became army chief of staff in July 1952, and was chairman of the joint chiefs of staff between February 1959 and May 1960. He retired from the army following the April uprising. Yang became a lieutenant general in July 1959.

45. An example is Gen. Ch'oe Yŏng-hi, director of the army personnel bureau; Ch'oe became army chief of staff following the April uprising and served as minister of defense in Park Chŏng-hi's government.

46. Song was army chief of staff between February 1959 and May 1960.

economic change." In this respect, the Korean military leaders resembled those of the "older nations" where, according to Janowitz, social origin and training reinforce their "conservative" thinking.[47] But they were far from having a strong puritanical outlook. The rather self-oriented nature of the top military leaders, and the availability of abundant funds and material, contributed greatly to pervasive corruption among the high officers of the Korean military.[48]

Finally, the top military officers shared an "anti-politics" outlook only in the sense that they spent much of their energy disassociating themselves from the politicians opposing Syngman Rhee. Rhee kept them under very close surveillance lest they establish contact with opposition politicians. In 1957 Gen. Yi Hyŏng-gŭn, the first to join the Korean Constabulary, was relieved from his post as army chief of staff after being admonished several times by Rhee that he should not see Vice-President Chang Myŏn.[49] The generals were certainly not "unpolitical" with regard to Syngman Rhee or the Liberal Party. In fact, "politics" had more to do with the successful career of most top military officers than any other factor.

A third characteristic of the Korean military was an absence of cohesion among the high-ranking officers and between the higher and lower officers. Factionalism grew between officers of different professional backgrounds and of different regional origins. Cliques and factions were formed among the "Tokyo group," "Manchurian officers," officers of non-Japanese Army origin, northerners, southerners, and so forth. President Rhee's method of playing major military groups off against each other and encouraging struggle among themselves further aggravated factional cleavages within the Korean armed forces.[50] Cohesion was absent not only between factions and groups, but also within them. Rivalries and alliances were made on personal and calculated grounds. No senior officer could, in fact, claim the absolute and strong loyalty of any number of his subordinate officers. This explains why, in May 1961, only about 250 officers and some 3,500 men out of a 500,000-man army could stage a successful coup d'état. The great effectiveness of the officers' "organizational weapon" testifies to the disorganization of the military as well as the society as a whole.[51]

47. Janowitz, *The Military in the Political Development of New Nations*, p. 64.

48. Between 1953 and 1960, an average of 35 percent of the national budget was spent on defense (Chŏn Pyŏng-wŏn, "Defense Budget," p. 101).

49. Kim Sŏk-yŏng (ed.), *Kyŏngmudaeŭi pimil* [Secrets of the Presidential Mansion: Despotism for Twelve Years], pp. 102–110.

50. *Henderson*, p. 345.

51. For their organizational efforts, see Korean Government, *Han'guk kunsa hyŏngmyŏngsa* [History of the Korean Military Revolution], I, 197–205.

The generals were also separated from the majors and colonels on ideological grounds. Among the junior officers whose military experience began after the Korean liberation, those most conspicuous in terms of ideological commitment were the pre-Korean War graduates of the Korean Military Academy.[52] Officers in this group generally distrusted their senior officers and often expressed the view that many of the generals had to be removed before the Korean military could stand on more effective and solid ground. It was not accidental that this issue initially united the original core group of nine colonels who later engineered the 1961 coup.[53] These colonels and majors, who represented an "indigenous" military background, had more "ideological" content in their outlook than their superiors. Among these men, it was possible to observe the "nationalistic, puritanical, collectivistic, and pragmatic" themes which Janowitz attributes to military officers of the new nations.[54]

From the above discussion of some of the salient characteristics of the Korean military, it is possible to draw a few conclusions concerning its role in politics. In the first place, it appears that the United States, through its high-ranking officers and "advisers" stationed throughout the Korean armed forces, could exercise a considerable amount of influence on the Korean military officers. It is debatable whether the United States could, on its own initiative, have influenced the Korean military to overthrow the government of Syngman Rhee. However, it was certainly in a position capable of inducing the top Korean military leaders to refrain from doing their best to rescue him in April 1960, when he had no other coercive mechanism left except the military. The United States was also capable of preventing any conscious efforts on the part of the top Korean military officers to take over power themselves at the time.

Secondly, it is erroneous to conceive of the Korean military as a monolithic entity susceptible to mobilization by one or a few top leaders for any "political" causes. The absence of military leaders who could appeal to a wide general public, as well as within the military itself, is attributable to the generally poor calibre of the senior officers and to Syngman Rhee's conscious effort to prevent the emergence of any military heroes, the subordination of the Korean armed forces to the United Nations Command, and pervasive factionalism among the

52. Before the Korean War, training in the Military Academy lasted for only one year, as compared with four years after the war. For an excellent study on the Korean military, see Se-jin Kim, *The Korean Military Government.*

53. *Han'guk kunsa hyŏngmyŏngsa,* pp. 196–197.

54. For example, "An Interview with Kim Chong-p'il," pp. 220–229; also *Han'guk kunsa hyŏngmyŏngsa,* pp. 204–205.

top officers. In the 1950s Korea did not have the equivalent of Turkey's Ismet Inonu or Indonesia's A. H. Nasution. In addition, the sheer size of the Korean armed forces made a coordinated effort for political purposes very difficult.

Lastly, few of the top-ranking officers were so committed to any specific and systematic values—except for opposing Communism—that they would risk their lives and fortunes in order to realize their ideological goals. From the earliest period, opportunism prevailed among the top military officers in the Korean Army, and they generally accepted the social status quo. Furthermore, few generals could avoid cooperating with the Liberal Party in election rigging within the armed forces, so most of them were not in a position to boast of their moral uprightness. Nor were any significant factions bonded together with a common and strongly felt outlook which would have enabled them to resort to determined action to achieve their political objectives.

Lt. Gen. Song Yo-ch'an, who was the key military man during the April uprising, belonged to a small group of "volunteers" who had joined the Japanese Army without particular educational background and thus had no significant factional ties. In a sense General Song represented the transition between the faction-ridden, opportunistic, and America-dependent senior officers and the relatively more self-assertive, ideological, and nationalistic junior officers. He was appointed army chief of staff on February 23, 1959, following a series of scandals concerning corruption and insubordination among high-level officers in the army. Song replaced Gen. Paek Sŏn-yŏp who, as a member of the "Manchurian officer" group, had been the first to become a four-star general in the Korean armed forces. General Song indeed made efforts to reduce corruption and factionalism within the Korean Army. He purged a number of high-ranking officers as part of the reduction of the army by some 100,000 men.[55] In this man we find a rare combination of strong anti-Communist and pro-American attitudes, military professionalism, a sense of self-righteousness, and lack of a personal group or faction of his own.[56]

This analysis of the Korean military and Gen. Song Yo-ch'an, whom Syngman Rhee appointed Commander of the Martial Law shortly before his resignation, provides a basis for analyzing the military's behavior during the Hŏ Chŏng period following Rhee's fall. The nonideological, nonpolitical, America-dependent, and incohesive nature of the top Korean military officers kept them from political action during

55. Song, "Memoirs," pp. 343–344; Henderson, p. 355.
56. Song, "Memoirs," *passim*.

a period when power appeared to be absent. The military was capable of preventing a radical change in the status quo, suppressing the rise of any significant leftist or other revolutionary groups, and assisting basically conservative politicians to eventually take over the government and maintain the existing political structure. Thus the military should be considered to have played a crucial role in post-Rhee Korean politics.

IV

THE INTERIM GOVERNMENT OF HŎ CHŎNG AND THE FALL OF THE LIBERAL PARTY

Syngman Rhee was forced to announce his resignation on April 26, 1960, in the face of a new wave of demonstrations touched off by the "professors' march," pressure from the United States, collapse of the police force, and, above all, lack of support from Gen. Song Yo-ch'an and the army. Hŏ Chŏng, whom Rhee had appointed foreign minister only two days before, became head of the interim government.

HŎ CHŎNG AND THE INTERIM GOVERNMENT

Hŏ Chŏng had enjoyed an unusually close relationship with Syngman Rhee. He was also on reasonably good terms with the old faction of the Democratic Party; he had attended Posŏng High School and was one of the original members of the anti-leftist KDP. Hŏ had worked with Rhee in the United States intermittently for more than ten years, between 1921 and 1932, in connection with such organizations as the Unified Koreans' Association (*Hanin Kongdonghoe*).[1] During this period, Syngman Rhee trusted Hŏ for his consistent support, and Hŏ respected Rhee's "intelligence, patriotism, and determination."[2]

1. Hŏ first met Rhee in 1912 at the age of sixteen at Hansŏng (Seoul) YMCA School, in which Rhee was a superintendent. (Hŏ Chŏng, "Memoirs," *Sasirŭi chŏnburŭl kisulhanda,* p. 195.)

2. When the Hŭngsa-dan members attempted to prevent Rhee from assuming leadership of the Korean residents in the United States during the early 1920s, Hŏ was instrumental in bringing Rhee from Hawaii back to the mainland. (Personal interview with Hŏ Chŏng by Chong-sik Lee, May 10, 1967.)

Hŏ joined Rhee's Cabinet in October 1948 as minister of transportation,[3] and was one of the most trusted among Rhee's associates.[4] Hŏ subsequently served as Rhee's minister of health and welfare and acting prime minister during the Korean War. Despite his close association with both Rhee and the KDP group, Hŏ refused to affiliate himself with either the DNP (later the Democratic Party) or the Liberal Party. Thus Hŏ left the government shortly before the 1952 "political crisis," criticizing the excesses of the newly-created Liberal Party. Hŏ stayed away from official positions, in spite of repeated offers by Rhee, except for the two years 1958 and 1959, when he served as mayor of Seoul (appointed by Rhee) and later as the chief Korean delegate to the Korea–Japan talks.[5]

Following the April uprising, Hŏ assumed the foreign ministership with a sense of sacrifice, upon Rhee's insistence. After Rhee's resignation it became clear that the power base of the Hŏ Chŏng government was highly precarious. Hŏ did not have the active support of any sector of the society. As far as the students and the masses were concerned, Hŏ represented a mere continuation of the Syngman Rhee government. He also lacked any organized political force behind him, such as the Democratic Party or the National Youth Corps.[6] Gen. Song Yo-ch'an considered Hŏ too meek and unprepared to cope with the revolutionary situation,[7] and no other military leader did or could provide a full weight of support for Hŏ's government.[8] One possible source of power for Hŏ was the governmental structure of the Rhee regime, including the bureaucratic apparatus and the police. In fact, Hŏ was

3. Hŏ did not enter Rhee's cabinet at the time of its formation in August, apparently because of his affiliation with the KDP. See his "Memoirs," p. 201.

4. Hŏ was present in a top-level military conference between Korean and American officials held during the early days of the Korean Republic. Brig. Gen. William L. Roberts, Chief American Advisor to the Korean Army, reportedly asked President Rhee why the transportation minister, who did not have direct military responsibility, was present. According to Ko Chŏng-hun, who was an interpreter in that conference, Rhee replied, "I trust him. I need him here as an observer." (Ko Chŏng-hun, *Pirok: kun* [The Military: An Unofficial Record], pp. 48–52.)

5. Concerning this appointment, Hŏ stated later: "I accepted this position only because of my 'personal relationship' with Dr. Rhee. During our days in Washington, D.C., I had sometimes shared the same apartment with him and we had often taken long walks to the park. I simply could not refuse him." (Hŏ, "Memoirs," pp. 202–203.)

6. Hŏ's relative independence from the existing political groups was of course an important reason for his acceptability to them as the head of the interim government.

7. Song Yo-ch'an, "Memoirs," in *Sasirŭi chŏnburŭl kisulhanda,* p. 347.

8. Hŏ's defense minister Yi Chong-ch'an agreed to accept the cabinet position only after a good deal of persuasion and entreating by Hŏ himself and other members of his cabinet. See *Kyŏnghyang Shinmun,* May 3, 1960, p. 1.

given the contradictory task of destroying those very political forces that represented the only basis for his power.

Hŏ was acceptable to both the Democratic Party and the Liberal Party because he did not belong to any political organization and seemed to lack any strong desire for political power. The Liberal Party did not anticipate any radical change in the sociopolitical structure, because of Hŏ's past close association with Rhee and his government. Hŏ's refusal to take over the government after Rhee's resignation would have meant serious political chaos, threatening the safety of most Liberal Party members. To them, Hŏ was preferable to any other person or group, including the military.

At the same time, the Democratic Party did not feel prepared to assume power, primarily because it lacked internal cohesion and unity. Chang Myŏn had already resigned from the vice-presidency, and there was no normal procedure by which the party could take over the government. Neither of the two factions in the party was willing to resort to extralegal means to achieve that end. Since the party seemed well assured of victory in the next election, they saw no reason to assume the burden of carrying out the "revolutionary task" which would earn many enemies and few friends.[9] Therefore, on April 26, leaders of both parties in the National Assembly urged Hŏ Chŏng to stay as head of the interim government, despite his reluctance to assume that thankless and difficult task.[10] Hŏ Chŏng sought the participation of the Democrats in his cabinet, but they wanted instead to exercise influence over his administration without actually joining it.[11]

The cabinet that Hŏ Chŏng finally formed consisted of men who showed little interest in the perpetuation of their political power; there was little incentive on their part to be responsive to either the general public or organized political forces.[12] Most of these men, prominent citizens who "individually had some proven, distinguished past performances in their respective spheres and commanded individually the confidence of the community," [13] had had little previous experience in political life and thus lacked a political organizational base. As Table 4 indicates, they also lacked radical views or revolu-

9. Personal interviews with Kim Yŏng-sŏn (new faction), November 2, 1968, and with Kim Yŏng-sam (old faction), July 30, 1969.

10. Kim To-yŏn, *Naŭi insaeng paeksŏ* [A White Paper of My Life], p. 351. Also Ho, "Memoirs," p. 218.

11. Hŏ "Memoirs," p. 219; also, Kim To-yŏn, *op. cit.*, pp. 351–352.

12. When Hŏ was criticized by the National Assembly for certain problems of his administration, he replied that he was always willing to step down. *Minŭiwŏn hoeŭirok* [House of Representatives Record], 35th session, no. 24, p. 20.

13. Hahn-Been Lee, *Korea: Time, Change, and Administration*, p. 113.

tionary inclinations. Indeed, their well-publicized slogan, "Revolution with nonrevolutionary methods," best reflected the character of the Hŏ Chŏng government.[14]

In a statement issued on May 3, the Hŏ Chŏng government made known to the public what its policy directions would be on a number of major issues. In internal affairs, main emphasis was placed on minimizing the effect of the uprising on daily routine and the basic structure of legal and social organizations. The task of maintaining law and order was closely linked with South Korea's anti-Communist struggle, and disruptive activities were warned against.[15] In foreign relations, the interim government made clear its intention to continue a strong anti-Communist line and maintain close ties with the United States. However, it opened the way to liberate Korea from the international isolation imposed by Syngman Rhee and his regime, especially regarding Korea's relations with Japan and the "neutralist countries" in Asia and the Middle East.

Government policy on these issues, of course, had a direct bearing on its ability to maintain its own power as well as on the relative power positions of various political groups in South Korea during and after the interim period. During its administration, the Hŏ Chŏng government had to deal with the military, the police, the business community, the students, the Liberal Party, the Democratic Party, and reformist or leftist politicians, and assume the role of balancing their conflicting interests and demands.

The Hŏ Chŏng government had to pursue a series of contradictory objectives during its existence. The government was expected to eliminate corruption and punish past election irregularities in the armed forces, but it could not offend high-ranking military officers or give them excuse or impetus to intervene in politics. It had to respond to demands from the students and the press for immediate and severe punishment of former Liberal officials and those who had accumulated illegal wealth during the Rhee regime, but such measures were to cripple the effectiveness of the police force and destroy the foundations of South Korea's economic structure. It was expected to help establish the basis of a two-party system in South Korean politics, but could not tolerate either the revival of the Liberal Party or the rise of the leftist parties. The Hŏ Chŏng government, overwhelmed with these conflicting tasks, handled them in the most cautious and moderate way. The interim government's unwillingness and inability to offend any sector was to have a serious effect upon the performance of its successor regime led by Chang Myŏn.

14. *Ibid.*, p. 113.
15. *Kyŏnghyang Shinmun,* May 3, 1960, evening ed., p. 1.

By his own admission, Hŏ Chŏng was most seriously concerned about the problem of how to handle the army.[16] He recognized the need for a purge, as many of the top-ranking military officers had cooperated with the Liberal regime in election irregularities and had been involved in numerous cases of scandal and corruption. Hŏ's first action regarding the armed forces was to appoint Gen. Yi Chong-ch'an, commandant of the Korean Defense College, as minister of national defense. Yi, a graduate of the Japanese Defense College in Tokyo and former army chief of staff during the 1951–1952 period, had lost Syngman Rhee's favor because of his opposition to Rhee's use of the army in the 1952 political crisis in Pusan. Therefore he was one of the few top military officers not closely identified with the Rhee regime, and he was respected by other military officers of all ranks.[17]

As defense minister, Yi Chong-ch'an regarded keeping the army out of politics as his primary task. In his first press conference following the appointment, Yi stressed most of all the need for the military to maintain political neutrality. On July 17, toward the end of the Hŏ Chŏng administration, chiefs of the various branches of the armed forces were thus asked to read and sign in front of the whole cabinet a pledge which declared: "As a member of the chiefs of staff of the Korean armed forces, I solemnly pledge that I shall maintain strict neutrality in politics and shall pay undivided attention to the sacred task of defending our country from our enemies." [18]

Hŏ was worried about a hostile reaction from the military to any drastic measure to reform it or purge its members. Therefore he chose to pursue an extremely moderate policy toward past mistakes of the top military officers. His view that a premature attempt to purge the military officers would not only provoke them but also seriously compromise the combat capability of the Korean armed forces was shared by both the American ambassador and the United States Army commander in Korea. Hŏ conferred with these American officials often and regularly during his three-month period as head of the interim government.[19] Gen. Carter B. Magruder, the U.S. Eighth Army commander, told Hŏ that a reorganization of the Korean Army had to be postponed until the existing instability and chaos were over.[20]

Hŏ Chŏng was more concerned about the possibility of political action by top-ranking military officers than by those in the lower ranks. He therefore conferred individually with a dozen top military officers

16. Hŏ, "Memoirs," p. 214.

17. Kim Sŏng-chong, "Gen. Yi Chong-ch'an's Refusal to Dispatch Troops to Pusan."

18. *Kyŏnghyang Shinmun,* July 17, 1960, p. 1.

19. Hŏ, "Memoirs," pp. 214–216.

20. *Ibid.,* p. 215.

and tried to persuade them to withdraw from the military voluntarily, promising that they would be given diplomatic positions abroad, commensurate with their ranks and achievements in the armed forces, after their discharge.[21] This approach met with some success, and a number of generals, including Chairman of the Joint Chiefs of Staff Gen. Paek Sŏn-yŏp and Commander of the First Korean Army Lt. Gen. Yu Chae-hŭng, resigned from the army. Paek Sŏn-yŏp and Yu Chae-hŭng were subsequently appointed ambassadors to the Republic of China and Thailand, respectively. Gen. Chŏng Il-kwŏn, who also enjoyed much prestige in the army, was already serving as ambassador to the United States. Lt. Gen. Song Yo-ch'an resigned from the army on May 20, stating that his duty as martial law commander had been fulfilled and that he felt an obligation to leave, since he had originally been appointed to the position by the ousted president.[22] Song temporarily ceased to be an important factor in Korean politics, as he immediately left for the United States for "study" after his resignation. General Magruder had arranged for General Song's admission to George Washington University as a special student, and Song accepted the arrangement.

There is no doubt that Hŏ Chŏng's moderate and indirect approach in dealing with the top military officers contributed considerably to their relatively docile attitude toward their civilian superiors. It is also true, however, that those qualities discussed in the preceding chapter—their America-dependent, non-ideological, opportunistic, and factional characteristics—were also responsible for their failure to participate directly in South Korean politics during the interim period.

Although Hŏ was primarily worried about the political role of the top military men, a considerable amount of unrest arose in the army from persistent and strong demands made by the lower-ranking officers (mostly majors and colonels) for radical reform and clean-up of the armed forces by removing the "corrupt and incapable" officers at the top.[23] These lower-ranking officers, many of them early graduates of the Korean Military Academy,[24] were dissatisfied with the lukewarm and ineffectual manner in which the Hŏ Chŏng government tried to reform the armed forces;[25] they urged Minister of National Defense Yi Chong-ch'an and Army Chief of Staff Lt. Gen. Ch'oi Yŏng-hi, who

21. *Ibid.*

22. Song, who was apparently disappointed by Hŏ's designation of Yi Chong-ch'an as defense minister, later intimated that his resignation was prompted by the suspicious attitude of the Hŏ Chŏng government (*Ibid.*, p. 214.).

23. See Chapter Two of this book. Also, *Han'guk kunsa hyŏngmyŏngsa,* p. 198.

24. Most of these officers participated in the military coup d'état of May 1961.

25. Hŏ, "Memoirs," p. 214.

had succeeded General Song on May 23, 1960, to take much more positive steps toward that end.[26] Defense Minister Yi proved to be relatively more receptive to the views of the lower-ranking officers than was Hŏ Chŏng himself. Yi stated repeatedly that no one could deny that illegal activities had taken place in the army in connection with the March 15 elections and that many corrupt officers in the armed forces should be severely punished, without exception.[27] However, Yi was caught between the conflicting demands of the reformist officers and the prime minister, who wanted to proceed slowly and cautiously. Frustrated in his effort to carry out radical reform of the army, Yi expressed his intention to resign from his cabinet post in June.[28] Although he was persuaded to remain, and the reformist officers were asked "to stay calm until the problems could be removed in a gradual and unprovocative manner," [29] the wave of dissatisfaction among these officers did not disappear, and remained as a potent and explosive issue throughout the Hŏ Chŏng and Chang Myŏn periods.

Another important area of political action for the Hŏ Chŏng government concerned punishment of the chief conspirators in the election irregularities, and members of the police who were responsible for illegal and oppressive acts under Rhee. In handling this matter, the basic position of the interim government was that it would operate only by means available within existing legal boundaries. Therefore the government brought the former leaders of the Rhee government and the Liberal Party to public trial in accordance with "existing laws" and attempted to "rectify" the police department through its personnel policy.

Those arrested during the Hŏ Chŏng administration included nine members of the Syngman Rhee cabinet and fifteen leading members of the Liberal Party, who were charged with having conspired to perform illegal activities in the presidential and vice-presidential elections of March 15; the presidents of various banks, for illegally providing large sums for election funds to the Liberal Party; Rhee's chief bodyguard Kwak Yŏng-ju and a number of other top-ranking police officers implicated in the shooting of the demonstrators during the April uprising; a number of low-ranking police officers involved in the torture and atrocious treatment of the demonstrating students prior to April 19; former mayor of Seoul Im Hŭng-sun and former minister of internal affairs Yi Kŭn-jik, in connection with the 1956 attempt to assas-

26. *Ibid.*
27. *Kyŏnghyang Shinmun,* May 9, 1960, p. 3; May 14, 1960, p. 1.
28. *Ibid.,* June 4, 1960, p. 1.
29. Hŏ, "Memoirs," p. 215.

sinate Vice-President-elect Chang Myŏn; and the ringleaders of the political gangsters who terrorized the business, cultural, and political communities in collusion with the Liberal regime.[30]

The trials of these individuals opened on July 5, less than one month before the National Assembly elections scheduled for July 29. In the trials, the Hŏ Chŏng government had no choice but to rely very heavily upon the existing officials of the Justice Department and the Prosecution Office, most of whom themselves had been forced to serve the political interests of the Rhee regime. Notwithstanding the fact that they had also operated as an effective political arm of the Liberal administration, they were given the task of prosecuting their colleagues in other branches of the government as if they had been outside of the Rhee system. Since the Hŏ Chŏng government was determined not to destroy South Korea's basic political, ideological, and legal structure, such a contradiction was inevitable. Thus the trials could not be carried out or terminated in "revolutionary" fashion, and consequently failed to give satisfaction to the students and masses, who urged more severe punishment of the defendants than was plausible within the given legal boundaries. The trials were carried over to the next government, led by Chang Myŏn, presenting a cause for considerable agony to his administration.[31]

Conspicuously absent among those being prosecuted during the interim period were those people who had illegally accumulated wealth in collusion with the power-holders in the government and the Liberal Party. Despite repeated proclamations concerning its intention to punish those with illegal wealth,[32] the government merely asked a few selected wealthy individuals to voluntarily report their past improprieties and pay their debts to society. During the month of July, the government released a list of 18 individuals and 66 business activities during the Rhee regime and announced its intention to investigate them. Because of the complex nature of the problem itself, action could not be taken against them until long after the inauguration of the Chang Myŏn government.

There were of course other reasons for the government's slowness to punish those with illegal wealth. Illegal business activities were rooted in all aspects of the Rhee government, and a complete investigation would have been impossible from a practical point of view. Even had it been possible, such an action would have been devastating for the

30. *Haptong yŏn'gam,* 1961, pp. 155–158.

31. This point will be discussed in further detail later, especially in Chapter Eight.

32. For example, *Kyŏnghyang Shinmun,* May 13, 1960, p. 1; July 5, 1960, p. 2; July 20, 1960, p. 1.

preservation of the very fabric of the South Korean government as well as the economic structure itself. Certainly the Hŏ Chŏng government was not prepared or willing to take that risk.

Most of those who illegally or improperly amassed wealth under the Rhee regime did so through one or more of the following means:

Illegal or improper purchase of government property which had belonged to the Japanese government and its citizens prior to August 1945 (estimated at about 80 percent of the wealth in Korea at the time)

Receiving bank loans at interest rates far below the inflationary rate

Purchase of government dollars obtained from foreign aid or other sources at an official rate far below the current market rate

Illegal or improper acquisition of concessions and privileges, or engaging in illegal monopoly or smuggling activities

Acceptance of graft and bribes

Tax evasion or illegal or improper tax exemption or reduction.[33]

It is evident that many of these activities required the acquiescence, cooperation, or active participation of leaders and officials of the government. A thorough treatment of the matter by the Hŏ Chŏng government would have affected a very high percentage of government officials of all ranks.

In the area of "de-politicizing" and "democratizing" the national police, the Hŏ Chŏng government again applied its basic policy of making only necessary and possible changes while maintaining its existing basic structure. The interim government thus attempted to achieve its objectives regarding the national police through legislation and personnel policy. While the National Assembly was considering a "police neutralization law," it set out to dismiss or relegate to less desirable positions top police officers responsible for election irregularities and police terror. However, given the basically conservative and moderate approach of the Hŏ Chŏng government, it achieved little success in satisfying the general public or changing the authoritarian nature of the police department.

The Hŏ Chŏng government aroused a great deal of hostile reaction from the public and the Democratic Party in early May, when it announced the names of those officers newly appointed to top positions in the national police headquarters and provincial police departments.

33. "Problems of Handling the Illegal Wealth."

The newspapers and anti-Rhee politicians argued that many of these police officers had been ardent servants of the Rhee regime. Some of them had records of oppressing opposition politicians and giving orders to shoot the demonstrating students. Protest against the appointments were heard even within the police department itself.[34] In an unprecedented move, the minister of internal affairs rescinded all the new appointments only twenty hours after the initial announcement. Two days later, on May 6, the government announced another series of new appointments. Of the eighteen top positions newly filled, only one went to an individual from outside the police department. This serves to illustrate the difficulties facing the Hŏ Chŏng government in its attempt to carry out "revolution with nonrevolutionary methods."

The interim government subsequently tried to "democratize" the police and "rectify its past misbehavior" by shifting and exchanging its personnel between and within various provincial departments. Extensive personnel change was clearly not possible, because of the short time available to the interim government. To perform all-out surgery on the police department throughout the nation would have seriously endangered the existing conservative political structure. The only possible alternative—filling vacant key police positions with military officers—was unacceptable to the Hŏ Chŏng government; it would have been against Hŏ's temperament and belief in the separation of military and civilian administrations. Later in this study, we will discuss the unsuccessful attempt of the Chang Myŏn government to undertake major police reform.[35]

In the above discussion, we have seen that the Hŏ Chŏng government did not succeed in achieving "revolutionary goals" during its brief period of administration. At the same time, it steadfastly maintained its position of fulfilling these tasks through "nonrevolutionary" means. As a result it left for its successor regime the difficult task of completing the "revolution" with limited freedom of action, since it was forced to operate within the context of nonrevolutionary methods set forth by the Hŏ Chŏng government. We will discuss this point in detail in later chapters.

One political development of significance in which the Hŏ Chŏng government played an important part was the disintegration of the

34. *Kyŏnghyang Shinmun,* May 4, 1960, evening ed., p. 1.

35. According to *Haptong yŏngam,* a total of 16,486, or 80 percent of the total police force, were given new posts by the end of November 1960. During the same period 4,520 officers were removed from the police force (p. 152). Of course most of these personnel changes were made by the Chang Myŏn government.

Liberal Party as a political group. The demise of the once-powerful Liberal Party will be analyzed in the remainder of this chapter.

THE COLLAPSE OF THE LIBERAL PARTY

With the resignation of Syngman Rhee and the demoralization of the police force, the Liberal Party quickly disintegrated after the April uprising. It seems, however, that the party did have the support of many actual social leaders of many localities so that, as a political force, it did not disappear completely. In fact, the revival of this group was started slowly under the Chang Myŏn regime, and many actually joined the government after the fall of the Second Republic. The pro-Rhee elements, representing the "administrative" and "authoritarian" direction of the Korean polity, were removed only temporarily from the political scene. Furthermore, it seems that even the institutional collapse of the party was not inevitable under the governments of Hŏ Chŏng or Chang Myŏn. In fact, had there been firm determination by its leadership and a reasonable degree of cohesion within it, the Liberal Party could have played the role of a major opposition party in the Second Republic. In this section, therefore, we will discuss the reasons and significance of the Liberal Party's disintegration during the interim period.

An interesting phenomenon during this period was a recurrent collusion between the Liberal Party and the old faction of the Democratic Party in their respective efforts to make the best of the existing chaotic situation. With remarkable speed and effectiveness, they succeeded in persuading the political elite and the general public that the most important task of the "revolution" was to adopt a new constitution with a cabinet system of government; that such a constitutional revision had to be passed by the existing National Assembly, and it therefore had to remain as the only legitimate legislative body of the nation until that task was achieved; and that any attempt to prevent such a constitutional revision or any demand for the dissolution of the National Assembly would be against the goals of the revolution. These were by no means unanimously accepted views during the first days of the interim period.

Many politicians and newspapers initially demanded the immediate dissolution of the National Assembly and the election of a new one to consider constitutional revision. Kwak Sang-hun, a member of the Democratic Party's supreme council, stated in late April that the only responsible thing for members of the National Assembly to do was to resign from it, so that new elections could be held. This was in recognition of the fact that the existing National Assembly was still dominated by Liberal Party members, many of whom had been elected in 1958 under questionable circumstances. Such a National Assembly, it was argued, did not have the moral justification to pass a constitutional amendment.[36] Even *Tong-a Ilbo,* a paper that consistently supported the position of the Democratic old faction, repeatedly stated in its editorials that the first order of the day was to dissolve the National Assembly and elect a new one.

The newly revived *Kyŏnghyang Shinmun,* a pro-new faction newspaper, agreed that the existing National Assembly did not have the right to amend the constitution. It claimed that the most acceptable solution for the nation would be first to hold new elections for president and vice-president, under the existing constitutional system.[37] This doubtless reflected the view of those members who were convinced that the presidency could be easily won by the new faction.[38]

However, the Liberal Party was intent upon using the issue of constitutional revision to protect the interests of its members. By reiterating that a constitutional amendment was the only way for Liberal Pary members to "redeem their unclean past," they tried to identify the constitutional amendment with the "revolutionary goal" itself.[39] At the same time, Liberal Party members saw that it was to their advantage to prolong passage of the constitutional amendment as long as possible. Many Liberal Party members felt particularly uneasy about the fact that the Democratic leadership was planning to pass the amendment bill by June 14, one day before the end of the prescription period concerning the crimes of the March election.[40]

The old faction of the Democratic Party also strongly preferred to change the constitution before elections of any kind could be held. A cabinet system of government was not only its most important trademark since the early days of the First Republic, it was also the only way to check the strong possibility that the new faction would monopolize political power in the future.

36. *Minŭiwŏn hoeŭirok,* 35th session, no. 8, pp. 4–5.
37. *Kyŏnghyang Shinmun,* April 27, 1960, p. 1.
38. *Minŭiwŏn hoeŭirok,* 35th session, no. 9, p. 1.
39. In a debate concerning the arrest of six Liberal members in connection with their "anti-state activities," a Liberal Party member argued that, since the existing National Assembly had been given the task of amending the constitution, there was no reason to approve their arrest. He also stated that those six members, as well as all others, should be respected as legitimate National Assembly members as long as its existence was maintained. (*Minŭiwŏn hoeŭirok,* 35th session, no. 20, pp. 6–8.) This statement suggests the Liberals' intention to use the constitutional amendment as a pretext for their protection.
40. *Minŭiwŏn hoeŭirok,* 35th session, no. 34, pp. 18–26.

By the end of April, the retention of the National Assembly became an agreed-upon fact by members of both parties, although new-faction Democrats accepted the *fait accompli* reluctantly. *Kyŏnghyang Shinmun,* in its April 29th issue, completely reversed its earlier position, and now supported the decision to achieve the Constitutional amendment by the existing National Assembly.[41] The *Tong-a Ilbo* did likewise by early May. Concerning this issue, Kim Yŏng-sŏn, a leading member of the Democratic new faction, wrote in the June issue of the influential *Sasanggye Monthly:* "Regardless of its validity, it has become the firm belief of the people that Korea has to have a cabinet system of government. Therefore the Democratic Party is determined to adopt such a system, despite the possibility of political uncertainty and instability." [42] Once the Democratic Party became committed to a constitutional amendment by the existing legislature, the Liberal Party had considerable bargaining power in the National Assembly. After all, it still held a majority in the Assembly.

The Liberal Party of the post-Rhee period was a more or less "reformed" one whose leadership had been transferred to its relatively "moderate" members in the aftermath of the April uprising. This moderate group was led by Yi Chae-hak, vice-speaker of the National Assembly, who had maintained a working relationship with the opposition party even during the Rhee period. Yi was one of the organizers of the Parliamentary Liberal Party in 1952, but joined Rhee's Liberal Party in 1954 instead of participating in the organization of the Democratic Party as did many PLP members. As vice-chairman of the central committee and a potential political rival of Yi Ki-bung, Yi Chae-hak often defended the views of the dissidents within the Liberal Party. Thus he successfully dissociated himself from the more unpopular activities of his "hard-line" colleagues.

In the 1956 election, Yi chae-hak was known to have been instrumental in preventing large-scale fraud in the ballot counting in the city of Taegu, thereby preventing the illegal election of Yi Ki-bung in the vice-presidential race.[43] According to Yi Chae-hak himself, he held a high respect for Cho Pyŏng-ok, leader of the Democratic Party, and helped him in various indirect ways, such as providing funds for his political and personal use.[44] Yi was also responsible for the unsuccessful proposal of the Liberal Party to amend the constitution to a cabinet system of government in collaboration with the old faction

41. *Kyŏnghyang Shinmun,* April 29, 1960, p. 1.
42. Kim Yŏng-sŏn, "Essential Elements of the Democratic Party Platform."
43. Yi Chae-hak, "Memoirs," in *Sasirŭi chŏnburŭl kisulhanda,* p. 149.
44. "Yi Chae-hak," in *Chŏnggye yahwa,* pp. 321, 331; also Yi Chae-hak, "Memoirs," pp. 190–191.

of the Democratic Party.[45] His friendliness toward the opposition party was at the same time cause for his unsatisfactory relationship with Yi Ki-bung, who suspected that Yi Chae-hak intended to take over the leadership of the party, and ultimately the government, by allying himself with the opposition.

Yi Chae-hak also played a bridging role between Yi Ki-bung's "mainstream" faction and the opposing faction, led by the Liberal dissidents who had rebelled against Yi Ki-bung after his defeat in the 1956 election. Members of the "anti-mainstream faction" protested again in 1960 against the excesses of the Liberal regime in the March election. The rebellion was led by the provincial chairmen, who felt that they had simply been ignored and bypassed by the party leadership, which let the ministry of internal affairs "elect" Syngman Rhee and Yi Ki-bung almost single-handedly. In a meeting held in Seoul on March 28, those "anti-mainstream" members declared that since most of the voters had personally experienced the police interference in the election process, there was no way to deny election irregularities; that with police meddling in the March election, the Liberal Party lost whatever popularity it had had among the voters; and that deterioration of world opinion concerning Korean democracy would have grave consequences for Korea, which depended upon foreign assistance for its defense and economic survival.[46] They demanded the resignation of the members of the party steering committee, consisting mostly of the "hard-liners" and members of the Rhee cabinet who had either acquiesced or actively participated in the election rigging. This protest by some Liberals was intended to place the blame for the obviously unpopular actions of the Rhee regime on the police and the Rhee administration. At the same time, with Yi Ki-bung now elevated to the vice-presidency, the "rebels" wished to capture the speakership of the National Assembly which would shortly become vacant.

Yi Chae-hak was not directly involved in this protest, but he expressed his support of the dissidents. On March 23, Yi Chae-hak declared publicly that the administration and the party steering committee should answer for the unjustly managed elections.[47] When the party leadership decided to "punish" those members who openly criticized the handling of the March elections, Yi even stated that he would leave the party if other members were to be expelled. Although some personality conflict was certainly involved in this crisis, it also represented a confrontation between those who recognized the importance of a strong party for the maintenance of the Liberal regime and those

45. Yi Chae-hak, "Memoirs," *op. cit.*, pp. 157–158.
46. *Tong-a Ilbo*, March 28, 1960, p. 1. 47. *Ibid.*, March 24, 1964, p. 1.

who looked to Syngman Rhee and his administration as the ultimate and only resort to the maintenance of power. The authoritarian and absolute nature of Rhee's leadership in the Liberal Party was demonstrated again when the protest "movement" met a sudden death through his announcement that disagreement within the Party had to cease at once.[48]

The dissidents now became the core of the Liberal Party which remained active after the fall of the Liberal regime. Following Rhee's resignation, Yi Chae-hak, who was one of the two vice-speakers, called the National Assembly into session and helped it pass a resolution which stated that it would not be dissolved until the constitution could be amended as a "last service" to the people and the nation.[49]

Despite the appearance of total subjugation to the dictates of the Democrats, the Liberal Party maintained a considerable amount of leverage in the National Assembly in its effort to minimize and harness the impact of the "revolution." The first sign of the Liberal Party's recalcitrance was given at the time of the election of a new National Assembly speaker to succeed Yi Ki-bung.[50] Although the Liberal Party at no time expressed desire to elect a Democrat, its leadership naturally preferred an old-faction Democrat, and many privately supported Yun Po-sŏn, a member of the Democratic Party's supreme committee, for the speakership.[51] However, when the Democratic Party nominated Kwak Sang-hun, a former vice-speaker and one known as an independent figure in the factional struggle within the party, Liberals expressed dissatisfaction and suggested that they could support Kwak only if Yi Chae-hak was to be kept in the position of vice-speaker.[52]

Although it is impossible to confirm whether or not a concrete deal was made between Kwak's supporters and the Liberals, later developments indicate the strong possibility of such an understanding. On May 2, Kwak was elected speaker with 137 votes, over Kim To-yŏn and Yun Po-sŏn who received respectively 0 and 7 votes.[53] A few minutes later Kwak, now presiding officer of the National Assembly, declared

48. *Ibid.*, April 1, 1960, p. 1.

49. Yi Chae-hak, "Memoirs," p. 170.

50. Yi Ki-bung committed suicide with his family on April 29, making it unnecessary to take a vote on his seat. The resignations of other members were all approved by the National Assembly by overwhelming majority votes. The dissenting votes ranged between 15 and 25, presumably cast by loyal Liberal Party members. See *Minŭiwŏn hoeŭirok,* 35th session, no. 13, pp. 7–20. One of the two Liberal vice-speakers, Im Ch'ŏl-ho, tendered his resignation on April 27, and it was accepted by the National Assembly by a vote of 149 to 25. (*Ibid.*, 35th session, no. 10, p. 5.)

51. *Kyŏnghyang Shinmun,* May 1, 1960, p. 1.

52. *Tong-a Ilbo,* May 1, 1960, p. 1.

53. *Minŭiwŏn hoeŭirok,* 35th session, no. 12, p. 1.

the Assembly's "unanimous" decision to reject Yi Chae-hak's resignation as vice-speaker, which had been submitted earlier. Kwak's declaration of "unanimity" ignored some dissenting voices and was sharply criticized later by independent members who argued that Kwak's action constituted an intolerable collusion between the two parties.[54] Kwak continued to keep a close relationship with the Liberal vice-speaker until Yi Chae-hak's arrest on May 26 by the interim government.[55]

The Liberals, using their majority in the National Assembly, were able to block moves of more militant members of the Democratic Party to penalize officials who had actively cooperated with the Rhee regime. On May 9, the National Assembly defeated by a vote of 62 to 73 a proposal to dismiss a number of prosecutors who had accused many of Rhee's political opponents as Communists.[56] A week later Liberal members threatened to withdraw from the National Assembly before passage of the constitutional amendment, unless the government and the Democratic Party would stop taking "retaliatory actions" against pro-Liberal Party officials in the localities and stop increasing the number of individuals to be punished for their activities during the Rhee administration. Although this threat received wide criticism from the public and Democratic members, the interim government complied with the demand of the Liberal Party, declaring that further retaliatory actions on minor matters would not be tolerated.[57]

The Liberals in the National Assembly chose as their new leader Cho Kyŏng-gyu, who had been alienated from the "mainstream" leadership of the Liberal Party under Yi Ki-bung and had not participated actively in key decisions of the party. As floor leader of the majority party within the Assembly (about 120 members), he came to occupy a critical position in the political situation during this period. But unfortunately for the Liberal Party, his power was to be severely circumscribed by the internal party split.

As already noted, the most important and immediate goal of the Liberals in the National Assembly was to use their majority and their status to protect former members and supporters of the Liberal Party. As this objective appeared to be reasonably well accomplished, however, they began to turn their attention to their future political opportunities under the new constitution. On this latter goal, Cho Kyŏng-

54. *Ibid.*, 35th session, no. 13, May 3, 1960, pp. 1–5.
55. Even after Yi's arrest, Kwak tried to assist Yi to get a release. (Yi, "Memoirs," p. 171.)
56. *Minŭiwŏn hoeŭirok*, 35th session, no. 15, p. 10.
57. *Kyŏnghyang Shinmun*, May 13–May 15, 1960.

gyu and his supporters of the so-called "revival faction" reasoned that if the Liberal Party could be saved from total collapse, it could have a great deal of political influence in future parliamentary politics. This seemed especially plausible in view of the serious factional strife within the Democratic Party and the Liberal Party's relatively cordial relationship with the old faction. The Party leadership was confident that the Liberal Party could elect "at least 40 to 50 members to the National Assembly in the forthcoming legislative elections." [58]

Encouragement for maintaining the basic structure of the Liberal Party also came from the United States embassy in Seoul, which hoped that the Liberal Party could function as an alternative to the Democratic Party in a future two-party system. Apparently the American Embassy anticipated that Chang Myŏn's new faction would assume power in the Second Republic, and that the Democratic old faction—Liberal alliance could serve as a loyal opposition to the Chang government.[59]

However, those opposed to Cho, known as the "reform Liberals," feared that their continuous affiliation with the discredited Liberal Party would jeopardize their fortune in future elections. These Liberals, who had most loudly criticized their party before the April uprising, argued that the best and only chance of electing many individual members of the Liberal Party was to dissolve the party immediately. These two groups, known respectively as the "revival faction" and the "reform faction," opposed each other on the issue of holding a party convention. Cho Kyŏng-gyu and his supporters in the "revival faction" felt that such a convention would provide them with an opportunity to test the remaining strength of the Liberal Party, and possibly to affirm their continuing solidarity. On the other hand, the "reform faction" Liberals argued against such a convention on the ground that it would again focus national attention on the Liberal Party and make it an easy target of hostility and criticism. Reform Liberals were joined in their opposition to a party convention by still another group of Liberals who kept personal loyalty to Vice-Speaker Yi Chae-hak. They agreed with the reform Liberals that such a convention would be impractical and meaningless at the time.

The lines that separated the different groups in the Liberal Party were neither strict nor clear-cut, but in the absence of a unifying force such as a strong leader or benefits from government power, the internal division of the Liberal Party could no longer be controlled.[60] Its dis-

58. Yi Chae-hak, "Memoirs," p. 172.
59. *Ibid.*, p. 168.
60. *Kyŏnghyang Shinmun*, June 2, 1960, p. 1.

unity was most clearly shown when the National Assembly was requested to approve Yi Chae-hak's arrest. On May 23, the Hŏ Chŏng government requested National Assembly approval of its plan to place six more Liberal assemblymen (eight had been arrested earlier), including Vice-Speaker Yi Chae-hak, under arrest, claiming that such an arrest was necessary for proper investigation of the March election irregularities. This request was received with a mixed reaction in the National Assembly.

As mentioned above, Yi had maintained a much more cordial relationship with the old faction of the Democratic Party than with the new faction. In fact, members of the new faction feared that a coalition between Yi's forces and the old faction, following the parliamentary election, might give the old faction a majority in the National Assembly. For this reason, the new faction was interested in complete destruction of the Liberal Party and the elimination of Yi Chae-hak from the political scene. It is not clear to what extent they were responsible for the interim government's decision to arrest Yi, but Yi himself did not doubt that his arrest was in fact prompted by the new-faction Democrats.[61] On the other hand, old-faction members expressed the hope that Yi Chae-hak could be exempted from arrest.[62]

Interestingly, the Liberal Party itself failed to present a unified front in defense of their leading member. The revival faction, led by Cho Kyŏng-gyu, expressed the view that the Liberal Party should refrain from taking an official position and leave it to individual members to decide. The reform faction argued instead for dissolution of the party on this occasion, so that they could act free of their bond with the Liberal Party. It was clear that Cho was willing to sacrifice the six Liberal members, including Yi Chae-hak, for the sake of the remaining members of the party. Supporters of the vice-speaker, like old-faction members of the Democratic Party, argued the necessity of selective approval—that is, to vote on the six members individually.

In the absence of a dependable political force to defend him, Yi together with five other Liberals "voluntarily" withdrew from the National Assembly and subjected himself to eventual arrest.[63] This case served to demonstrate the *potential* power of the Liberal Party had it been more united. But such was not the case. On June 1, eleven days before the scheduled provisional party convention, 105 of the 138 Liberal members of the National Assembly withdrew from the party, stating that with actual destruction of the leadership and the drasti-

61. Yi Chae-hak, "Memoirs," p. 172.
62. *Kyŏnghyang Shinmun*, May 24, 1960, p. 1.
63. *Minŭiwŏn hoeŭirok*, 35th session, no. 22, p. 11.

cally changed political environment, the existence of the Liberal Party as a parliamentary group was meaningless.[64] This action marked the actual disintegration of the party, and it was never again able to "revive" its organizational structure.

The Liberals' withdrawal from their party took place only three days after Syngman Rhee's secret departure for Hawaii. Many Liberal Party members' indecisiveness during the month of May concerning their affiliation with the party, and the timing of their final withdrawal, indicated that there had been some hope that Rhee—or some other figure such as Yi Pŏm-sŏk, with Rhee's backing—might be able to recapture power and make it profitable for the Liberals to remain in the party. Syngman Rhee's departure decisively put an end to their hope for the revival of a Liberal regime and the party.

The Liberal Party "convention" which was held on June 12 thus served in effect as a final rite for the demise of the party. It was attended by a total of 657 delegates, or about half of the 1,215 delegates invited, with all the "reform Liberals" and supporters of Yi Chae-hak boycotting it. In contrast to previous party conventions, there were no flowers or congratulatory addresses. The meeting was held in the party's political training center, where the delegates sat on the floor instead of chairs. In the convention, delegates adopted the principle of collective leadership for the party.

The Liberal Party nominated a total of 11 candidates for councillors' seats and 54 for the National Assembly, far fewer than originally expected by the party leadership, which had hoped to nominate at least 150 candidates for both houses of the National Assembly. Many potential candidates with some chance of winning the election preferred not to be identified with the Liberal Party, and the party leadership voluntarily withdrew its candidates from some districts in which leaders of the Democratic Party were running, as a gesture of deference to the future rulers.

The Liberal Party as a political group finally lost its significance after the July election, as it captured only 2 out of 233 seats in the House of Representatives and 4 in the 58-member House of Councillors.[65] This final and easy collapse of the Liberal Party as an institution reflected the spurious and superficial nature of its past strength and unity. Most of the Liberals had joined the party because of its attraction as a government party, and thus did not find it difficult to abandon it when it no longer had government power behind it. In the localities, according to newspaper reports, those who had been working

64. *Kyŏnghyang Shinmun,* June 2, 1960, p. 11.
65. Korean Government, *Taehanmin'guk sŏn'gŏsa,* pp. 436, 444, 448.

for the Liberal Party now flocked to the Democratic Party, which appeared certain to become the government party.

The Liberals failed to demonstrate either cohesion or purpose in their behavior following the collapse of the Rhee government. They were prepared to join any other political force which might provide them with protection and power. Furthermore, without the intervention of the government through police power, all but a few of the officially nominated Liberals and former Liberals who ran under different party names were defeated in the July election.

Although the complete collapse of the Liberal Party has often been attributed to the Hŏ Chŏng government for its decision to arrest Yi Chae-hak and the timing of the "revolutionary trials" that opened a few weeks before the elections, the Liberal Party collapsed due to its internal weaknesses as much as external pressures. There existed no ideological bond that would have held it together. Party organization, both in the center and in the localities, could be maintained only through the lure of power and assistance of the police. The London *Economist* observed rather perceptively at the time of the April uprising that no leader of the party exhibited Cromwellian qualities of self-righteousness, chivalrous spirit, or personal energy.[66] Thus, despite favorable external political conditions—the split within the Democratic Party, the nonrevolutionary nature of the Hŏ Chŏng government, the United States embassy's hope of developing the Liberal Party into a strong opposition, and the generally conservative nature of the political elite, all of which gave the Liberal Party considerable room to maneuver—the Liberal Party was unable to capitalize on these conditions, and quickly sank into oblivion.

One significant aspect about most politicians of the period was that "private" considerations weighed far more heavily than "public" ones in their political activities. The interest of a political party received higher priority than that of the political system as a whole. The interest of a faction was more important to its members than that of the party of which the faction was a part; similarly, factional interest was often sacrificed for the sake of simple personal ties or individual interests.

The Liberal Party therefore found it relatively easy to make its members accept its scheme of election rigging (although some did so reluctantly) by the implicit premise that the interest of the Liberal Party would be served through such means. Similarly, it was Hŏ Chŏng's personal loyalty to Syngman Rhee that made him accept the task of heading the interim government, rather than his sense of public

66. *The Economist*, April 20, 1960, p. 26.

duty or his desire to realize his policy objectives through that position. It is not surprising, therefore, to find an implicit collusion between the old faction of the Democratic Party and the Liberal Party during the interim period—or, for that matter, the internal division of the Liberal Party itself, which contributed decisively to its disintegration.

One factor which contributed to the supremacy of personal and private considerations in South Korean politics was the conservative monopoly of the political scene and the resultant ideological consensus among the contending politicians. The orthodoxy of uncompromising anti-Communism was never questioned, leaving no ideological alternatives. The presence of large armed forces constituted a major block to successful disruption of the existing social and political order by ideological dissenters such as the leftists. The only serious ideological difference among the conservative politicians related to the question of distribution of political power. However, as the group supporting an autocratic framework (the Liberals) met a temporary setback on their question, there now came to be a prevailing consensus in favor of a pluralistic, limited system of government.

A second factor that can be held responsible for the private nature of South Korean politics was the tradition of intense factionalism which is often attributed to the high degree of centralization, social homogeneity, and ideological consensus in dynastic Korea (especially during the Yi dynasty).[67] Among conservative politicians, factions and personal ties were formed on the basis of provincial origin, school ties, common experience in the past (such as sharing an apartment or a prison room), or a common patron who had assisted the members in financial and other matters (as in the KDP group). These alliances proved to be much longer-lasting and cohesive than either political parties or any other formal political groupings.

The Democratic Party and its members represented the prototype of a major political grouping consisting of various levels of personal ties and loyalties. Not only factions were "parties within a party,"[68] but also small personal groupings were parties within a faction. These factions and small groupings went their separate ways to further their private interests, frequently at the cost of hurting the interest of the larger body of which they were a part. Our discussion in later chapters (especially Chapters Six and Seven) will further elaborate this point.

67. This point has been forcefully argued by Gregory Henderson in his perceptive book, *Korea: The Politics of the Vortex, passim.*, esp. Chap. 9, "Factionalism and the Council Pattern."

68. R. A. Scalapino, *Democracy and Party Movement in Prewar Japan.*

The network of personal ties around Syngman Rhee was much more centralized and hierarchical than that in the opposition Democratic Party. Rhee had maintained personal contact with, and therefore received loyalty from, leading members of the Liberal Party on an individual and hierarchical basis. Yi Ki-bung, Yi Chae-hak, Chang Kyŏng-gŭn, Im Ch'ŏl-ho, and Yi Kŭn-jik were all "personally" loyal to Rhee. Similar personal ties had been established with the leading members of the cabinet (such as Ch'oi In-gyu) and military officers and other individuals not currently occupying government positions (such as Hŏ Chŏng and Pyŏn Yong-t'ae). With Syngman Rhee's fall, the central "pin" linking these different groups and individuals was lost, and temporary disintegration took place between and within various groups of the ruling structure. These groups, however, did not disappear completely; rather, they remained dormant, ready to be mobilized with appropriate motivation and timely leadership.

Even when these groups were not actively involved in politics, they were able to act as a powerful force (especially the armed forces) capable of checking the possible rise of leftist elements. Hence the Hŏ Chŏng administration did not really operate "in a vacuum," as many observers assumed. Hŏ was given the task of heading the interim government because of the Democratic Party's inability and unwillingness to assume power following the fall of Syngman Rhee's Liberal regime. But his freedom of action was sharply circumscribed not only by his own conservative ideological orientation but, more importantly, by the presence of various powerful political sectors with a strong conservative bent, by the internal split of the Democratic Party, and by the opportunism of its "private groups," which made the Democratic Party susceptible to manipulation by former Liberal elements. This was true despite dissension and division among Liberals themselves.

In the next chapter, we will analyze the unsuccessful attempts of "reformist" (i.e., leftist) parties to become a major political force in South Korean politics during the interim period.

V

THE POLITICS OF THE REFORMISTS [1]

During the twelve years of the Syngman Rhee government, South Korea provided an extremely inhospitable soil for leftist political movements of any kind.

The rivalry and hostility between leftists and rightists was intensified after Korean Liberation in 1945, in part because of the United States–Soviet conflict over the Korean issue and in part because of the sure prospect that either the "nationalists" or the leftists would assume

1. This is a translation of the Korean word *hyŏkshin'gye*. Most of those who considered themselves "reformists" were in fact "radicals," in the sense that they rejected the basic socioeconomic structure of South Korean society. The Korean leftists could not call themselves either socialists or radicals because of the strongly anti-Communist bias of the state. Thus, "reformists" included socialists, democratic socialists, and anarchists, as well as labor interests ("trade unionists") who were neither Communists nor socialists. The term is often so broadly applied that it may merely refer to individuals who did not belong to either the ruling party (the Liberal Party) or the conservative opposition party (the Democratic Party).

In this study, the terms "reformist," "leftist," and "radicals" will be used interchangeably. As we discussed in Chapter One, a reformist (leftist) in South Korea at the time of the April uprising could be characterized by rejection of capitalism and the existing socioeconomic order in Korea, which he believed endorsed and perpetuated economic inequality; advocacy of peaceful unification of Korea and belief in the necessity for accommodation with the North Korean Communists for that purpose; a negative attitude toward South Korea's heavy dependence upon the United States; and ambivalence toward the world conflict between the Communist and non-Communist camps. On the other hand, a "rightist" or conservative could be characterized by his belief in the imperative nature of anti-Communism at all costs; endorsement of basic capitalist principles for the Korean economy, belief in the necessity of dependence on the United States for South Korea's economic and political survival, and unequivocal support of the "free world" in its struggle with the Communist world.

power in an independent Korea. In South Korea, the rivalry ended with the total victory of the anti-leftists, led by Syngman Rhee, and the eventual elimination from the political scene of leftist and pro-leftist politicians. Rhee's successful bid for power during the post-liberation period can be attributed largely to the deadlock between the United States and the Soviet Union over the Korean unification issue; the leftists' alienation from United States occupation authorities by their intransigent and terroristic activities; and the support Rhee received from former Korean members of the Japanese bureaucracy, police, and military, who feared that socio-political revolution in South Korea would result from a leftist takeover.[2] The North Korean invasion of the South in 1950, and the bitter experience under Communism of many South Koreans during the war, deprived leftist movements in South Korea of legitimacy, effectiveness, and even legality.

Furthermore, South Korea lost many of her leaders of moderate liberal political persuasion (such as Kim Kyu-sik and Cho So-ang) during the Korean War, because they chose not to leave Seoul during Communist occupation of the city and were subsequently taken to the North by the Communists. Those who went to North Korea during the war included 27 of the 210 members of the Second National Assembly.[3] The Korean War also served to liquidate a large number of leftists and their supporters who failed to leave the South with the Communist forces during their retreat. As a result, South Korea lost most of its "centrist" political leaders who could have led a progressive political movement without the stigma of being Communist or pro-Communist. A handful of nationalists who held what might be called "progressive" views were subject to a great deal of pressure from the government to stay out of the political arena.

It is therefore not surprising that whatever political dissent existed under the Syngman Rhee regime was mostly non-ideological in nature, the opposition differing from the ruling regime only in how a liberal democratic and socioeconomically conservative system could best be adapted to Korean society within a strongly anti-Communist framework, and in who should control the government. Neither the Democratic Nationalist Party (1949–1955) led by Shin Ik-hi, nor the Democratic Party (1955–1961) under the leadership of Cho Pyŏng-ok and Chang Myŏn, offered the Korean people any ideological alternative in opposing the Syngman Rhee group.

2. McCune, *Korea Today,* p. 76.

3. Pak Mun-ok, *Han'guk chŏngburon* [A Study of the Korean Government], p. 527.

THE PROGRESSIVE PARTY MOVEMENT (1956–1958)

Given a political climate extremely hostile to any form of ideological dissent, the short-lived Progressive Party movement of Cho Pong-am must be viewed as an extraordinary phenomenon in South Korean politics. The fact that the party was organized at all, and had a considerable following, is attributable largely to the ideological appeal and personal charisma of its leader.

Cho Pong-am received his education in Japan and the Soviet Union and was active in the late 1920s as a leading member of the Korean Communist Youth League and the Korean Communist Party in Shanghai. He was arrested by the Japanese police in 1930 and was in prison at the time of Korean Liberation.[4] Following his release, Cho organized and led a "people's committee" in the Inch'ŏn area in support of Yŏ Un-hyŏng's People's Republic. In the meantime, he worked with Pak Hŏn-yŏng, a well-known Communist leader, in an effort to rehabilitate the Korean Communist Party, which had been all but completely destroyed by the Japanese. In 1946, however, Cho left Pak Hŏn-yŏng's Communist Party, bitterly criticizing it for its sectarianism and subservience to the Soviet Union.[5] From then on, Cho attempted to work with the conservative politicians, including the political forces of Syngman Rhee and the KDP. Cho even served Rhee as his first minister of agriculture. Even after he resigned from Rhee's cabinet, Cho maintained a strong anti-Communist position and kept close to the rightist politicians. As a result, he received the nomination of the pro-Government Korean National Party in the 1950 legislative election and was elected to the Second National Assembly from his Inch'ŏn district. Cho was elected vice-speaker and retained that position until 1954, with the support of the relatively progressive members of the National Assembly.

Nevertheless, it is clear that Cho never accepted the rightist views of Rhee or the opposition Democratic Nationalist Party. In 1952 Cho

4. Kim Chong-bŏm, *Che-i-dae minŭiwŏn ŏpchŏkkwa inmulgo* [A Review of the Achievements and Personalities of the Second National Assembly], pp. 482–504.

5. Yun Ki-jŏng, *Han'guk kongsanjuŭi undong pip'an* [A Critical Study of the Korean Communist Movement: A Record of the Progressive Party Incident], pp. 382–383. In two of his widely-read essays entitled "My Discovery of the Contradictions in Communism," and "I Speak to thirty Million Koreans," Cho denounced Pak Hŏn-yŏng and the Korean Communist Party for their subjugation to outside forces and for the Party's internal contradictions. In these essays, Cho stated that he had joined the Communist Party for the sole purpose of fighting Japanese imperialism and achieving liberation for the oppressed Koreans, and that he had worked closely with the Soviet Union because of its anti-Japanese policies and geographical proximity to Korea. Contents of the two essays can be found in *Chŏnggye yahwa* [Behind-the-Scenes Stories of Korean Politics], I, 491–493.

ran for the presidency on a progressive platform against both Syngman Rhee, the incumbent, and Yi Shi-yŏng, the candidate of the opposition DNP. Cho campaigned without a strong organizational base and was defeated by Rhee by a wide margin of 5.2 million to 0.8 million votes. However, Cho received a considerable amount of popular support in Pusan, then the nation's temporary capital, taking 35 percent of the votes cast there, compared to Rhee's 45 percent and Yi Shi-yŏng's 17 percent. This was by no means a small achievement, considering Rhee's deployment of the police, army, and other administrative apparatus for his reelection.

In 1956, Cho again startled the conservative politicians by receiving more than 30 percent of the valid votes in the presidential election and a majority of votes cast in such major cities as Taegu, Chŏnju, Monkp'o, Chinju, and Chŏngŭp. In most other major cities, he ran second to Rhee by only a very slight margin.[6]

After his defeat in the 1952 election, Cho tried desperately to join the DNP, the only national organization other than the Rhee supporters. In this effort, he "clarified" his position in a pamphlet entitled "The Tasks We Are Facing Today." Although it presents a diluted version of his "progressive" ideas, it is worthwhile to introduce a few important points of this essay, as it represented the most progressive views one could possibly express in South Korea at the time without being persecuted.

In this pamphlet, which he ostensibly wrote "for the victory of the anti-Communist struggle," Cho called for realignment of all anti-Communist and anti-authoritarian political forces, in preparation for eventual unification of the country.[7] He argued that the most effective struggle against the Communists could be waged not through suppression alone, but through strengthening and organizing the democratic political forces. It would then be possible to win in a peaceful battle against the Communists, through an all-Korea election. Cho underscored the importance of a major alliance among existing political forces by stating that at a time when South Korea was being threatened, militarily and ideologically, by the North Korean Communists, political leaders could not allow their "minor ideological differences to get in the way of building a united democratic front."[8]

Cho placed special emphasis on the need for bringing youth back to the political arena. He contended that Korean youth were unable to get healthy political inspiration and motivation from their elders.

6. *Taehanmin'guk sŏn'gŏsa* [History of Elections in Korea], pp. 659–665, 680.
7. Cho Pong-am, *Uriŭi tangmyŏn kwaŏp* [Our Tasks Today].
8. *Ibid.*, pp. 34–35.

That is why young people could be easily moved by Communist propaganda during the immediate post-liberation period; most youths who had demonstrated against the signing of the Korean armistice in 1953 did so without firm conviction. Young people, Cho argued, should be heard, understood, enlightened, mobilized, and organized, instead of being intimidated and regimented.[9]

Despite Cho Pong-am's persistent effort to ally himself with anti-Rhee conservative politicians, they refused to accept him into their group. In December 1954, while preparations were being made by the anti-Rhee forces to form an opposition party, its chief organizers refused Cho's admission to the new party on the grounds that his political views were not at all conservative.[10]

It was evident that most of the political leaders within and outside of the government feared admitting to the new party ideologically oriented leaders, whether of the right or the left, who had a considerable following among the youth. Neither Yi Pŏm-sŏk, a nationalist with rightist inclinations, nor Cho Pong-am, his leftist counterpart, were acceptable to the organizers of the Democratic Party, because of their apparent popularity among the youth. Significantly, in his 1954 essay, Cho Pong-am made special reference to the tragic fate of the Nationalist Youth Corps (Chokch'ŏng) in the Liberal Party. Cho deplored the government party for purging those affiliated with the Corps as Communists, despite their crucial role in the initial organization of the party.[11] As a man who had a particularly deep interest in the youth movement, Cho must have found himself in sympathy with the leaders of the National Youth Corps, despite the ideological distance that separated them.

Failing to join the anti-Rhee politicians of the conservative ranks, Cho set out to organize an exclusively leftist party, consisting of progressive and youthful intellectual elements. Leading figures in the preparatory stage of organization of the Progressive Party were Cho Pong-am himself and Sŏ Sang-il, who had recently joined the "progressives" after spending most of his life as a member of the conservative KDP group.

While preparation was underway for organization of the Progressive Party, Cho Pong-am ran for the presidency in May, 1956, hoping to energize the Progressive Party movement and its organizing effort. In that election, held nine days after the death of Shin Ik-hi, Cho was defeated by Syngman Rhee, receiving 2,164,000 votes compared to

9. *Ibid.*, pp. 81–82.
10. Kim To-yŏn, *Naŭi insaeng paeksŏ* [A White Paper of My Life], p. 269.
11. Cho Pong-am, *op. cit.*, pp. 78–80.

Syngman Rhee's 5,046,000. But he led Rhee in 25 of 181 electoral districts throughout the nation, 11 of them in Kyŏngsang Puk-to Province, which had 29 electoral districts.[12] Kyŏngsangpuk-to had been the site of many anti-government demonstrations and leftist riots since 1945, and many hard-core members of the Progressive Party came from this area.

The election results showed that support for Cho was concentrated in the urban areas of the traditionally rebellious Kyŏngsang Puk-to and Chŏlla Nam-do regions. In Seoul itself, however, the "invalid votes," most of which were presumably cast for the deceased Shin Ik-hi, far outnumbered the votes for either of the living candidates.[13] The fact that at least 15 percent of the voters in the nation and more than 40 percent of those in Seoul voted for the deceased conservative candidate rather than voting for Cho Pong-am [14] indicated that Cho's "progressive" ideas and his "Communist past" were far from being favorably accepted by a great majority of the voters, except in certain localities.

Cho Pong-am's rather weak showing in major urban areas reflected the relatively strong anti-Communist feelings of the urban dwellers. Either because of forceful government propaganda against leftist views during the preceding decade or because of their experience under Communism during the Korean War, urban voters seemed fearful of the prospect of a drastic shift toward the left in Korean politics.

Following the presidential election, the Progressive Party was beset with internal conflict between the Sŏ Sang-il faction, which advocated an alliance with the nonreformist politicians, and the Cho Pong-am faction, which insisted upon creation of a leftist party consisting of "pure" elements dedicated to the cause of a socialist, unified Korea. The Cho Pong-am faction concluded after the election that there was no longer a need to cooperate with the "fellow-traveling" Sŏ Sang-il faction, and declared in early October that it would organize the Progressive Party independent of the Sŏ Sang-il faction.[15]

Shortly thereafter, reformists who feared the consequences of participating in an extreme leftist movement led by ex-Communist Cho

12. Taehanmin'guk sŏn'gŏsa, pp. 680–688.

13. In Seoul, there were 284,349 "invalid" votes. Rhee received 205,253 votes and Cho 119,129 votes. (*Ibid.*, pp. 680–695.)

14. The percentage of Shin's votes in the nation and in Seoul have been obtained by subtracting the percentages of "invalid" votes in the vice presidential election (4.7 percent in the nation and 3.6 percent in Seoul) from those in the presidential election (20.5 percent and 46.2 percent, respectively). (*Ibid.*, pp. 680–688.)

15. A few members of the Sŏ Sang-il group commented later that the conflict between Cho and Sŏ arose primarily from their personal struggle for leadership rather than from their ideological differences. This view may be correct. However, it appears that such a personal power struggle was greatly intensified by their different world views. See Im Hong-bin, "The Death of Cho Pong-am."

Pong-am joined Sŏ Sang-il's Democratic Reformist Party, which was dedicated to the broadly defined goal of achieving a democratic, unified, and progressive Korea and creating a welfare state. Thus, after its promising start in 1955, the reformist movement was again split into two competing groups. In order to gain a better understanding of the reformist movement during this period, however, it is necessary to examine briefly the ideological orientation and organizational framework of the Progressive Party, which constituted the only challenge to the existing sociopolitical structure in South Korea.

Although the Progressive Party rejected both the "Communist dictatorship" and "capitalistic corruption," its basic ideological assumptions were essentially Marxist in nature. The Progressive Party manifesto pointed out that the suffering and oppression of the masses were the result of the internal contradictions of capitalist societies and their *laissez-faire* principles. It went on to reject the idea that the capitalist system could be maintained by piecemeal changes; a true welfare state could be built only by positive action of the revolutionary forces representing the working masses, and not through the self-correction of capitalism itself.[16] The party thus called upon the workers, peasants, working intelligentsia, and those engaged in small-scale business and industry to work for realization of the interests of the working masses in a democratic welfare state.[17]

As for the unification issue, the party proposed "peaceful unification" through an all-Korea election supervised by the United Nations "under the sovereignty of the Republic of Korea." [18] It then called for the creation of a planned economy in which there would be no exploitation of the peasants. Large-scale industrial and mining enterprises would be given "the right to participate in the management of the enterprises in which they worked."

Thus the ideological orientation of the Progressive Party was far more "socialistic" than any other political group to be found in South Korea during the Rhee period.[19] This also represented a significant

16. The full texts of the manifesto and the platform of the Progressive Party can be found in Yun Ki-jŏng, *op. cit.*, pp. 462–489.

17. *Ibid.*, p. 464.

18. The prosecution argued that Cho helped the cause of the North Korean Communists in their effort to subvert the South Korean government by treating the North Korean regime on equal terms with the South Korean government in his unification proposal. (*Ibid.*, pp. 327–360.)

19. The platform of the Democratic Reformist Party led by Sŏ Sang-il mentioned only such broad and relatively innocuous goals as "the realization of reformed politics," "the establishment of a rational and systematic economy," and "the achievement of national unification through democratic methods." (Ibid., pp. 291–292.)

change of tactics for Cho; for the first time since his defection from the Communist Party in 1946, he was expressing his leftist views in unequivocal fashion. Given the political climate in Korea during the second half of the 1950s, the Progressive Party's ideological orientation came very close to violating the limits of permissible expression.

The Progressive Party was also unique among the major parties in another important area, its organization—a "general organization," known to the outside world, and a "special organization," to be kept hidden from all but hard-core members of the party. On the surface the party was to operate on the basis of democratic principles, with emphasis on mass participation in party matters. Thus its platform statement declared:

> In the twentieth century, genuine democracy can be realized only by representing the views and interests of a broad spectrum of the working people. For this purpose we have to possess highly sophisticated scientific knowledge and the capacity for energetic social and political action. Such knowledge and capacity cannot be expected from one person or a small group of persons. Only a political grouping based on the working masses—i.e., a genuinely democratic party—can analyze and absorb the knowledge and experience of the human race. Thus, only through *democratic and constructive organization, mobilization, and utilization* of the creative energy of the broad masses can we hope to overcome the transitional chaos and difficulties of backward Korea. . . .[20]

In actuality, however, key decisions were made by the top members and communicated through the "special organization." Except for the publicly known leaders of the party, all those involved in the special organization were secret members, many of them recent college graduates or students; they numbered perhaps 400 out of a total membership estimated at 10,000.[21] The two most important units of the special organization, namely the "Seven-man Circle" and the Morning Star Society (*Kyemyŏng-hoe*), consisted almost entirely of these young members. The Seven-man Circle operated as the highest cell committee (analogous to the Politburo of a Communist Party), with direct lines of command to the cell committees of the provinces, cities, and counties.

20. Quoted in Yun Ki-jŏng, pp. 463–464. Emphasis mine.

21. Cho, in a message intended for Yang Myŏng-san, allegedly a North Korean agent who operated between Cho and the Communist regime, asked Yang to deny the prosecution charges so that the political life of "more than 10,000 Progressive Party members" could be saved. (See Im Hong-bin, "The Death of Cho Pong-am and the Judicial Power.") South Korean investigators estimated that there were about 400 secret party members in responsible positions (Yi Ki-ha, *Han'guk chŏngdang paltalsa,* p. 268).

The kyemyŏng-hoe also operated secretly in major university campuses under the direction of the party's central organization. They were special organizations of students who would surface when their active participation was required. Such special and latent organizations were also envisaged in other sectors of the society—among artists, writers, educators, religious, military and police veterans, service and health organizations, farmers, workers, fishermen, policemen, military personnel, and women.[22]

The Progressive Party's tight organization, youthful membership, and radical ideology constituted a major threat to both the Liberal Party and the Democratic Party. Realizing the potential capacity of Cho Pong-am and his Progressive Party—especially after the 1956 presidential election in which Cho ran a reasonably strong second—the Rhee government tried to suppress the movement. Throughout the year 1957, successive provincial organizational meetings of the Progressive Party were broken up by terrorists and sometimes by the police. A final blow was dealt to the party when its top leaders were arrested in January 1958 on the charge of making illicit contact with North Korean agents.

Cho was charged with engaging in espionage activities, and others with violating various aspects of the National Security Law. Cho was accused of receiving funds in the amount of about 20 million hwan (approximately $30,000) from North Korea between 1955 and 1956 through Yang Ri-sŏk, a former acquaintance of Cho's, who was acting as a double agent between the North and South Korean intelligence organizations. Through Yang, Cho was allegedly told that the North Korean regime now regretted that Cho had been expelled from the Communist Party in 1946, following his dispute with Pak Hŏn-yŏng, and that ever since Pak's execution it had been hopeful of cooperating with Cho for the common socialist cause. The prosecution argued that Cho subsequently agreed to help the North Korean regime and in return received funds for his presidential election campaign and to purchase a newspaper which would be used as an organ of the Progressive Party. The prosecution also claimed that the Progressive Party platform, which called for peaceful unification through an all-Korea election, and for unity of the working masses, was in close accord with the North Korean line and thus violated South Korea's national principles.[23] In July 1958 the district court ruled that the Progressive Party platform did not violate the fundamental principles of the Republic of Korea, but it sentenced Cho to a five-year prison

22. Yun Ki-jŏng, p. 91.
23. For a text of the prosecution charge, see *ibid.*, pp. 449–461.

term for his contact with a North Korean agent. Most of the other defendants were acquitted.

One month later, however, an appellate court sentenced Cho to death, while each of Cho's close associates, Pak Ki-ch'ul, Kim Tal-ho, and Yun Kil-chung, were sentenced to three-year prison terms. The key evidence in this decision was a message from Cho intended for Yang. In the message, which Cho allegedly wrote in jail and gave to the jailer for delivery, Cho simply asked Yang to testify that Cho had had no knowledge of Yang's trips to North Korea. Cho's death sentence was upheld by the Supreme Court in February 1959, and he was executed on July 31, 1959, one day after his appeal for retrial was denied, and less than eight months before the presidential election of March 1960.[24] The Progressive Party itself was outlawed by the Rhee government shortly after Cho's arrest in April 1958, and now, with the death of Cho Pong-am, the reformist movement was effectively silenced.

The tragic end of Cho Pong-am and his Progressive Party made it unequivocally clear that a serious leftist movement could not be openly promoted in South Korea without falling victim to violent suppression by the government. The Progressive Party purported to be the champion of the oppressed and representative of the working masses. Its penetration into various functional groups, especially college students and recent graduates, was well under way. Most of the strong supporters of the party were either old "revolutionaries" who, like Cho himself, had participated in the leftist movement before 1948, or younger members who had a deep sense of deprivation and frustration from what they considered pervasive inequality in South Korean society, and South Korea's excessive dependence on the United States. There is little doubt that the Progressive Party movement was growing rapidly, although mostly underground, when it collapsed with the death of its leader. The 1958–1959 Progressive Party trial revealed that many of its younger members were deeply committed to the necessity of changing the existing social and economic order.[25]

24. There has been some controversy (far less than there should have been) over the fairness of the Supreme Court's ruling in the Cho Pong-am case. See, for example, the accusations and counter-accusations of Im Hong-bin, a progressively oriented columnist of *Han'guk Ilbo,* and Kim Kap-su, former Supreme Court judge who had written the court's opinion on the Cho case, in the August, October, and December 1955 and February 1966 issues of *Shin-dong-a*. It is difficult to determine the extent of Cho's contact with the North Korean regime. However, it seems certain that the evidence produced by the prosecution was not sufficient to prove that Cho was in fact a Communist agent.

25. It is no mere coincidence that most of its student members were from relatively low-ranking schools rather than from Seoul National University, in which

From the point of view of the South Korean government, these were indeed subversives and had to be silenced completely before they could gain a broader basis of support. During the remainder of the First Republic following the Cho Pong-am trial, even the relatively moderate parties, such as the Democratic Reformist Party, had to remain completely silent and inactive.

REFORMIST POLITICS DURING THE INTERIM PERIOD

The collapse of the Rhee regime gave immediate impetus to the rise of various reformist and leftist political movements. To many who did not accept the prevailing conservatism in South Korea, the new political atmosphere seemed to provide an opportunity to organize and advocate their views without the kind of repression they would have received from the Rhee government. Despite the relatively free political atmosphere during this period, however, the leftist movement was to suffer from a number of difficulties: conflict among different factions, direct and indirect harassment by the government, and absence of a leader capable of bringing the reformists together and attracting a large segment of the population.

The most important "reformist" party, and the first one to be organized during the interim period, was the Socialist Mass Party (*Sahoe Taejung-dang*), organized by former members of the Progressive Party and joined by Sŏ Sang-il and Yi Tong-hwa, leaders of the former Democratic Reformist Party. This reunion of the leaders of the Progressive Party and the DRP [26] seems to have been possible because of the absence of Cho Pong-am, whom Sŏ would not have wished to work with. Other reformist parties, chief among them the Korean Socialist Party led by "trade-unionist" politician Chŏn Chin-han, were also formed with a limited grass-roots organizational basis.

The immediate and obvious objective of the reformist parties was to win as many seats in the National Assembly (especially the lower house) as possible. As long as the Democratic Party itself was split between the new and old factions, it was felt, they had a good chance of gaining significant power, even with only a small number of representatives in the National Assembly. At the same time, only by elect-

---

the "ideological leftists" were most likely to be found. Among those in the leadership of the party most came from the Hamgyŏng-do, P'yŏngan-do or Kyŏngsang-do Provinces—areas which had been traditionally discriminated against by the central regions. See Yun Ki-jŏng, pp. 390–443.

26. For a discussion of the split between the Progressive Party and the DRP in 1956, see Yi Ki-ha, p. 289.

ing their own men to the National Assembly could they obtain a political forum from which to make their views known and felt in national politics. Their long-term objective was to bring about a two-party system in which the reformists would constitute the major opposition party.

Not all the reformist parties, however, were willing to operate within the general framework designed by conservative Democrats and Liberals in the National Assembly. From the beginning, the Socialist-Reformist Party led by Ko Chŏng-hun, a former member of the Progressive Party and later of the DRP, had as its primary aim the mobilization of youth and realization of the "real goals" of the April revolution. For this purpose the party demanded complete eradication of the past sins of the old politicians of both the Liberal Party and the Democratic Party.

Only one week after Rhee's resignation, Ko and a few of his youthful colleagues (mostly former military officers of lower ranks) [27] announced their intention to organize a "Young Guardians of the Republic" Party, declaring that "the ultimate goal of establishing a democratic Second Republic could not be achieved without the wisdom and passion of the young." [28] In this sense the party inherited much of the militant spirit of Cho's Progressive Party. But it was clear that the party was more interested in immediate subversion of the existing political framework than winning in future elections. In its declaration, the party stated:

> What were the old politicians doing when young students were braving the bullets and bayonets of the police, when the bones of our brothers were being broken and their flesh torn by police torture, and when all the students were going through a death march for fair elections and political freedom? Why did they not throw away their disgraceful seats in the National Assembly? What have they done to provide the constitutional foundations of the Second Republic? . . . . We cannot leave the future of Korea to these cowardly and corrupt politicians.[29]

Ko, a former army intelligence officer and formerly editor of the respected *Chosŏn Ilbo,* argued that the full story behind the assassination of Kim Ku in 1950 and the execution of Cho Pong-am in 1959 had not been told. He demanded that those responsible in the two cases—some of whom were still in the National Assembly—should be brought to trial and punished. Since those accused by Ko of having committed

27. *Myŏngin okchunggi* [Celebrities Write About Their Life in Prison], p. 27.
28. *Kyŏnghyang Shinmun,* May 3, 1960, p. 1.
29. *Ibid.*

various "sins" during the Rhee administration included important conservative politicians such as Kim Chun-yŏn, a former leading member of the Democratic Party and at that time leader of the Unification Party, and Yu Chin-san, one of the top members of the old faction of the Democratic Party, most political leaders reacted to Ko's accusations with overt scorn and hostility.

Ko further irritated many politicians by proposing a "nonpolitical" exchange between North and South Korea, and the legalization of Communist activities in South Korea. The Democratic Party promptly struck back, arguing that such proposals would "only serve to provide the Communists with a fine opportunity to destroy the Korean Republic." [30] Ko's short political career as a reformist-agitator and as a self-appointed crusader against the "sins" of the old politicians ended abruptly on July 2, when the Hŏ Chŏng government arrested him on charges of "slandering through published materials" and obstructing official actions of the Speaker of the National Assembly.[31] He was imprisoned, not to be released until late November, well after the National Assembly election and the formation of the Chang Myŏn government.

Ko's experience as a maverick reformist provides a few interesting observations that illuminate the nature of the political situation during the interim period. Ko obviously believed that the conservative politicians in the National Assembly and the Hŏ Chŏng government were not capable of carrying out the "revolutionary tasks" presumably called for by the April uprising. He thought that by demanding the withdrawal of the old politicians—not only the Liberal and Democratic politicians, but also many of the old-time "reformists"—and exposing their past "sins," he would be able to mobilize the support of the younger generation, especially the students. Rather than operating within the political framework provided by the Democrats and other conservative politicians, as most other "reformists" chose to do, Ko attempted instead to obstruct their scheme. Ko not only denied the authority of the National Assembly (elected during the Rhee regime) to change the constitution, but also opposed the adoption of a parliamentary cabinet system.

Ko did not have the opportunity to test his strategy among the young people and students, because the interim government did not allow him to do so. However, the consequences of his political work indicate the boundaries for radical political activities in Korea, even

30. *Ibid.,* May 27, 1960, p. 1.
31. *Kyŏnghyang Shinmun,* June 3, 1960, p. 1.

during the "free" interim period.[32] His bold and seemingly reckless approach to politics was unacceptable to most politicians, so much so that he was kept away from the political scene during the crucial six months, while a new National Assembly was elected and a new cabinet was formed.[33] The conservative political leaders in the government and the National Assembly, being unable to enlist the support of the ideologically oriented young people, felt very much threatened by those with the determination and ability to mobilize them, and succeeded in removing such individuals from the political arena.

Other reformist parties—particularly the Socialist Mass Party and the Korean Socialist Party—were also subject to considerable discrimination and harassment by the Hŏ Chŏng government and the conservative-dominated National Assembly. An early indication of the interim government's unfavorable attitude was given on May 7, when reformist leaders were denied a permit to hold a meeting to discuss forming a reformist league. The meeting, held despite the denial, was interrupted by the government's order to disperse.[34] Concerning this incident, a spokesman for the reformists stated that "the conservative reactionary camp, which was startled by the persistent efforts of the reformist forces to form a unified front, now tries to obstruct these efforts by blocking assemblies of the reformists and through false accusations." [35]

The government kept a particularly vigilant eye upon policy pronouncements and membership composition of the reformist parties. As we can see in Table V-1, the reformist platforms did not differ significantly from those of the Democratic Party or the Liberal Party in many policy areas.[36] It was with regard to the "private" views expressed by leading members of the reformist parties that the govern-

32. In terms of ideology, Ko could not be considered a "radical leftist." His goal was "to establish a political party resembling either the British Labour Party or the Social-Democratic Party of Germany." He regarded himself as a "democratic socialist" with more emphasis on democracy than on socialism. See *Myŏngin okchunggi*, pp. 40–45; also, Ko's *Kut'o: purŭji mothan norae* [Songs I Could Not Sing: Politics, Prison, and I), *passim*.

33. This raises the question how much influence the Democratic Party actually had over the Hŏ Chŏng government. There is no question that Hŏ Chŏng worked very closely with the Democrats. All members of the Democratic Party whom I interviewed agreed that the leaders of both factions of the party had considerable influence in Hŏ Chŏng's administration. However, it is not clear what actually prompted Ko Chŏng-hun's arrest. It seems highly probable that leaders of the Democratic Party did urge privately that the Hŏ Chŏng administration do something about Ko.

34. *Kyŏnghyang Shinmun*, May 8, 1960, p. 1.

35. *Ibid.*

36. For the respective platforms of the different parties, see *Taehanmin'guk sŏn'gŏsa*, pp. 344–348.

Table V-1

MAJOR PARTIES' POLICY STANDS ON CERTAIN ISSUES IN JULY, *1960*

	Democratic Party	*Socialist Mass Party*	*Korean Socialist Party*
Unification	Free Elections under UN supervision in accordance with the South Korean Constitution (i.e., separate election in the North)	Peaceful unification through an all-Korean election under UN supervision on one-man, one-vote basis	An all-Korea election under UN supervision on one-man, one-vote basis
Economy	Long-term plans; eradication of privileged monopoly	Long-term plans; nationalization of major industries and financial organizations	Long-term plans; nationalization of major industries
Military Service	Two-year universal service; consolidation of professional service system	Two-year universal service; one-year service for students	Two-year service; emphasis on the conclusion of status-of-forces agreements with allies
Labor Relations and Welfare	Guarantee right to organize, and engage in collective bargaining and strike	Cooperatize small and medium industries; establish close ties with international labor organizations such as ILO; public ownership of medical facilities	Establish social insurance and security system; cooperatize small and medium industries; tax-exemption for low-income families
Korea–Japan Relations	Normalize diplomatic relations	Normalize diplomatic relations	Normalize diplomatic relations; establish welfare funds for Korean residents in Japan

Source: Kyonghyang Shinmun, July 6, 1960, p. 1.

ment, National Assembly, and mass media reacted with sensitivity, insinuating that those views were pro-Communist in nature.

We have already mentioned how much Ko Chŏng-hun's proposals for the legalization of Communist activities in South Korea and initiating nonpolitical exchange between the North and the South irritated the conservative politicians. On July 4, Sŏ Sang-il suggested the desirability of an all-Korea election under the supervision of certain "neutralist countries." [37] Since a similar proposal had been made by the Communists in the 1954 Geneva Conference concerning the Korean unification problem,[38] his proposal was received in many quarters with disdain and suspicion. Sŏ, now the senior director of the Socialist Mass Party, also emphasized the necessity of an exchange of reporters, scholars, and students with North Korea.[39] Ten days later, Chang Kŏn-sang, one of the organizers of the General League of Reformist Comrades, stated that the issue of Communist China's admission to the United Nations should be seriously considered, since it might facilitate the unification of Korea.[40] A few days later, Pak Ki-ch'ul, another leader of the SMP, stated that Korean armed forces should be drastically reduced, to perhaps the 50,000- to 100,000-man level, adding that Korea would have to be neutralized, should the United Nations fail to guarantee its security.

Early in July, the prosecutor-general's office announced it had obtained information that more than 60 percent of the membership of the reformist parties consisted of former members of the South Korean Workers' Party, and this percentage was still increasing; and that it had ordered the police departments throughout the country to investigate the membership and activities of these parties.[41] On July 20 the vice-minister of justice stated that Chang Kŏn-sang's earlier statement concerning Communist China's admission to the United Nations clearly reflected a pro-Communist view and that he was examining whether such a statement violated the National Security Law.[42] Although no other reformist leader besides Ko was actually arrested during this period, the intimation by the authorities that most of the reformists were former Communists and were expressing pro-Communist views effectively served to check the expansion of reformist power at the grass-roots and to arouse suspicion among the voters as to the sin-

37. *Tong-a Ilbo*, July 4, 1960, p. 1.
38. See U.S. Dept. of State, *The Korean Problem at the Geneva Conference, April 26–June 15, 1954*, pp. 10–13.
39. *Kyŏnghyang Shinmun*, June 18, 1960, p. 1.
40. *Ibid.*, July 15, 1960.
41. *Ibid.*, July 7, 1960.
42. *Ibid.*, July 20, 1960.

cerity of their anti-Communist façade. This was to have a serious bearing upon the National Assembly election of July 29.

The reformists further weakened their chances in the July elections by internal and inter-party rivalries. The most conspicuous struggle was that of the Progressive Party faction within the Socialist Mass Party.

On June 8, only a few weeks after the initial organizational meeting, representatives of the non-Progressive Party faction announced their decision to "expel" Kim Tal-ho for his obstructionist activities in the new party. They claimed that Kim, one of the original organizers of the SMP and former vice-chairman of the central committee of the Progressive Party, conspired with a number of other members to expel some of the nonmembers of the SMP. As soon as the announcement was made, former Progressive Party members lined up behind Kim and accused the Sŏ Sang-il group of engaging in the same kind of divisive maneuver that he had employed in 1957, when he left the Progressive Party to form the Democratic Reformist Party. Kim also declared that Sŏ and his supporters were engaging in "a political conspiracy arising from their jealousy and inferiority complex toward former Progressive Party members." [43] Kim's "expulsion" proved to be only temporary. He was permitted to remain in the party following a series of negotiations between the Sŏ group and the Progressive Party group.

The struggle between the two factions erupted into an open quarrel at the party convention held on June 18, in which Sŏ Sang-il was elected head director of the SMP. Members of the Progressive Party faction argued that Sŏ was not qualified to lead the SMP because, in the past, he had accused the Progressive Party of being "red." [44] Although the SMP survived this particular crisis through further negotiations, it was clear that the party had neither the ideological commitment nor leadership strong enough to hold it together for any length of time.

Despite internal disharmony, the SMP was still by far the most important group among the reformists. In preparation for the July elections, it started building local branches earlier than any other reformist parties, taking advantage of the former Progressive Party organization. But its early success in local organization made it reluctant to form a common front with other reformist parties against the conservatives. As a result, they were unable to coordinate their campaign efforts in the July election. Often a number of reformists competed for the non-

43. *Ibid.*, June 9, 1960, p. 1.
44. *Ibid.*, June 18, 1960, p. 1.

Table V-2

RELATIONSHIP BETWEEN URBANIZATION OF THE DISTRICT AND REFORMIST CANDIDACY IN THE ELECTIONS OF JULY 29, 1960

Largest Urban Area *	*Total Districts*	*With Reformists*	*Without Reformists*	*Percentage of Reformist Districts*
Over 50,000	45	33	12	73.3%
30,000–50,000	21	14	7	67.8
15,000–30,000	43	25	18	58.1
SUB-TOTAL	109	72	37	66.1
Less than 15,000	124	51	73	41.1
TOTAL	233	123	110	52.0%

* The classification scheme of urbanization has been adapted from Yun Ch'ŏn-ju, *Han'guk chŏngch'i ch'egye*, pp. 366–367.

conservative votes in the same district, especially in those areas in which the reformists seemed to have a fair chance of winning.[45]

Tables V-2 and V-3 show the distribution of reformist candidates for the House of Representatives by different regions and different degrees of urbanization. Predictably, reformist candidates were concentrated in the more urbanized districts and in the Kyŏngsang Puk-to and Chŏlla Nam-do areas. Table 2 indicates that the reformist parties had candidates in 33 of the 45 highly urbanized districts, 14 of the 21 relatively urbanized districts, and 25 of the 43 semi-urban districts. Only 51 of the 124 rural districts had reformist candidates.[46]

At the same time, there was a considerable degree of regional variation in the distribution of reformist candidates. In Kyŏngsang Puk-to and Chŏlla Nam-do Provinces, the reformists had candidates in more

45. For understandable reasons, the reformist parties placed very little emphasis on the House of Councillors elections. Having only limited resources and organization, they concentrated on the elections for the lower house, which would have the real power in forming the new cabinet and other important matters. The reformist parties had only 9 candidates for the upper house elections. (*Haptong yŏn'gam*, 1961, p. 141.)

46. *Kyŏnghyang Shinmun*, July 3, 1960, appendix; also, July 3–July 4, 1960.

Table V-3

DISTRIBUTION OF REFORMIST CANDIDATES IN THE ELECTIONS OF JULY *29, 1960*

Province	*SMP*	*KSP*	*SRP*	*Other*	*Total*	*(A)*	*(B)*	*(C)*	*(C/B)*
Seoul	10	6	1	0	17	3 *	16	10	.625
Kyŏnggi	8	2	0	0	10	1	25	9	.360
Ch'ungbuk	5	1	0	0	6	1	13	5	.385
Ch'ungnam	2	1	1	0	4	0	22	4	.182
Chŏnbuk	8	1	0	2	11	1	24	10	.418
Chŏnnam	22	0	0	1	23	0	32	23	.717
Kyŏngbuk	32	0	1	3	36	6 †	38	29	.761
Kyŏngnam	32	4	0	7	43	12 ‡	40	27	.675
Kangwŏn	4	1	0	0	5	0	20	5	.250
Cheju	0	1	0	0	1	0	3	1	.333
TOTAL	123	17	3	13	156	24	233	123	.571

Source: Tabulated from the list of candidates in *Kyŏnghyang Shinmun,* July 3, 1960, appendix; also, July 3, evening ed.—July 4, 1960.

* In one district (formerly that of Cho So-ang), 3 reformists competed against each other.

† Includes one district with 3 reformists and another with three SMP candidates.

‡ Includes three districts in which 2 SMP candidates competed against each other. One district had 4 SMP candidates.

(A) Districts in which reformists competed among themselves.

(B) Total number of districts.

(C) Districts which had one or more reformist candidates.

than 70 percent of all electoral districts. The capital city of Seoul and Kyŏngsang Nam-do Province had reformist candidates in 62.5 percent of their districts.[47] This can be contrasted with Ch'ungch'ŏng Nam-do's 18.2 percent, Kangwŏn-do's 25.0 percent. Kyŏnggi-do's 36.0 percent, and Ch'ungch'ŏng Puk-to's 38.5 percent.[48] Such uneven distribution of reformist candidacies in different regions suggests that the reformist

47. In the city of Taegu, 7 reformist candidates ran in all five of its electoral districts. In Pusan, 15 candidates ran in nine of its ten districts.

48. It is beyond the scope of this study to conduct a thorough investigation of the reasons for the relative strength of the reformist forces in certain regional areas. However, this presents a very important area of inquiry, and only tentative explanation can be given here.

The "progressivism" in Taegu can be explained by its traditional anti-government sentiment and the highly politicized nature of the city. As of 1960, Taegu had more newspaper circulation per capita than any other city in the nation. It also had a higher degree of educational accomplishment, a higher percentage of factory workers and low-income families, and a higher level of population inflow from the surrounding rural areas than most other cities. (For an informative

parties found it possible only in the more urbanized areas and in areas with a history of previous anti-government activities to quickly organize local party branches and solicit support for their candidates.

Tables V-2 and V-3 also show that reformists competed against each other in 24 of the 123 electoral districts which had at least one reformist candidate. In a number of districts, especially in the Kyŏngsang Nam-do area, three or more reformist candidates ran at the same time. In five districts, candidates from the SMP competed among themselves. This is indicative of the inability of different reformist parties to coordinate their efforts for a common cause. It also shows that even within the SMP itself, such coordination was not possible; it was unable to exercise effective control over its own members who wished to run for the office, regardless of nomination by the party. A total of 26 candidates ran in various districts under the SMP banner without its endorsement, hurting the winning chances of the officially nominated candidates of the party.

In the July election itself, the reformist parties experienced decisive defeat at the hands of Democratic and other conservative candidates. From the 123 districts in which they had candidates, the reformist parties managed to elect only 5 candidates—4 from the SMP and 1 from the Korean Socialist Party. Although reformist candidates ran second in 25 other districts, most of them received far fewer votes than the winning candidates, many of whom were Democrats. Chŏn Chin-han, leader of the Korean Socialist Party, was also defeated in a district in Seoul by a wide margin.[49] The SMP and the Korean Socialist Party

---

sociological study of Taegu, see T'ak Hi-jun and Yi Chŏng-jae, "An Analysis of Taegu Society.") In addition, Taegu had not been occupied by the Communists during the Korean War, and thus left-leaning activists had not been "weeded out" as in most other areas. Pusan had many things in common with Taegu except for the latter's "anti-government" tradition.

The situation in the Chŏlla Nam-do area was quite different from that of Taegu, Pusan, and the areas around these cities. Chŏlla Nam-do had been the scene of a bloody reign of terror during the Korean War and was far less urbanized than either Kyŏngsang Puk-to or Kyŏngsang Nam-do. For example, approximately 3.2 percent of the total combined population of Kyŏngsang Puk-to and Kyŏngsang Nam-do were living in cities of 50,000 or more people in 1962, while the corresponding figure for Chŏlla Nam-do was 1.7 percent. (Tabulated from Korean Government, *Taehanmin'guk chipang haengchŏng kuyŏk pyŏnnam* [Handbook of Local Administrative Districts in Korea], pp. 433–476. People living in cities of 50,000 or more were 1.5 percent of the population in 1959, according to *Haptong yon'gam,* 1960). However, the people in this province had been highly politicized and also had a long and persistent record of anti-government sentiment and activity. In addition, wealth was very unevenly distributed in this province; about half of the farmers owned less land than could support their families and themselves. (*Haptong yon'gam,* 1961, p. 372.)

49. *Kyŏnghyang Shinmun,* July 30, 1960, p. 1.

received only 6.0 percent and 0.6 percent, respectively, of the votes cast. This can be compared with 42.7 percent for the Democratic Party and 46.8 percent for the "Independents," most of whom were Democrats running without party nomination. In the House of Councillors election in which the reformists captured 2 seats out of 58, the SMP received 2.4 percent of votes cast, and the Korea Socialist Party, 0.9 percent.[50]

Reformist party leaders attributed their defeat to the lack of funds, identification of reformism with Communism by many voters, and the "Democratic boom," which led the voters to believe that the Democratic Party was the only possible successor to the Liberal regime.[51] Shin Sang-ch'o, a political scientist who ran for a National Assembly seat in a Seoul district and was defeated, remarked that Korean voters could still be influenced by money and intimidated by authority, and that this was one of the most important reasons for the reformists' near-complete defeat.[52]

However, these arguments do not adequately explain the fact that the reformists did extremely poorly in the highly urbanized areas like Seoul and Pusan. Besides, if the "Democratic boom" (resulting from the desire of many voters to reward the party for its past sufferings) was a major factor in the reformists' defeat, how can one account for the fact that the Democratic candidates received less than 50 percent of all votes? [53] It would appear that Korean voters, in the cities as well as in the rural areas, were securely indoctrinated in anti-Communism and well taught to fear the consequences of supporting leftism. The July election rather dramatically reflected such anti-leftist, conservative views. Thus voters seemed more concerned with the external Communist threat than with social injustice and economic oppression at

50. *Taehanmin'guk sŏn'gŏsa,* pp. 848–849.

51. For example, Chŏn Chin-han in *Kyŏnghyang Shinmun,* July 30, 1960, p. 1, and Chang Kŏn-sang, "Memoirs," in *Sasirŭi chŏnburŭl kisulhanda,* p. 319.

52. Shin Sang-ch'o, "Fifteen Years of Socialist Movement in South Korea."

53. See *Taehanmin'guk sŏn'gŏsa,* pp. 848–849. There are no systematic studies currently available which deal with the relationship between the reformist parties and the nationalist and leftist-oriented organizations among the students and labor unionists. Preliminary studies of Taegu revealed that there was a very close link between the SMP and labor unions such as the teachers' union, as a pressure group during the Hŏ Chŏng and Chang Myŏn administrations (see Chapter Seven of this book) and the nationalist student groups such as the Student National Unification Front. (T'ak Hi-jun and Yi Chŏng-jae, *op. cit.,* pp. 169–170.) Similarly, many students were accused by conservative politicians of campaigning for reformist candidates when college students in Seoul organized into a number of teams and went to the countryside in an attempt to "enlighten and educate the farmers about the significance of the July elections." See *Kyŏnghyang Shinmun,* July 6, 1960, p. 3; July 7, 1960, p. 4; July 7, 1960, evening ed., p. 4.

home. They rejected Syngman Rhee's dictatorial rule, but not his conservatism.

The reformist parties were at an even more severe disadvantage in non-urban districts, where the attitudes of the electorate were basically "pre-modern."[54] In the first place, most of the non-urban voters, lacking in stable party affiliation or national issue orientation, participated in the voting in order to "conform" with others and "ratify" the existing authority structure, rather than to make a conscious and "rational" choice between the contending parties.[55] This observation is supported, in part, by the fact that voter turnout and the degree of support for the ruling party systematically were higher in rural than in urban districts.[56] In the July election itself, most voters considered the victory of the Democratic Party a foregone conclusion, and the party was in fact acting like the party in power even before the election. For most rural voters, therefore, voting for the Democratic candidate meant "endorsing" the government party.

A second characteristic of the rural voters, closely related to the first, was that they had had no strong emotional ties or lasting affiliation with any existing political parties. Table V-4 shows the results of a survey conducted in July 1960 among rural and semi-rural voters of Sangju, Kyŏngsang Puk-to, which indicated that only about 7 percent of the respondents (voters) supported the same party in the elections of 1954 and 1958.[57] The fact that the parties themselves were relatively new, and that their rise and fall had been abrupt and erratic, was of course largely responsible for the lack of any stable party affiliation among the voters, as is shown in Table V-5. Thus the rural voters could easily transfer their support from one ruling party to another.

Third, the rural voters not only lacked any stable party loyalty, but also were quite indifferent to issues (especially on the national level) raised and discussed by the candidates, and showed little interest in candidates' positions on the issues. Tables V-6 and V-7 indicate that issues in general, but particularly the issue of national unification strongly emphasized by the reformist parties, were largely ignored by the voters.

54. I have adopted in this instance the distinction between "traditional" and "modern" political behavior given by Scalapino and Masumi, who consider that (in the Japanese context) voting on the basis of factors other than parties or issues (i.e., because of intimidation by authority, personal ties, small group pressure, etc.) reflects "traditional" behavior. (*Parties and Politics in Contemporary Japan*, pp. 118–120.)

55. For a discussion of voting as a "ratification of authority," see *ibid.*, p. 120.

56. Yun Ch'ŏn-ju, *Han'guk chŏngch'i ch'egye*, p. 378; for a similar observation on Japan, see Scalapino and Masumi, p. 109. See also Oh Byŏng-hŏn, "An Analysis of the July 29th General Election."

57. See Tables V-4 and V-5.

Table V-4

NUMBER OF NATIONAL ASSEMBLY ELECTIONS IN WHICH RESPONDENTS SUPPORTED SAME PARTY, *1954–1960*

Number of Elections	*Number of Respondents*	*Percent*
In all three elections	28	6%
Twice	50	11
1954 and 1958	25	7
1958 and 1960	19	4
1954 and 1960	6	1
Two different parties in all three elections	163	40
Don't know	77	17
No answer	86	19
TOTAL	454	101 *

Source: Adapted from Yun Ch'ŏn-ju, *Han'guk chŏngch'i ch'egye,* p. 410.
* Rounding error.

Table V-5

PARTIES WHICH RESPONDENTS CONSIDER TRUSTWORTHY

Parties	*Number*	*Percent*
Democratic Party (DP) *and* Socialist Mass Party (SMP)	89	22%
DP *and* Liberal Party	2	0
DP and no other	64	16
DP *and* "other parties (unspecified)"	16	4
SMP *and* "other parties (unspecified)"	5	1
DP *and* independents	6	1
SMP *and* independents	3	1
SMP and no other	17	4
None	19	5
Don't know	150	37
No answer	34	8
TOTAL	405	99% *

Source: Adapted from Yun Ch'ŏn-ju, *Han'guk chŏngch'i ch'egye,* pp. 390–391.
* Rounding error.

Table V-6

REASONS GIVEN BY VOTERS FOR SUPPORTING A CANDIDATE IN THE *1960* NATIONAL ASSEMBLY ELECTION

Reason	*Number*	*Percent*
Because I think the candidate is a good man	278	69%
Because I support his party	24	6
Because I like both the candidate and his party	74	18
Because I am indebted to the candidate	2	0
Because the candidate has good educational background	8	2
Because the candidate has done much for our locality	3	1
Because the candidate is related to me	0	0
Because I support the candidate's platform	4	1
Don't know	6	1
No answer	3	1
TOTAL	402	99% *

Source: Adapted from Yun Ch'ŏn-ju, *Han'guk chŏngch'i ch'egye,* p. 414.
* Rounding error.

It would appear that these "pre-modern" characteristics of Korean voters discussed above were not unique to rural areas, although they were more salient there than in more urbanized areas. In urban areas the Democratic Party was heavily supported by the voters because of the voters' generally anti-Communist orientation and relatively strong sense of Democratic Party identification fostered during the Rhee regime.[58] Given the basic characteristics of the behavior and attitudes of South Korean voters in both the urban and rural areas, it is not surprising that reformist parties were unable to mobilize support for their cause among the voting public. Consequently they experienced almost total defeat in the July election and shifted their attention from parliamentary to nonparliamentary politics.

The experience of the reformists during the interim period helped to reveal a significant gap in Korean politics—between the ideas of

58. See Chapter Two of this study. This is of course only an impressionistic statement, as to my knowledge a systematic survey of urban voter behavior during the period is not available.

Table V-7

TASKS WITH WHICH VOTERS WISH TO ENTRUST THEIR REPRESENTATIVES (NATIONAL ISSUES ONLY)

Tasks	*Number*	*Percent*
Lay foundation for democracy in Korea	74	16%
Establish social welfare	63	14
Achieve economic growth	26	6
Eliminate dictatorship	22	5
Establish fair government personnel policy	19	4
Accomplish national unification	18	4
Create "clean" politics	15	3
Eliminate coercion and corruption	8	2
Establish "orderly diplomacy"	4	1
Other tasks (fair elections, protection of human rights, etc.)	12	3
Don't know or none	203	44
TOTAL	464	102% *

Source: Adapted from Yun Ch'ŏn-ju, *Han'guk chŏngch'i ch'egye,* p. 401.
* Rounding error.

the ideologically oriented activist students, on the one hand, and the conservative politicians and a great majority of the voters, on the other. As pointed out earlier, the conservative politicians were most sensitive about reformist proposals concerning a North–South cultural exchange program and Communist China's admission to the United Nations. These issues, suppressed by the government and ignored by the voters, were precisely the ones that the politically active radical students and schoolteachers and a few urban intellectuals were much concerned about. The main significance of the near-complete collapse of reformists at the grass-roots level—especially in Taegu—was that the ideologically oriented students in major universities were left without significant representation in the National Assembly.

As we shall see in later chapters, the economic disturbances of the student groups and many labor organizations (particularly the teachers' unions), which provided good excuse for a strong rightist reaction, could be attributed largely to the utter failure of the reformists and their sympathizers to secure a respectable position on the national political scene through the electoral process.

The April uprising resulted in effective paralysis of the Liberal Party and the national police. However, no effective political organization came into being to replace them until the fall of the Second Republic in May 1961. The Hŏ Chŏng government lacked both the incentive and ability to build a durable political machine to perpetuate its power. The Democratic Party complacently assumed that it would inherit power without further organizational effort. It was unable, furthermore, to mobilize mass and student support, because of the leadership's preoccupation with internal squabbles and uninspiring political views. The forces that brought about the revolution—the students and the urban intellectuals—were never a cohesive group with any organizational base, and they could not develop into one within the short period of time available. The "reformists" came closest to soliciting and receiving the active support of the students and the highly politicized individuals in the urban areas. However, they were badly split into many groups and parties and were decisively rejected by the voters. Furthermore, their attempt to develop as a formidable political force, broadly organized with a firm ideological foundation, was blocked by a political system in which such activities would not be tolerated and could not be carried out freely.

VI

PARTY POLITICS IN THE SECOND REPUBLIC

In the general election held on July 29, 1960, the voters gave the Democratic Party an overwhelming majority of seats in the National Assembly. The initial results of the election showed that the party captured more than 160 lower house seats from the 220 districts in which the election returns were officially confirmed.[1] The decisive victory of the Democratic Party could be attributed to a variety of factors, some of the important ones being the party's position as the only nationally organized political force participating in the election; the disorganization of the reformist politicians and the unpopularity of their political views; and a desire on the part of many voters to reward the party for its difficult struggle against the Liberal regime during the past few years. The Democratic Party benefited most from the general expectation that it would control the government after the election, as government officials and police cooperated closely with the party and businessmen provided sufficient political funds.[2] However, the sure prospect that the Democratic Party would have control of the National Assembly—and therefore the next cabinet—also intensified the factional struggle within the party.

1. In 13 districts, election results were nullified and new elections were held because of violent incidents resulting largely from the favorable showing of the former Liberals.

2. Although it is difficult to document the exact extent of the financial contribution made by businessmen to the Democratic Party, there is little doubt that large sums went to both factions of the Democratic Party before and after the July 29 general election. A special committee set up by the National Assembly to investigate "illegal flow of political funds" revealed later that the Democratic Party had received "more than one billion hwan from leading businessmen prior to the election." See *Kyŏnghyang Shinmun,* October 1, 1960, p. 1.

THE FACTIONAL STRIFE IN THE DEMOCRATIC PARTY

The central issue which preoccupied both factions of the party during the month of June was the nomination procedure, which would have a direct bearing upon the balance of power between the two factions following the election. In an attempt to block the new faction's ascendence to power, the old faction, whose power position was weaker, sought to open ways for election of a number of independents and former Liberals who were leaning toward it. Thus the old faction demanded that the party should leave some 50 districts without official Democratic nominees, and that in those districts where competition between many different Democratic candidates was too severe, the party should support whoever appeared to be leading the field—even if he turned out to be a non-Democrat.

The new faction, on the other hand, attempted to make past loyalty to the party the main criterion of eligibility for the Democratic nomination. It particularly emphasized that the primary consideration in all contested districts should be whether the candidate had any record of past collaboration with the Liberal Party and how much he had worked for the Democratic nominee (Chang Myŏn) in the last vice-presidential election.[3] Undoubtedly the new faction was making an issue out of the fact that many old-faction members and their supporters had not campaigned for Chang Myŏn after the death of Cho Pyŏng-ok, the Democratic nominee for the presidency. From the different contentions made by the two factions, it was clear that neither was willing to cooperate with the other and that the only reason the two factions still remained in the same party was that the party was recognized as the heir-apparent to the interim government. When nominations were finally announced, the new faction came out with more candidates for the National Assembly than the old faction, 113 to 106, with 8 candidates not closely affiliated with either faction.[4] The party placed candidates in 227 of the 233 electoral districts; contrary to the old faction's proposal, only 6 districts were left without an official Democratic nominee.

Once the nominating committee's decision was announced, however, most of the candidates who failed to receive official nomination declared that they would run in their respective districts anyway, against the official nominee of the party; each faction implicitly encouraged the candidacy of its supporter against the official nominee, if he happened to be from the rival faction. The pervasiveness of

3. *Tong-a Ilbo,* June 14, 1960, p. 1.
4. *Ibid.,* July 3, 1960, p. 1.

intra-party competition was shown by the fact that 113 Democrats were "dismissed" by the party because of their candidacy for National Assembly seats without official party endorsement.[5] Supporters of the old faction were competing with the official party nominees in 55 assembly districts, and those of the new faction in 26 districts.[6]

In the campaign itself, the candidates publicly used such labels as "old-faction" and "new-faction" nominee. In districts where their own men received official nomination, each faction discouraged all other aspirants among its members from running. However, in districts where a faction failed to secure the nomination of its own man, it often helped the campaign of either its own faction's unofficial candidate or an independent candidate who opposed the rival faction of the Democratic Party. In Chŏlla Nam-do Province, the old faction placed candidates in all 10 districts where the new-faction candidates had the official party endorsement. New-faction candidates ran in 3 of the 22 districts which had officially nominated old-faction candidates.[7] Aspirants who failed to receive party nomination sometimes crossed the factional line in order to run against the party candidate.[8]

The antagonism and hostility between the two factions were based primarily upon personal links and consideration of immediate personal interests rather than on different ideological orientation or social and economic position. Much of the rivalry arose out of personal and emotional animosity. Therefore the two factions offered identical programs, operating within the same conservative framework.

Because of its non-ideological nature, the struggle between the two factions was carried out in the form of personal attacks on the integrity of the candidates and the sources of their political funds. Mutual slander commonly took place between the competing factions. One consequence of such rivalry was the absence of effective discipline within the Democratic Party. Since the party could never speak with one voice, there was no way to effectively censure a dissenting Democrat. He could always expect to receive the support of one faction as long as he was hurting its rival faction. Many observers reported during the campaign period that the Democratic Party's dismissal of those running without party nomination had only a minimal impact on the candidates themselves or the outcome of the election, as they continued to receive the full support of their respective factions.[9]

5. *Ibid.*, July 5, 1960, p. 1.
6. *Kyŏnghyang Shinmun*, July 6, 1960, p. 1.
7. *Tong-a Ilbo*, July 1, 1960, p. 1.
8. *Ibid.*, July 21, 1960, p. 1.
9. Similarly, those who were outside the hard-core circle in both factions had highly flexible attitudes toward both political groups, freely promising or with-

The problem of discipline could also be found *within* the factions themselves, but it was especially serious in the old faction. Following Cho Pyŏng-ok's death, no leader could claim that he was speaking on behalf of the faction as a whole. As will be seen in the following discussion, the new faction's strategy was to attempt to take advantage of the internal disunity of the old faction.

Another consequence of the intense rivalry was that both factions strove to bring external political forces into the party in an effort to overpower the opposing faction. As already mentioned, the old faction attempted to leave as many electoral districts as possible without official Democratic nomination, so that pro-old faction independents or former Liberal Party members could be elected. Furthermore, there were frequent reports that the old faction was contemplating an alliance with other political forces, such as those led by Hŏ Chŏng or a group of prominent lawyers who showed an interest in politics following the April uprising. Many former attorneys, judges, and prosecutors became candidates for National Assembly seats in the July election; they included individuals like former Chief Supreme Court Judge Kim Pyŏng-no. Some old-faction leaders such as Yun Po-sŏn subsequently denied that there had been an understanding with other groups on the formation of a new party. However, it was subsequently made clear that a few of the old-faction leaders such as Yu Chin-san—known as the "real" powerholder within the old faction, as opposed to "figurehead" leaders such as Yun Po-sŏn and Kim To-yŏn—had indeed attempted such an alliance with the lawyers' group.[10]

Meanwhile, members of the Democratic old faction, including Yu Chin-san and Sŏ Pŏm-sŏk, said that a two-party system would have to be established among conservative politicians "in order to prevent the dictatorial rule of one party that might result from the overwhelming victory of the Democratic Party, and to prevent the rise of the reformist elements" as a result. Such a statement was consistent with earlier pronouncements made by some leaders of the old faction, that they would form a separate party after the election.[11] One important purpose of the seemingly premature announcements of the old faction's intention to form a separate party was to help the campaign of many old-faction-supported candidates who were running without Democratic Party nomination. Sŏ Sŏn-gyu, another hard-core old-faction member, went so far as to state that the two factions would defi-

---

drawing support. Often they would pledge support to both factions. Yun Po-sŏn, *Kugugŭi kasibatkil* [Thorny Road Toward National Salvation], p. 53.

10. *Tong-a Ilbo*, July 7, 1960, p. 1.
11. *Ibid.*, July 22–24, 1960.

nitely split into separate parties in case either one of them proved capable of forming a majority in the National Assembly, with the cooperation of the independents.[12] Furthermore, Kim To-yŏn later said that those statements concerning the old faction's plans to form a new party were made with the concurrence of its top leaders.[13]

Following the July 29 election, additional factors gave the old faction impetus to secede from the Democratic Party. In the first place, while the party as a whole captured 160, or about three-fourths, of the National Assembly seats, it appeared that the old faction had elected more assemblymen than the new faction. Shortly after election returns were confirmed in most legislative districts, each faction held separate meetings of the assemblymen-elect on August 5, to reaffirm solidarity and discuss future strategy for capturing the government. The old faction claimed that its caucus was attended by 83 assemblymen-elect (including 9 who had not been officially nominated by the Democratic Party) and 12 successful candidates in the newly created House of Councillors. On the other hand, it was reported that 75 assemblymen-elect (including 7 who had been elected without party nomination) and 10 councillors-elect attended the caucus of the new faction.[14] The fact that more assemblymen-elect attended the caucus of the old faction boosted the morale and confidence of its leaders and encouraged their scheme to establish a separate party.

In the caucus itself, the old faction established a 23-man committee which was entrusted with the task of selecting candidates for president and prime minister. Under the new constitution of the Second Republic, the president was to have the power to "appoint" the prime minister, who in turn had to be approved by the National Assembly by a majority of the membership. The caucus also approved a declaration which stated:

1) There is ever-present danger of a one-party dictatorship if the Democratic Party is allowed to have a two-thirds majority in the National Assembly. Since it is desirable to have healthy competition of two major parliamentary parties under a parliamentary system of government, and since no other party can act as a major opposition party under the present circumstances, the Democratic Party has to split into two independent parties.
2) The Democratic Party has so far maintained an uneasy unity by distributing party positions to the two factions on an equitable and equal basis. However, present circumstances demand a strong party government which cannot be expected from a superficial alliance between two opposing

12. *Ibid.*, July 8, 1960, p. 1.
13. Kim To-yŏn, *Naŭi insaeng paeksŏ*, p. 361.
14. Sŏ Pyŏng-jo, *Chukwŏnjaŭi chŭngŏn*, p. 368.

factions. Therefore, we [the old-faction members] will strive to form a government consisting of individuals who share common political views and who would be responsible to the people on a collective basis.

3) We condemn all anti-democratic actions committed during the election period, including assaults, vandalism, arson, and illegal opening of the ballot boxes, and urge the authorities to conduct a thorough investigation of the situation.[15]

In addition, the caucus resolved to boycott the conference of the Democratic assemblymen-elect scheduled for the next day. With some 90 members of the National Assembly firmly supporting it, the old faction felt it a relatively easy task to induce the independents to support its own candidates for the two highest offices in the Second Republic.

In the meantime, the conference of elected members supporting the new faction decided to form a 13-man selection committee which would have exclusive power in nominating the candidates for president and prime minister. The new faction did not give up the idea of restoring party unity under its own control. Thus, in the name of a balanced distribution of offices, the 13-man committee decided to support Yun Po-sŏn for the presidency and Chang Myŏn for the prime minister. It was also resolved in the committee meeting that in case the old faction refused to come to terms with the new faction to this end, the "Yun-Chang line" would be reexamined.[16]

The new faction adopted the "Yun-Chang line" on the assumption that, since it could not hope to capture both of the top government positions, it would be easier to elect Chang prime minister if Yun, a leading candidate for high office among the old-faction members, were elected president and thus eliminated from contention for the real power position. Furthermore, such a strategy would serve to demonstrate the new faction's effort to compromise and to reconcile with the old faction.[17]

The old faction's claim of numerical superiority in the National Assembly seemed to be confirmed when the candidates they sponsored won in the contests for presiding officers in both houses of the National Assembly. In addition to a sense of confidence, the old-faction leaders had another important reason why they would not accept the new faction's proposal that the two share the presidency and prime ministership. Unlike the new faction, the old faction did not have an undisputed leader within the group. As discussed in Chapter Three, the Korean Democratic Party (KDP), and later the Democratic Nationalist

15. *Kyŏnghyang Shinmun,* August 5, 1960, p. 1.
16. *Ibid.,* August 7, 1960, p. 1.
17. Yun Po-sŏn, *Kugugŭi kasibatkil,* p. 84.

Party (DNP), had the characteristics of a party of notables, organized in a loose manner based on pluralistic principles. This became more conspicuous with the deaths of two of its popular leaders, Shin Ik-hi and Cho Pyŏng-ok. Following the July election, the old faction was faced with the problem of accommodating the conflicting wishes of Yun Po-sŏn and Kim To-yŏn, both of whom had been with the old-faction group since the earliest days of the KDP.

A brief description of the two leaders' past political activities will shed light on the nature of the old faction and its leadership. Yun Po-sŏn was born in Ch'ungch'ŏng Nam-do in 1897 to family of considerable wealth and social status, his ancestors having had high government positions during the Yi Dynasty.[18] Following graduation from an elementary school in Seoul which had been set up primarily to teach Japanese pupils, Yun went to Japan for further education. In Tokyo, he spent two years as an unsuccessful student at Keio Preparatory School. Having returned to Korea without any notable accomplishment in Japan, Yun now contemplated making a trip to Europe. For this purpose he first went to Shanghai in 1918, where he met a number of nationalist leaders such as Syngman Rhee, Kim Kyu-shik, and Shin Ik-hi. While in Shanghai, Yun became a member of the legislative council of the Korean Provisional Government because of his financial contribution to the nationalist movement.[19] In 1921, Yun went to England for study and returned home in 1932.[20] According to Yun himself, he went back to Korea "at the insistence of his father," and in order to collect funds to be used for the nationalist cause abroad.[21] However, Yun was unable to leave Korea again, and was not involved in any public activities until the Japanese defeat in 1945.[22]

Following the Japanese withdrawal from Korea in 1945, Yun was among the first to join the KDP as a political group of conservative individuals. Yun's primary value to the party was his wealth: he provided its meeting places and funds. Yun was appointed a consultant to

18. Much of the information concerning Yun's personal background is from his own memoir, *Kugugŭi kasibatkil.*

19. While in Shanghai, Yun was asked by Syngman Rhee to bring some of his family money for the independence movement. Yun went as far as Japan, but decided to leave the actual task of taking the money out of Korea to his brother who was then studying in Tokyo. (*Ibid.*, p. 26.)

20. Yun took pride in the fact that, while attending the University of Edinburgh, he had not exchanged one word with the Japanese students who were also studying there.

21. *Ibid.*, pp. 36–37.

22. This can be described as Yun's "silent period," as Yun literally kept his mouth closed in public, and never responded to visitors from the police or other government offices. See *Chŏnggye yahwa,* [Behind-the-Scenes Stories of Korean Politics], pp. 207–208.

the agricultural and commercial bureau by the U.S. Military Government in Korea. In the first general election for the National Assembly held in May 1948, Yun was defeated in his native district in Ch'ungch'ŏngnam-do. After establishment of the Rhee government, Yun was appointed mayor of Seoul by Syngman Rhee and subsequently served in the Rhee cabinet as the minister of commerce and industry until 1951. Yun resumed his party activities in 1952 by joining the DNP, and was elected for the first time to the National Assembly in 1954, from a relatively well-established district in Seoul.[23]

Despite his passive political manner, Yun was chosen floor leader of the DNP after the National Assembly elections in 1954. Yun's election to this position—in spite of his unwillingness to serve in that capacity—was indicative of the importance the party placed on length of affiliation. However, Yun was reluctant to accept the responsibility of waging an all-out struggle against the ruling Liberal Party, and declined to accept the position. According to Yun himself, the resignation was accepted "only because of his timely illness which required recuperation in Pusan." [24] Yun further wrote, "After my resignation was finally accepted because of the illness, I was assigned to the foreign affairs committee. This committee was always short of its full membership and consisted of a few elderly assemblymen and those who had been forced out of other committees and had nothing better to do." [25]

Yun was elected chairman of the Democratic Party's central committee in October 1957, and was reelected to the position following the general election in 1958. In November 1959, Yun was elected to the supreme council of the Democratic Party, replacing Kim To-yŏn, who had been a long-time enemy of the new faction for his active advocacy of the old faction's cause.

Although Yun had maintained close association with the old-faction members ever since establishment of the KDP in 1945, he was considered because of his reluctance to take the leadership to be much more acceptable to the new faction than Kim To-yŏn. The 1959 Democratic Party convention, in which the new faction had the superiority in numbers, thus chose to replace Kim with Yun.[26] Yun kept his posi-

23. He was elected from the First Chongno District, where his palace-like mansion was located. The residents in this area were generally well-to-do, and many of them had deep roots in the area by virtue of the fact that it had been a favorable residential area for the *yangban* (officialdom) class in Seoul for many centuries.

24. Yun Po-sŏn, pp. 66–67.

25. *Ibid.*

26. In the same convention, the old faction's Cho Pyŏng-ok won the presidential nomination over the new faction's Chang Myŏn. Cho's victory, despite the numerical inferiority of the old faction, could be attributed only to his own personal popularity. See Kim To-yŏn, pp. 330–331.

tion as a member of the Democratic Party's Supreme Council until after the July 1960 election. During this period the Supreme Council consisted of 5 members, of whom only 2 were from the old faction. Cho Pyŏng-ok, who had been a member of the Supreme Council, was dead, and Paek Nam-hun, the only other old-faction man, was kept in the Council for reasons not dissimilar to Yun's election to it. At the age of 75, Paek had never been elected to the National Assembly and therefore could not be considered a threatening figure as far as the new faction was concerned.[27]

Thus, as the result of a deliberate scheme on the part of the new faction and a series of accidents involving the death of other old-faction leaders, Yun became the highest-placed old-faction member in the party. Yun did not have an organized following within the old faction. At the same time, he had not seriously antagonized any political groups either in his own faction or outside of it. He was not the first choice for leadership of most party members, but few had strong objections to giving him a high position.

Kim To-yŏn's personal background shows certain differences from that of Yun, although their similarities are more striking. Kim was born to a reasonably wealthy farming family in a village near Seoul in 1894. He received his elementary education in Seoul and attended Po-sŏng High School, where he established his initial contact with the "Po-sŏng group." Kim went to Japan in 1913 at the age of 19 and completed his secondary education there. In Tokyo he became well acquainted with some of the future leaders of the KDP and the Kim Sŏng-su, Song Chin-u, Chang Tŏk-su, and Shin Ik-hi. In February 1919, during his second year at Keio University in Tokyo, Kim was arrested by the Japanese police for participating in a demonstration by Korean students protesting Japanese rule over Korea, and was imprisoned for nearly a year. Shortly after his unhappy experience in Tokyo, Kim went to the United States where, while working for a master's degree in economics at Columbia University, he came into close contact with Cho Pyŏng-ok, who was pursuing a Ph.D. degree in the same school.[28]

While in New York, Kim was active in organizations of Korean residents in the United States such as the Hŭngsa-dan, under An Ch'ang-ho's leadership, and the Korean Residents' Association, which supported Syngman Rhee. However, because of his affiliation with these rival organizations and his efforts to bring them together on peaceful terms, he came to be suspected by and alienated from both of them. Kim had joined Hŭngsa-dan while he was studying in Tokyo, and was

27. Paek Nam-hun, *Naŭi ilsaeng* [My Life], *passim*.
28. Kim To-yŏn, pp. 110–114.

also active in that organization during his school days in the United States. He was expelled from the group, however, when it was learned that he had also joined the Korean Residents' Association. At the same time, he was accused by the leaders of the Residents' Association of being a "traitor" for his efforts to maintain cordial relationships with members of Hŭngsa-dan even after his expulsion from it.[29]

Kim then attempted to organize another group with those Koreans who were not affiliated with either of the competing organizations. In this effort, Kim cooperated with a number of others in New York, including Chang Tŏk-su,[30] Ch'oi Sun-ju [31] Yun ch'i-yŏng,[32] and Hŏ Chŏng, to publish the *Sam-il Shinmun* (*March First Times*) in Korean. However, the newspaper came under attack from both the Hŭngsa-dan group—which resented Hŏ Chŏng, a close follower of Rhee—and Rhee, who would not tolerate any "neutral" position between him and his rivals.

Disillusioned with political activities, Kim went to Washington, D.C., in 1929 to concentrate on his studies. In 1932 he received a Ph.D. in economics from American University in Washington, D.C., and returned to Korea, where he established a business firm which subsequently engaged in land sale and development, lumbering, mining, construction, and fish processing. The firm, the Chosŏn Hŭng-ŏp Company, was first created by about a dozen promoters, most of whom had studied abroad, and some thirty stockholders who, according to Kim, consisted of mainly "land-owning intelligentsia." [33] Many of the original promoters of the firm became prominent politicians during the first Korean Republic. They included Yi Ki-bung, Yi In,[34] Ch'oi Sun-ju, Sŏ Min-ho,[35] and Kim To-yŏn himself.

In 1942 Kim was arrested by the Japanese police on charges of supplying funds to the Korean Language Association, which allegedly incited an independence movement through revival of the Korean lan-

29. *Ibid.*, pp. 113–114.

30. Chang was the leader of the KDP following the death of Song Chin-u in 1946.

31. Ch'oe was a leading member of Syngman Rhee's Liberal Party and Vice-Speaker of the National Assembly in 1956.

32. Yun Ch'i-yŏng was a close follower of Syngman Rhee after Korean Liberation in 1945. In 1969, Yun served as chairman of the central committee of the ruling Democratic Republican Party.

33. Kim To-yŏn, p. 126.

34. Yi In was an original member of the KDP, but later left the group to become the first minister of justice in Rhee's cabinet.

35. Sŏ was a member of the KDP and later the DNP. As an assemblyman, he was imprisoned in 1952 in connection with a shooting incident in which an army officer who attempted to harm Sŏ under orders of the Rhee regime was killed. Sŏ was released following the April uprising.

guage.[36] During his three-year period of confinement, first in the police jail in Hongwŏn, Hamgyŏng Nam-do, and later in the Hamhŭng Prison, Kim was subjected to severe hardships from torture and hunger until he was released on bail ten months before Korean Liberation.

Immediately after Japanese withdrawal from Korea, Kim joined the KDP and served as one of the original directors of the party. In December 1946 he was elected to the Interim Legislative Assembly from a Seoul district. In the Interim Legislative Assembly, Kim actively opposed the trusteeship plan of the four powers. Thus, in cooperation with a number of other KDP members and over the objection of a few moderate members close to the Assembly's Chairman Kim Kyu-sik, Kim To-yŏn was able to pass a resolution in the legislative assembly opposing the trusteeship plan and criticizing General Hodge for restricting the freedom of expression of those individuals and organizations opposing the plan.

Kim was chosen to serve as the first minister of finance and the only KDP member in Rhee's cabinet. Kim discharged his duties as finance minister with remarkable impartiality and honesty, though he was lacking in forcefulness and renovative spirit. During the two-year period in Rhee's cabinet, Kim's primary concern was prevention of the inflationary spiral which had characterized the Korean economy since Japanese withdrawal in 1945, and which developed into an extremely serious problem after establishment of the Rhee government. Kim's financial policy placed emphasis on reduction of government expenses rather than expansion of domestic industry. Kim's cautious approach to the national economy was largely responsible for his relatively long tenure in Rhee's cabinet, considering the rapid turnover of cabinet posts which characterized the Rhee government.

Kim returned to the National Assembly in 1954, as one of the 15 Democratic Nationalist candidates to be elected, and later assisted Shin Ik-hi and Cho Pyŏng-ok in the formation of the Democratic Party. He was one of the six directors—three from the DNP—who made major decisions concerning the shape of the new party. In the directors' meetings, Kim often clashed with Chang Myŏn, who represented the non-DNP group. According to Kim himself, he always bore the main burden of blocking the non-DNP group's demand on behalf of Shin Ik-hi, Cho Pyŏng-ok, and other members of the group, with the result of making himself the main target to the new faction's hostility and attack.[37] At the time of the April uprising, Kim was holding a

36. For a detailed discussion of the incident, see Yi Hi-sŭng, "The Korean Language Association Incident," in *Sasanggye,* August 1959 through May 1960.

37. Kim argues that this was the main reason for his inability to be elected to

nominal party position as vice-chairman of the central committee of the Democratic Party. Thus, in the mind of Kim and his supporters, he was being treated unfairly by the party because of the irreconcilable rivalry between its two factions.

The respective personal backgrounds of Yun po-sŏn and Kim To-yŏn help us understand better the different positions of the two men in the old faction. It appears that Yun's ascendance in stature in the political scene was primarily due to his wealth, some interest and ambition in politics, and his inability or unwillingness to undertake any other activities such as business or scholarly work. During Japanese rule, Yun had maintained his contact with the nationalist leaders without actually participating in any activities that might seriously endanger his safety or wealth. It is true that Yun persistently refused to cooperate with the Japanese rulers. However, his attitude during this period could be characterized as complete passivity and negativism. His record as an official in the Rhee government—either as mayor of Seoul or as a cabinet member—showed similar traits of the man, seemingly lacking in initiative, and unwilling to risk controversy in carrying out his own programs. Yun's unwillingness to be involved in controversies and to offend other people was an asset which helped his ascendance in the Democratic Party.

On the other hand, Kim showed more activism in public activities and was more willing to commit himself to a controversial course of action. Kim had maintained a close identification with the old faction and its leaders. His strong advocacy of the old faction's cause cost him his acceptability to the new faction. Furthermore, because of his loyal support of Shin Ik-hi and Cho Pyŏng-ok, he had to remain in the shadow of the well-known leaders. After the July election, Kim had many disadvantages; he was relatively unknown to the public, bitterly opposed by the new faction, and often referred to as an example of the factionalist politician. Kim's support came from a solid group of some 20 "hard-core" old-faction assemblymen who desired a permanent separation from the new faction at any cost.[38] Yun, on the other hand, lacked any solid following such as Kim To-yŏn had. For Yun, therefore, the maintenance of some kind of working relationship with the new faction was essential to keeping alive his hopes to become either president or prime minister.

---

the Supreme Council except for a brief period between July 1956 and January, 1958. See Kim To-yŏn, p. 271.

38. According to a *Kyŏnghyang Shinmun* breakdown, there were about 20 pro-Kim members and 66 pro-Yu Chin-san members who were less than categorical about the desirability of Democratic Party division (September 22, 1960, p. 1).

It appears, however, that there were certain similar elements in the two men which contributed to their rise to leadership positions in the Democratic Party, and which demonstrate certain significant aspects about the old faction and the party itself. Although Kim showed more willingness than Yun to risk personal danger and controversy, his political atttiude, like Yun's, was essentially negative and passive, lacking in personal dynamism and powerful leadership qualities. Neither of them could energetically move their fellow members of the Democratic Party or even of the old faction itself. It was widely assumed that the "real" power in the old faction rested with such skillful internal operators as Yu Chin-san and So Sŏn-gyu. Thus, the "top" leaders were more often objects of manipulation by individuals of lesser stature than the prime movers of their own faction or party.

Much of the passivity that we attributed to Kim To-yŏn and Yun Posŏn appears equally applicable to Chang Myŏn, leader of the new faction. When Chang was "drafted" by members of the Parliamentary Liberal Party (PLP) to become their leader in 1952, it was largely because of his stature as prime minister under Syngman Rhee, because of his good reputation among the American officials at the time—and, most importantly, because of the prospect that Chang could be easily influenced by them.[39] His election to the vice-presidency in 1956 was attributable primarily to the sudden death of Shin Ik-hi and the extraordinary unpopularity of the Liberal Party and its vice-presidential candidate, rather than to the vote-getting ability of Chang himself.

Chang's life-history also reveals qualities similar to those of Yun Po-sŏn and Kim To-yŏn: general passivity, moderation, and cautiousness. Chang was born to a reasonably wealthy Catholic family in Inch'ŏn in 1899, and attended an elementary school there which taught both the traditional and Western subjects. He later attended an agricultural school in Suwŏn,[40] from which he graduated at the age of 19.[41] Chang studied English at the YMCA institute for about three years after his graduation from the agricultural school, and shortly after the March First Movement he went to the United States to study education and religion at Manhattan College for five years. Following his return to Korea in 1925, Chang devoted himself to educational projects of the Catholic Church, first in Pyŏngyang and later in Seoul. For 17

39. Sŏnu Chong-wŏn, *Mangmyŏngŭi kyejŏl* [Season of Exile], pp. 25–27; also, interviews with Sŏnu, October 22, 1968, and with Kim Kŏng-sŏn, November 4, 1968.

40. This school was the predecessor of the present Agricultural College of Seoul National University.

41. The following discussion on Chang's personal background is primarily based on Chang Myŏn, *Memoirs*, pp. 25–61.

years, until the end of the Second World War, Chang served as superintendent of the Catholic Tongsŏng Commercial School in Seoul. Thus Chang had had little experience or contact with political activities when he turned to political life following the liberation of Korea in 1945. Chang's Catholic background and knowledge of the English language were instrumental in his appointment to the Interim legislative Assembly in 1946 by the American Military Government in Korea.

Following his election to the First National Assembly in 1948 from a district in Seoul, Chang was appointed by Rhee to serve as the first Korean ambassador to the United Nations and later to the United States. Chang received much credit for his successful effort to persuade the United Nations to render official recognition of the South Korean government in December 1948. His name grew more familiar among Koreans for his plea to the U.N. General Assembly to assist South Korea against the North Korean invasion in June, 1950. In February 1951, Chang was appointed prime minister by Rhee. This appointment was apparently motivated by Rhee's desire to reduce his difficulties with the opposition members in the National Assembly, as Chang was quite favorably regarded by most assemblymen. Through Chang, Rhee also attempted to improve his relations with the United States, which had been strained because of Rhee's dictatorial rule and maladministration. Like most other men who served as prime minister under President Rhee, Chang's record as the chief cabinet member was relatively undistinguished, although Chang claimed that he was instrumental in getting the 1951–1952 budget through the National Assembly and in dissolving the controversial National Defense Corps.[42]

Late in 1951, Chang was sent to Paris to represent South Korea at the 6th U.N. General Assembly. While in Paris, according to Chang, he had to be hospitalized because of hepatitis. Later he was brought back to Korea, but again he had to stay in a U.S. military hospital located in South Korea.[43] It was during this period of Chang's absence from the political scene that South Korea was experiencing the "political crisis" of 1952, which involved intimidation of the National Assembly by pro-Rhee mobs and the arrest of many opposition assemblymen by the military police and national police. Chang's disappearance at this time aroused speculations that Chang was secretly directing a movement to displace Rhee from the presidency, with the help of his American friends. Chang later denied the story, but it is difficult to determine the seriousness of Chang's illness or the true reasons for Chang's complete disappearance from the political arena.

42. *Ibid.*, pp. 32–33.
43. *Ibid.*, pp. 24–35.

In general, however, Chang showed a considerable degree of timidity and indecisiveness in situations which required strong determination and immediate action. According to Kim To-yŏn, Chang was scheduled to be the principal speaker and to read the main declaration against Rhee's scheme for a constitutional amendment at a meeting of anti-Rhee politicians in Pusan in 1951. Upon learning that the meeting might be disrupted by pro-Rhee terrorists, however, Chang simply failed to show up, and his absence delayed the reading of the declaration and the meeting itself, which was eventually broken up by unidentified invaders. Toward the end of the meeting, scores of terrorists attacked the participants, and anti-Rhee politicians such as Cho Pyŏng-ok, Sŏ Sang-il and Kim Ch'ang-suk were seriously injured.[44] Chang's complete withdrawal from the political scene during this period is very similar to his five-day disappearance following the military coup d'état of May 1961. As in the situation nine years earlier, Chang's whereabouts were unknown, and he took no action concerning the existing critical situation.

Chang's support within the Democratic Party came from the non-KDP-NDP group, many of whom had not actively participated in party politics before the Korean War. Many of his supporters had bureaucratic, financial, or judicial backgrounds.[45] Fortunately for the new faction, since the Democratic Party rejected the inclusion of all leaders of substantial calibre outside of the KDP-NDP group such as Cho Pong-am, Yi Pŏm-sŏk, and Chang T'aek-sang at the time of its organization in 1954, the new-faction members could rally around only one man, namely Chang Myŏn. In this sense, the new faction had less of the pluralistic characteristics of the "party of notables" than did the old faction. Instead, its members operated as a "team," with Chang Myŏn as their formal leader.

The leadership qualities of these three men Yun, Kim, and Chang, who were in serious contention for power, were more suitable for a stable and institutionalized situation requiring no major efforts than for a period which called for the building of new legitimacy and support after the fall of the Rhee regime. One might ask, "How did such men come to occupy leadership positions in the Democratic Party during such a critical period?" We have already discussed how factional rivalry made Yun acceptable to the new faction. At the same time, in

44. Kim To-yŏn, pp. 253–254. Incidentally, Yun Po-sŏn was not present at that meeting, and Kim avoided the attack because he "arrived at the meeting somewhat late." See also Cho Pyŏng-ok, *Naŭi hoegorok,* pp. 346–348, for a description of the incident.

45. See Chapter Three.

both factions of the party what counted most was how long and how faithfully one had been associated with the particular faction and what position one had occupied before (such as a cabinet post in Rhee's government), rather than the attractiveness of one's political views or popularity among the general electorate.

Self-assertive individuals with much personal dynamism were unable to endure the necessity for political self-negation and passivity within the Democratic Party. For example, Kim Chun-yŏn, a director of the original KDP and leading member of the DNP, left the Democratic Party in 1957 to form his own Unification Party, following his bitter argument with the new faction about the legality of Chang's vice-presidential nomination. Kim and his supporters argued that the new faction had packed the party convention with its own delegates and therefore Chang was illegally nominated by it.[46] At the same time, Sŏ Sang-il, also one of the original organizers of the KDP, refused to join the Democratic Party in 1954 when it did not admit Cho Pong-am and other progressives, and later took part in the organization of the Progressive Party, as we have seen in the preceding chapter.

The fact that all three men happened to display passivity in political action, lack of dynamism in personality, and considerable conservatism in ideology, also requires explanation in the context of the general political structure. With the police, judicial apparatus, and armed forces firmly in the hands of Syngman Rhee, a conspicuous display of popularity, personal dynamasm, or ideological radicalism would have made an opposition politician an easy and certain object of liquidation by the Rhee regime. In order to avoid destruction by the Rhee government, an opposition figure in Korean politics had to have the protection, or at least implicit support, of an external force, namely the United States. No domestic political force could provide a check against a determined attack from Rhee. At the same time, as became evident at the time of the April uprising, Rhee regarded America's moral support as essential for the maintenance of his regime. This situation in turn required moderation in ideological and personal orientation on the part of opposition politicians.

Let us now examine the competition and maneuvering that took place between the three leaders and their supporters involving the positions of president and prime minister in the Second Republic. The question how the key positions should be allocated among the three leaders could not be settled through the party apparatus, as the old

46. In that contest, most of the old-faction members actually supported Chang's candidacy for vice-president in return for the new faction's support of Shin Ik-hi for the presidential nomination. Kim To-yŏn, p. 277.

faction persistently refused to participate in all functions of the party. Informal negotiations brought no results either, because of the basic differences in the positions of the two factions.

A summit meeting of the two factions was arranged by Kwak Sang-hun, on behalf of the neutral Democrats, in order to seek possibilities for reconciliation between the two factions concerning selection of the president and prime minister. However, the meeting, which was attended by Chang Myŏn and Yun Po-sŏn, ended only 40 minutes after it was called because of Yun's refusal to reconsider the old faction's position.[47] Yun's inability to compromise the old faction's contention that it had to capture both top positions was due to the fact neither Yun nor Kim actually controlled the old faction.

Although the president was to be elected by a joint conference of both houses of the National Assembly, attention was focused on the House of Representatives because of its relative size and because of its power to approve the president's nominee for prime minister.

As of early August, members of the lower house were split into three broadly defined groups—the new faction of the Democratic Party, the old faction of the Democratic Party, and the independents. As noted earlier, 75 to 80 assemblymen were unequivocally committed to the new faction, while those clearly in the old-faction camp numbered approximately 80 to 85. About a dozen Democrats refused to join either of the two factions, claiming to be neutral in their struggle. The "neutral group" consisted of relatively young members, who on August 8 met separately and expressed their opposition to any scheme to divide the party in two. They also demanded that both factions nullify their respective choices for the presidential and prime ministerial candidates.[48]

In addition to these groups within the Democratic Party, over 40 assemblymen formed the "People's Politics Club" in order to function as a parliamentary group, a minimum membership of 30 being required to qualify as an official group in the National Assembly. This was a highly heterogeneous group, consisting of those lacking any political affiliation because of their previous absence from the political scene; those who had served in the previous National Assembly as "pure" independents; former Liberals who were elected without party affiliation; and members of the reformist parties who by themselves could not form a separate parliamentary group.[49] Of these, however,

47. *Kyŏnghyang Shinmun*, August 11, 1960, p. 1.

48. *Ibid.*, August 9, 1960, p. 1.

49. For a list of the 44 assemblymen who joined the People's Politics Club (*Minjŏng-hoe*), see *ibid.*, p. 1.

only about half remained in the group for a common course of action, the other half joining one of the factions of the Democratic Party within a few days.

The even distribution of assemblymen between the two factions of the Democratic Party; the relatively loose nature of the organization of the old faction, which had a slight numerical superiority in the House of Representatives; and the highly heterogeneous nature of the group of independent assemblymen—all these factors made it very difficult for either faction to form a winning coalition. The new faction, which was concentrating on the prime ministership, decided to support Yun Po-sŏn for the presidency, partly in order to remove him from competition with Chang and partly to demonstrate its generous intentions. Subsequently, on August 12, Yun was elected president at a joint conference of the National Assembly with the support of both factions of the party, after he decided to accept the position which was assured to him rather than risking defeat to Chang in a contest over the prime ministership.[50]

As president, Yun was given the power to nominate the prime minister to be approved by the National Assembly. After extensive consultation with the leaders of all political groups, including both factions of the Democratic Party and independents, Yun announced on August 16 his nomination of Kim To-yŏn, his rival in the old faction for first prime minister of the Second Republic. Although Yun contended that his decision was reached solely on the basis of an objective assessment of the relative support that each possible candidate seemed to have in the National Assembly,[51] he was widely criticized in and out of the National Assembly for this apparent factional choice.[52] Many youthful members of the old faction argued that Kim's nomination would finalize the split between the two factions, and that the choice was politically unwise as well as ethically impermissible, since it would be easier to block the nomination of the first candidate than the second one.[53] They argued that the appointment of Kim as prime minister offended the few "neutral" Democrats who were not clearly committed to either faction, and that the independents would be eager to demonstrate their position as the deciding power in the National Assembly by voting against his approval.

Prior to Yun's announcement of his choice for the top executive position, some 20 independent members of the National Assembly who

50. *Ibid.*, August 13, 1960, p. 1.
51. Yun Po-sŏn, pp. 90–91.
52. Min Kwan-shik, *Nakchesaeng* [The Flunkout], pp. 153–156.
53. Ibid., p. 156.

sought to take a common course of action had asked both Chang Myŏn and Kim To-yŏn to express their opinions concerning the composition of the new cabinet. While both candidates emphasized an "all-nation" cabinet, they differed on the issue of whether or not independents would be brought into the cabinet. Chang stated that his "all-nation" cabinet would include not only members of both factions of the Democratic Party, but also those "able individuals" among the independents. On the other hand, Kim virtually excluded the possibility that any independents would be chosen on the basis of the *principle of party government.*[54]

In retrospect, it would appear that Kim's insistence on "party government" cost him the National Assembly's approval. Although Kim's promise to have independents in his cabinet would not have turned all the independent members to his support, it could have changed at least two or three votes, by which margin Kim's nomination failed to be approved in the National Assembly two days later. However, most responsible for Kim's defeat in the National Assembly were his inability to hold all the old-faction members solidly behind him and his failure to deal with the independents collectively because of their heterogeneity. At the time of voting, it was estimated that the two factions had 90 and 95 "reliable supporters" in the National Assembly, as shown in Table VI-1. Of these, 5 to 7 old-faction members eventually defected to the new-faction camp, voting against Kim's approval.[55] It thus appears that actually less than half of some 30 "independent" assemblymen voted with the new faction in rejecting Kim's nom-

Table VI-1

NATIONAL ASSEMBLY VOTES ON KIM TO-YŎN'S CANDIDACY AUGUST *10, 1960* (SPECULATED)

	*Old-Faction Members **	*New-Faction Members **	*Independents*	*Total*
For Kim	91	0	21	111
Against	6	90	16	112
TOTAL	97	90	37	223 †

* Includes non-Democrats who were closely identified with either of the two factions.

† There were 3 absent assemblymen, of whom 2 were in jail and 1 reported as being ill. Also, there was 1 invalid vote.

54. *Kyŏnghyang Shinmun,* August 15, 1960, evening ed., p. 1; also Kim To-yŏn, pp. 366–367.

55. Yun Po-sŏn, pp. 90–91.

ination,[56] the critical votes being those of the old-faction defectors. The voting revealed that the old faction, being a loosely organized coalition of individual leaders and their respective followers, was quite vulnerable to disintegration by and defection to an outside force.

The difference between the two factions can be demonstrated more clearly by citing a typology of political parties introduced by David Apter. Apter distinguishes between a "political coalition" and a "party of representation," according to the degree of discipline and institutionalization of leadership in the political group. A political coalition comes into being by combining various factions and political groups during the pre-party period. India's Congress party in its founding period and Burma's Anti-Fascist People's Freedom League are given as examples of this type of political coalition, with more institutionalized leadership which operates the party in a more disciplined manner. Both types are to be distinguished from either "political movements" or "parties of solidarity" which ordinarily accompany strong ideological commitment on the part of the membership and/or the existence of a charismatic leader capable of arousing the masses and the party membership.[57]

It seems that while both factions of the Democratic Party were more than mere political coalitions, they had not reached the stage of being parties of representation. We could only say that the new faction had more characteristics of a party of representation than the old faction. This discussion makes it easier to understand the circumstances under which the defection of the old-faction members to the new faction took place, and why Kim failed to receive the approval of the National Assembly.

On August 19, two days after the National Assembly's rejection of Kim for prime minister, President Yun nominated Chang Myŏn, who subsequently received approval by a vote of 117 to 107. The breakdown of votes given in Table VI-2 indicates that the independents gave Chang about the same number of affirmative votes as they did Kim. It also appears that, contrary to expectation, most independents who had voted for Kim earlier also voted in favor of Chang.[58] The independents, of course, correctly observed little ideological difference between the two factions, and those who voted against the first nominee be-

56. *Kyŏnghyang Shinmun,* August 13–19, 1960.

57. For a discussion of the different types of political parties, see David E. Apter, *The Politics of Modernization,* pp. 179–222.

58. Those 20-plus independents who had earlier resolved to vote against Kim decided again to reject Chang's nomination as premier. (*Tong-a Ilbo,* August 19, 1960, p. 1.) During this period, according to leaders of both factions, many independents promised support to both of them.

Table VI-2
NATIONAL ASSEMBLY VOTES ON CHANG MYŎN'S CANDIDACY
AUGUST *19, 1960* (SPECULATED)

	Old-Faction Members	*New-Faction Members*	*Independents*	*Total*
For Chang	6	90	21	117
Against	91	0	16	107
TOTAL	97	90	37	224

cause of his conservatism and lack of leadership qualities also voted against Chang for similar reasons. In general, they included individuals who belonged to the "reformist" political groups, and other independent members who desired a greater share of influence for the non-Democrats in the operation of the national government and the National Assembly. Approval of Chang Myŏn as first prime minister of the Second Republic can be seen as the result of a coalition of the new faction, those Democrats who defected from the old faction, and independents whose action was based primarily upon their individual choice without reference to any political group. In his effort to form a parliamentary majority, Chang had a choice between attempting to consolidate this slim majority which approved his nomination as the prime minister by absorbing the independents, or soliciting support from the old faction by forming a coalition cabinet with it. Chang's difficulty lay in the fact that neither of the two political groups had the makings of a reliable ally. The independents could not be brought into stable coalition with his party because of its heterogeneity in membership and wide variety in political ambitions and views. At the same time, the old faction became extremely hostile to the new faction and was too hurt by the recent defeat to come under Chang's leadership. In this critical choice, Chang seemed to prefer to keep the old faction within the Democratic Party. Chang eventually failed in this effort, and he had to operate without a stable parliamentary majority for some two months.

PARTY POLITICS UNDER THE CHANG MYŎN GOVERNMENT

Following National Assembly approval of Chang Myŏn as prime minister, the old-faction assemblymen met on August 20, in preparation for the formation of a new party. In the meeting, they resolved that the old-faction members would immediately form a party separate from the Democratic Party; would refuse to join Chang's cabinet under any circumstances; would punish those old-faction members who defected to the new faction; and would begin consultations with individuals outside of the National Assembly concerning formation of a new party. However, Kwak Sang-hun, Speaker of the House elected with the support of both factions of the party, arranged a meeting of the leaders of the two factions at President Yun's residence, in an attempt to prevent a permanent split of the Democratic Party. In the meeting, held on August 21, in the presence of Chang Myŏn, Yun Po-sŏn, Kwak Sang-hun, and Yu Chin-san, Chang apparently agreed to admit at least five old-faction members to his cabinet.[59] However, Chang could not live up to this commitment, as he was faced with a strong objection from other new-faction members who rightly felt that, instead of forming a coalition government with the old faction, they could more easily form a parliamentary majority by gradually absorbing independents and individual members from the old faction, with Chang's government power as the main inducement.[60] In his meeting the next day with the old-faction leaders, including Kim To-yŏn and Yu Chin-san, Chang demanded that the old faction refrain from forming a separate parliamentary group if it wished to participate in the new cabinet.[61] Given the decisions made by the old-faction members concerning formation of a parliamentary group, Chang's demand meant that no deal was possible between the two factions.

The list of new cabinet members, as shown in Table VI-3, included 10 new-faction Democrats, 1 old-faction member who had supported Chang Myŏn in the parliamentary voting for prime minister, and 2 individuals who were not members of the National Assembly.[62] In the first Chang cabinet, at least 7 ministers were former members of the Parliamentary Liberal Party (PLP) which first "drafted" Chang to become their leader. This was the same group which formed the inner circle to advise Chang in the formation of his cabinet.[63] Those names Chang especially mentioned for their assistance, and their respective positions in the new cabinet, were: Kim Yŏng-sŏn (finance), O Wi-yŏng (cabinet secretary), Hyŏn Sŏk-ho (defense), Cho Chae-ch'ŏn (justice), and Yi Sang-ch'ŏl (communication). Generally speaking, the composi-

59. Yu Chin-san, "Kyŏngmudae hoedamŭi chŏnmo" [A Complete Picture of the Kyŏngmutae Conference], pp. 13–15; also Yun Po-sŏn, pp. 92–93, and Kim To-yŏn, pp. 369–370.

60. Interview with Kim Yŏng-sŏn, November 4, 1968.

61. Yu Chin-san, *op. cit.*, and Kim To-yŏn, pp. 369–370.

62. See Table VI-1.

63. Chang Myŏn, pp. 65–66.

tion of Chang's first cabinet was a faithful reflection of what a Korean scholar called the "bureaucratic bent" of the new faction itself.[64] At the same time, the new cabinet failed to represent those individuals whose careers could be characterized as exclusively or primarily "political" in nature.[65] Neither did it include individuals representing such important political groups as the military leaders or reformist intellectuals.

According to Professor Hahn-Been Lee, those represented in the cabinet were the "program-oriented elements" who were more interested in the general thrust for development than in enjoying power. Those power-oriented elements, it was observed, still remained in the National Assembly.[66] Let us investigate the circumstances under which such a one-sided cabinet came to be born.[67]

Kyŏnghyang Shinmun, which had excellent connections with the new faction of the Democratic Party, reported that the Chang Myŏn faction in the National Assembly consisted of some 20 members from the old PLP group, about 10 members closely affiliated with Hŭngsa-dan, about 20 members who joined it after the April uprising, and some 40 members who belonged to what was known as the "junior group." [68] As already observed, Chang's "inner circle" consisted exclusively of the first group (PLP), which also occupied a majority of the cabinet positions. Some concession had been made to the Hŭngsa-dan group by giving them the positions of ministers of reconstruction and of education. The group which was left out most conspicuously, and was thus

64. Hahn-Been Lee, *Korea: Time, Change, and Administration,* p. 135. According to Lee, the old-faction members demonstrated a "rural-conservative bent."

65. See Chapter Two of this book.

66. Hahn-Been Lee, p. 136.

67. A brief explanation of the term "power-orientation" seems necessary here. Professor Lee uses the term to describe those elements "who represented mostly the rural constituencies and whose policy was oriented more towards their particular communities than towards the economy and society as a whole." He also considers them as "basically more interested in enjoying power than in a general thrust for development" (Lee, pp. 135–136). In this book, it is assumed that the "power orientation" of the politicians serves as a motivation to build support and legitimacy for the party and government to which they belong. In this sense, we can argue that power-oriented persons are support-consumers. The power-oriented (or politically oriented) are more concerned with the management of power than are program-oriented individuals, whose primary interest resides in the management of specific programs such as economic development. "Power-oriented" leaders should also be distinguished from what Eisenstadt calls the "solidarity-makers." Although the latter are power-oriented, simple power orientation does not necessarily accompany the ideological and charismatic quality normally associated with the solidarity-makers. For the above discussion, see S. N. Eisenstadt, *Modernization: Protest and Change;* Herbert Feith, *The Decline of Constitutional Democracy in Indonesia,* pp. 32–33; Apter, *The Politics of Modernization,* p. 49.

68. *Kyŏnghyang Shinmun,* September 22, 1960, p. 1.

Table VI-3

COMPOSITION AND BACKGROUND OF THE FIRST CABINET OF CHANG MYŎN

Cabinet Member (Year of Birth; Age)	*Position*	*Field of Study* (Schooling)	*Principal Non-Political Career*	*Party Affiliation* (Faction)
Chang Myŏn (1899; 61)	Premier	Education Religion (M.S.—U.S.)	Educator	Democratic (New)
Chŏng Il-hyŏng (1904; 56)	Foreign Affairs	Sociology (Ph.D.—U.S.)	Educator	Democratic (New)
Hong Ik-p'yo (1911; 49)	Home	Law (Seoul, Imperial Univ.)	Civil Servant †	Democratic (New)
Kim Yŏng-sŏn * (1919; 41)	Finance	Law (Seoul, Imperial Univ.)	Civil Servant †	Democratic (New)
Cho-Chae-ch'ŏn * (1912; 48)	Justice	Law (Japan)	Lawyer †	Democratic (New)
Hyŏn Sŏk-ho * (1907; 53)	Defense	Law (Seoul, Imperial Univ.)	Civil Servant †	Democratic (New)
O Ch'ŏn-sŏk (1901; 59)	Education	Education (Ph.D.—U.S.)	Educator	None
Chu Yŏ-han (1900; 60)	Reconstruction	Literature (Shanghai)	Journalist/Business	Democratic (New)
Pak Che-hwan (1905; 55)	Agriculture	Law (Japan)	Agricultural Association Worker	Independent

Yi Tae-yŏng (1909; 51)	Commerce and Industry	Law (Seoul Imperial Univ.)	Civil Servant †	Democratic (New)
Shin Hyŏn-don (1904; 56)	Health, Social Science	Medicine (Seoul, Medical Inst.)	Doctor	Democratic (New)
Chŏng Hŏn-ju (1915; 45)	Transportation	Law (Japan)	Education/Business	Democratic (Both) ‡
Yi Sang-ch'ŏl * (1893; 67)	Communication	Politics (Japan)	Journalist	Democratic (New)
Oh Wi-yŏng (1902; 58)	Cabinet Secretariat	Commerce (Japan)	Banker	Democratic (New)
Kim Sŏn-t'ae	No portfolio	Law (Japan)	Lawyer †	Democratic (New)

Sources: Sŏ Pyŏng-jo, *op. cit.*, pp. 378–379; Hahn-Been Lee, *Korea: Time, Change, and Administration*, p. 137; *Gendai Chosen Jinmei Jiten* (1962), *passim;* Chang Myŏn, *Memoirs*, pp. 65–66.

* Individuals who, according to Chang Myŏn, constituted the "inner circle" in formation of the cabinet.

† Individuals who had passed the Higher Civil Service Examination.

‡ Chŏng supporter Chang Myŏn for the premiership as an old-faction member, and subsequently joined the new faction.

most bitter about the composition of the new cabinet, was the junior members, who believed that their contribution had been most crucial in Chang's triumph over the old faction.[69]

The younger group, it should be noted, were distinctly more "power-oriented" than their elders in the new faction, by virtue of the fact that most of them had been active in student and other youth organizations during the pre-Korean War period. The personal background of Yi Ch'ŏl-sŭng, a representative figure in this group, clearly demonstrates this. Yi, a student at Korea University at the time of Korean Liberation in 1945, organized the National League of Students and, as its chairman, campaigned against the Trusteeship Plan in 1946. This organization, consisting largely of anti-Communist students, was instrumental in fighting leftist youth organizations on behalf of the rightist political parties such as the KDP and Syngman Rhee's National League for the Rapid Realization of Independence. During this period, Yi established close ties with other rightist youth organizations such as the Sŏbuk (Northwest) Youth Corps organized by North Korean refugees. Yi's student group later acted as the core organization in the formation of the All-Nation Student Association (*Hagyŏn*), which waged a bitter struggle against its leftist counterpart, the All-Nation League of Students (*Haktong*).

After the Korean War, Yi was elected to the National Assembly from a district in Chŏnju, Chŏlla Puk-to, and became vice-chairman of the Democratic Party's organization committee. Together with a number of other youthful members of the Democratic Party, he became the main source of energy in its battle against the undemocratic practices of the Rhee government and the Liberal Party. He was widely known to the public for his fight in the National Assembly and his leadership role among many students on college campuses, especially Korea University. Many of those who had been active in rightist student organizations during the post-Liberation period later joined the Democratic Party and the new faction. Others, such as Pak Yong-man and Son To-shim, chose the Liberal Party as their arena of political activities.[70]

By completely leaving out all the critical elements in the Democratic Party which could be considered politically oriented rather than program or task oriented, Chang Myŏn was in effect inviting serious difficulties in generating support and legitimacy for his cabinet, both within and outside of the National Assembly. His new cabinet would contribute little either to strengthening the solidarity of the new fac-

69. Interview with Yi Ch'ŏl-sŭng, November 15, 1968.

70. For a discussion of the junior groups in the respective factions, see *Tong-a Ilbo*, September 4, 1960, p. 2.

tion itself or to a reconciliation with the old faction. It is difficult to determine why Chang took this seemingly unwise course of action. It probably represented the triumph of O Wi-yŏng, known as a hard-liner toward the old faction, over some other close associates of Chang who recommended reconciliation.[71] Although the hard-liners led by O Wi-yŏng and soft-liners represented by Kim Yŏng-sŏn agreed on the desirability of strengthening the new faction at the expense of the old, O Wi-yŏng wished to achieve this goal by isolating the old faction through the new faction's superior position in political funds and patronage, while Kim thought their goal could best be achieved by bringing the old faction into the government.

Announcement of the formation of the new cabinet was followed by the registration as a parliamentary group of 84 old-faction members in the National Assembly, and their subsequent resolution to boycott all meetings of the Democratic Party. Under these circumstances, the junior members in both factions attempted to persuade the elder members to come to terms with one another for the preservation of the Democratic Party. Thus, while the younger members of the new faction, led by Yi Ch'ŏl-sŭng, insisted that the central committee meeting of the Democratic Party be postponed, as demanded by the old faction, their counterparts in the old faction, represented by Min Kwan-sik, urged their elders to attend the central committee meeting and participate in the party machinery.[72]

While the elder members of the two factions were arguing about the status of the Democratic Party, it did not take Chang himself long to realize that the cabinet he had formed had only limited usefulness to strengthen his political power. Thus, only two weeks after its formation, Chang persuaded four cabinet members—including O Wi-yŏng (director of the secretariat), Hyŏn Sŏk-ho (minister of defense), Yi T'ae-yŏng (minister of commerce and industry), and Hong Ik-p'yo (minister of internal affairs)—to resign.

This critical move by Chang Myŏn demonstrated his lack of self-assurance and the unstable state of power distribution around him. The cabinet reshuffle was mainly the work of Kim Yŏng-sŏn, who had served Chang as his closest advisor for a long time.[73] By reopen-

71. Interview with Kim Yŏng-sŏn, November 5, 1968.

72. Min Kwan-shik, *Nakchesaeng*, pp. 155–158.

73. The *Tong-a Ilbo* reported that the decisive force behind Chang Myŏn's decision to undertake a major cabinet reshuffle at that time was the pressure of the businessmen, who felt that a division in the Democratic Party would make it difficult for Chang to protect them because of the stepped-up criticism of him by the old-faction members. For this interesting and significant revelation, see *Tong-a Ilbo,* September 10, 1960, p. 2.

ing the opportunity for old-faction members to join the Chang cabinet, Kim wished to weaken the position of those within the old faction who were advocating immediate and permanent division of the Democratic Party; to make it easier for the accommodationists in the old faction to join the new faction; and to make the younger members within the new faction less "indispensable" in forming a parliamentary majority. Kim further reasoned that since the old faction lacked a strong leader, many of its members would slip into the Chang camp and that, in due time, Chang would not need the full cooperation of the old faction as a whole.[74] Chang was to achieve the third objective—that of making the junior members in his own faction less important—as the support of the junior group continued to be crucial for a parliamentary majority and they continued to be highly critical of the Chang administration.

With four vacant cabinet posts, Chang approached the old faction with the hope that a type of coalition government could be formed with their support. However, the old faction responded by offering a list of "available" members for cabinet posts, largely from the middle-level leadership. The failure of the top old-faction leaders to participate in the coalition cabinet demonstrated their unwillingness to cooperate with Chang's overall scheme.[75] Instead, their primary goal remained overthrowing the Chang government at the earliest possible date. Hence, a reliable parliamentary majority, which alone could have given Chang's government effectiveness and stability, could not be achieved. This was to have a serious effect on the fate of the Second Republic, as we shall see in the next chapter. Ultimately the old faction formed the New Democratic Party (*Shinmin-dang*) in early November, with the support of 65 assemblymen.[76]

After 5 old-faction members accepted cabinet positions in the Chang government "with the understanding that they could be recalled at any time by their faction leaders," [77] two different political groups within the old faction itself expressed interest in joining the new faction under certain conditions. One was a loosely associated group of some 60 members—that is, practically all old-faction members, with the exception of those under Kim To-yŏn's leadership—who could be persuaded to rejoin the Democratic Party if they were given good justifications and attractive rewards. It was believed that the most powerful man in this group was Yu Chin-san, a man noted for his

74. Interview with Kim Yŏng-sŏn, November 5, 1968; also *Tong-a Ilbo,* September 10, 1960, p. 2.

75. Chang Myŏn, pp. 66–67; Kim To-yŏn, pp. 570–571.

76. Kim To-yŏn, pp. 370–371.

77. *Ibid.,* p. 370.

skillful behind-the-scenes political maneuvers. Recognizing that a significant number of the "junior members" were seeking ways to get on Chang Myŏn's bandwagon at an appropriate opportunity, Yu made it known to Chang that he was willing to reconcile with him if Chang would remove himself from the control of key political groups within the new faction and undertake a complete personnel overhaul in the party and the government.[78] Ultimately, Yu was unable to achieve a political alliance with Chang Myŏn because of the latter's inability to free himself from the PLP and Hŭngsa-dan groups. This episode demonstrated the fluidity of the situation resulting from the absence of unity and leadership in the old faction, on the one hand, and Chang's irresolute nature, on the other.

While Yu Chin-san was conducting high-level negotiations with Chang Myŏn in a quiet and indirect manner, the younger group of the old faction, consisting of over 30 members, publicly made the following demands to Chang Myŏn as a first step toward reconciliation with the new faction: (1) establishment of a political consultation committee with an equal number of representatives, including Prime Minister Chang Myŏn himself, from each of the two factions; (2) unconditional admission to the party of those assemblymen elected without official nomination or those independents who had joined either of the two factions; and (3) retaining in the party those members who favored the establishment of a separate party.[79]

It would appear that a variety of motivations led the junior members to make the above move. They had undergone severe difficulties as opposition members during the Syngman Rhee government, and now they were again turned away from power positions simply because they happened to belong to the "wrong" faction. By preventing permanent and complete division of the Democratic Party, they wished to enjoy the consequences of belonging to a ruling party. At the same time, many of them regarded the action as a convenient stepping stone before finally changing their factional affiliation.[80]

With the gradual alienation of the junior members from their elders in the old faction, the new faction was now assured of the support of nearly 30 more assemblymen simply by giving verbal approval of their demands. Actually, neither the leaders of the Democratic Party (new faction) nor most of the old-faction junior members took the demands

78. These proposals were not made in public. However, the behind-the-scenes contact between Yu and Chang alarmed Kim To-yŏn's group sufficiently that Kim announced his plans to organize a separate party without a faction-wide consultant. (*Kyŏnghyang Shinmun*, September 22, 1960, p. 1.)

79. Min Kwan-shik, pp. 158–159.

80. *Ibid.*, p. 160.

seriously. Most of the junior members in fact chose to join the ruling party and remain in it, regardless of the status of their demands. With the official admission of 21 (a few had already joined the ruling party) to the Democratic Party on November 22, Prime Minister Chang Myŏn now had a total of 124 members under his leadership.[81] This was 7 more than the number of assemblymen needed to form a majority in the parliament.

This "parliamentary majority," however, was to prove to be true more in name than in reality. The old-faction "cooperationists" who joined the Democratic Party, and junior members of the new faction under Yi Ch'ŏl-sŭng's leadership, became increasingly hostile to the party leadership, consisting of the "elder members," as it was becoming clear that they were not going to be given a large share of either the government or the party.[82]

Having failed to win cabinet positions in the Chang government, members of the junior group now turned to a struggle to bring the party under their control. For this purpose, they demanded that an early party convention be held so that a comprehensive party reorganization could be carried out. During this period the Democratic Party had a number of vacancies in key positions as a result of the split in the party. Thus, by early January the next year, the members of the junior group declared that they could not cooperate with the legislative efforts of the Chang cabinet unless the party leadership called a convention immediately.

The key legislative matter at this time involved a supplementary budget, necessitated because of a drastic revision of the hwan-dollar exchange rate (from 650 to 1,300 Korean hwan to one U.S. dollar) and a new 32-million-dollar National Construction Project.[83] As soon as the government made public the contents of the supplementary budget, the junior group severely attacked the budget on a partisan basis, arguing that it had been formulated by the "bureaucrats and the elder members without any prior consultation with other members of the Democratic Party," and that "it completely failed to reflect the views of the Party." They further argued that the Chang cabinet had been irresponsible and incompetent in carrying out its duties, and declared that they would not "act like a rubber stamp" for the Chang government.[84] Since the new Democratic Party was already critical of the new supplementary budget, the junior group's threat to act indepen-

81. *Kyŏnghyang Shinmun,* November 22, 1960, p. 1.

82. *Ibid.,* November 6, 1960, p. 1. For a discussion of the conflict between the senior and junior groups, see *Han'guk hyŏngmyŏng chaep'ansa,* I, 194–200.

83. These problems will be discussed in detail in the next chapter.

84. *Tong-a Ilbo,* January 6, 1961, evening ed., p. 1.

dently of the party leadership constituted a major problem for the Chang government and the cabinet system of government.

The leadership of the party correctly felt that it lacked the ability to mobilize support in local party organizations at the time, and that it would not be able to assume control of the party in an early party convention. Thus members of the senior group wished to postpone the party convention for at least four to five months, during which period they hoped to consolidate their position in the localities with the help of government power.[85] In the meantime, they attempted to bring about a disintegration of the junior group by inducing some of its members to denounce its "factionalist and destructive nature." [86] This negative effort on the part of the elder members only served to arouse a more hostile reaction from the junior members, who subsequently formed the "New Wind Society" (*Shin p'ung-hoe*) for a common course of action in the National Assembly.[87] Furthermore, the "cooperationists," who had maintained their loose organization since their defection from the old faction, now joined the junior group in the latter's attack on the party leadership.[88]

The pressure from the younger members within the Democratic Party thus forced Chang to carry out another major cabinet reshuffle at the end of January 1961—this time by ousting the old-faction ministers from their cabinet positions. By this time, the old faction had ceased to be a partner with the Chang government, despite the fact that its own members were serving in his cabinet; the only reason for Chang to have kept them in the cabinet until that time was that he was reluctant to undertake too frequent cabinet changes.

The third Chang cabinet, made public on January 30, failed however to reduce the dissatisfaction and hostility of the junior group. The reshuffle involved the appointment of two key individuals of the senior group, Hyŏn Sŏk-ho and O Wi-yŏng, to the positions of minister of defense and minister without portfolio. Another member of the group was appointed minister of reconstruction. Two other cabinet positions, health-social affairs and communications, vacated by the old-faction ministers, went respectively to Kim P'an-sul, a member of the former "cooperationist" group, and Han T'ong-suk, a Democratic member of the House of Councilors. Chang offered only two viceministerial positions—in foreign affairs and reconstruction—to the junior group.[89]

85. *Ibid.,* January 5, 1960, p. 1.
86. *Han'guk hyŏngmyŏng chaep'ansa,* I, 197.
87. *Tong-a Ilbo,* January 24, 1960, evening ed., p. 1.
88. *Ibid.,* January 18, 1960, evening ed., p. 11.
89. *Kyŏnghyang Shinmun,* January 30, 1960, p. 1.

Chang's refusal to respond to the wishes of the junior group served to further alienate its members, who continued to demand immediate convening of a party convention. The junior group had been urging Chang from the early days of the Democratic government to appoint its leader Yi Ch'ŏl-sŭng to the position of either national defense or home affairs minister. Chang and his advisors, concerned about the prospect that Yi could use these key positions for his own political advantage, offered instead cabinet positions which carried less weight and political opportunity, such as minister of health and social affairs or minister without portfolio.[90]

On the other hand, Yi Ch'ŏl-sŭng and his junior group declined to exchange their freedom to oppose the Chang government for what seemed to be inconsequential government positions. They thus sought to consolidate their position within the party outside of the government, rather than by serving in it. Contrary to the view of the senior members that the junior group should feel gratified by the mere fact that it had been offered cabinet positions at all,[91] its members were deeply hurt by what they considered the contempt and insult the senior members showed them.

At the same time, the former "cooperationists," who were given one cabinet post in the new reshuffle, also expressed serious dissatisfaction with the fact that the cabinet post—health and social affairs—was offered to them only after it was rejected by Yi Ch'ŏl-sŭng. They also claimed, as did the junior group, that those who entered the Chang cabinet did not receive the group's endorsement, but did so as individuals only. Subsequently they formally organized a political circle of their own, with the vow that they would henceforth act as a "powerful opposition group within the Democratic Party."

The loss of the assured support of these two groups, which had a combined membership of some 40 members—approximately 25 in the junior group and 15 "cooperationists"—thus represented a serious threat to the stability and effectiveness of the Chang government. In their struggle against the leadership of the party, the junior group went so far as "exposing" serious instances of corruption within the Chang government. In a speech before the National Assembly, a member of the group charged that the Chang government had accepted at least a million dollars in commission from a Japanese company, in return for entrusting it with the sale of Korean tungsten, a major

90. Interview with Yi Ch'ŏl-sung, November 15, 1968.

91. Interview with Hyŏn Sŏk-ho, in *Kyŏnghyang Shinmun,* January 30, 1961, evening ed., p. 1.

export item amounting to nearly half a million dollars annually.[92] The primary culprit, according to this charge, was O Wi-yŏng, who negotiated an arrangement with the Japanese company during his earlier trip to Japan. The allegation resulted in a National Assembly investigation and the resignation of the government-appointed president of the Korean Tungsten Company, and marked a decisive rift between the junior and senior groups of the Democratic Party, comparable to an earlier one between its old and new factions.[93]

Until the final days of the Second Republic, therefore, the Chang government did not have a reliable majority in the National Assembly. His difficulties with the Democratic Party and the National Assembly even caused Chang to declare at one point that he would leave the party if internal dissension did not cease.[94] The inability of Chang's third cabinet to command parliamentary support resulted in another major cabinet reshuffle early in May, less than two weeks before the collapse of the regime by a military coup d'état. Even in this third major reshuffle, however, Chang refused to meet the wishes of the junior group, failing to allocate even a single cabinet post to it.[95]

One may wonder about the reasons for the persistent refusal of Chang and his associates to meet the desires of the junior group. It seems that members of the senior group were convinced that the junior members, and especially Yi Ch'ŏl-sŭng, would turn into a direct and serious challenge to their power once the juniors were allowed to occupy key positions in the government or the party. It appears to have been their intention to postpone as long as possible the inevitable party and governmental reorganization so that, in the meantime, they could build solid political machinery of their own, taking advantage of their close association with Chang Myŏn and their control of the government.

At the same time, close advisors of Chang Myŏn felt—as did Chang himself—that what the cabinet needed most in the Second Republic were hard workers who could serve Chang and the country as a "team," rather than individual heroes who would cause more problems than assistance in "getting the work done." [96] Such a view resulted in successive cabinets which had little ability to command the loyalty of either a stable majority of the National Assembly or the support of the nation as a whole.

92. See *Han'guk hyŏngmyŏng chaep'ansa,* I, 199–200.
93. *Minŭiwŏn hoeŭirok,* 38th session, no. 30.
94. *Kyŏnghyang Shinmun,* March 4, 1961, p. 1.
95. *Han'guk hyŏngmyŏng chaep'ansa,* I, 200–201.
96. Interview with Kim Yŏng-sŏn, November 5, 1968.

It thus seems that Chang's highly defensive attitude toward political power and his heavy reliance on "task-oriented" associates were primarily responsible for his failure to cultivate a reliable parliamentary majority. Furthermore, he gave the general public the distinct impression that he was basically lacking in leadership and self-assurance. The notion that he was not his own man, but instead susceptible to the pressure of his close associates, seemed to have been confirmed.

In this chapter, we have discussed the processes by which Chang Myŏn and his new faction came to occupy power over the competition of the old faction. We also examined how his government succeeded in forming a parliamentary majority in the National Assembly. It was then pointed out that the parliamentary majority that Chang so painstakingly created proved to be neither cooperative nor reliable. In the course of the above discussion, we analyzed the composition, ideological orientation, and power position of various political groups within the Democratic Party.

Those who occupied key positions in the major political parties professed beliefs in liberal democracy and economic conservatism. Despite this consensual nature of the political scene (or because of it), however, Chang was unable to create an effective parliamentary majority to back his post-revolutionary programs. This was partly the result of circumstances over which Chang had no control, and partly his and his close associates' own doing.

The incohesive and disorganized nature of all political groups in national politics, including his own faction, was primarily responsible for the difficulty Chang had in forming a stable and reliable parliamentary majority. He could not readily count on the support of his own faction because of the rebellious and demanding attitude of the members of the junior group. Nor could he form a coalition-type government with different political groups, because of both the exclusivistic and bureaucratic orientation of his own associates and the lack of unity within those groups from which he sought support. The situation was made worse by Chang's passivity and lack of confidence in his own actions. He vacillated between a cabinet consisting exclusively of his closest associates and one which included enough "outsiders" to make it a coalition cabinet. Such vacillation seems to have been a major factor in Chang's failure to mobilize the support of either the old faction or the dissenting group within the new faction itself.

As an intellectual participant in the Democratic Party observed after the collapse of the Chang government, Chang lacked firmness in his personnel policy, "offering positions to whoever caused enough trouble for him." [97] With regard to both the old faction and the junior group, however, Chang's concessions were invariably too little and too late, enough to expose his weaknesses, but not enough to receive co-operation and support. That such a policy (of making piecemeal concessions in a passive fashion) would eventually have the self-defeating effect of inviting more "troubles" and "trouble-makers" has been perceptively pointed out by Myron Weiner in his study of Indian democracy.[98]

Unfortunately for the Democratic government and the Second Korean Republic, Chang always followed such a passive and self-defeating course of action. He would systematically alienate the political forces around him without making any new allies. Chang's failure to perceive his own role as a cultivator of power in the chaotic and uncertain days of the post-revolutionary period was also evident in areas outside of party politics as well as within it. In the next two chapters, we shall examine the relationships between the Chang government and other major political forces in the Second Republic, and how these forces affected the power position of the Chang government itself.

97. Shin Sang-ch'o in "Former Politicians Speak Out," p. 147.

98. Myron Weiner, *The Politics of Scarcity,* Chap. 9, "Political Demands and Modernization," pp. 216–240.

VII

CAUGHT IN THE MIDDLE:
The Chang Myŏn Government Between the "Revolutionary" and "Anti-Revolutionary" Forces

When we described the Korean situation in 1960 as "revolutionary," in Chapter Two, it was in the sense that there was a considerable discrepancy between the behavior of the Syngman Rhee government and the value system of a significant part of the political public, including the students. It was also pointed out that the April uprising could be considered a revolutionary attempt by those with liberal-democratic orientations to destroy the "power-dependent" pro-government forces allied with Syngman Rhee. This is not to say, of course, that the South Korean population could be neatly classified into these two clearly definable categories. Most of the people did not belong to either of them, and even those who could be identified with one or the other category differed among themselves in terms of degree and motivation.

It is clear, however, that many people regarded the political upheaval favorably—both for practical and ideological reasons—while many others feared that they had more to lose than gain from the changed situation. Generally speaking, the liberal-democratic, anti-Rhee forces included most of the university professors and students, members of the press, and many professional politicians, while the pro-Rhee forces included those in the "police-bureaucratic nexus," the highest layer of the military, and the business community. The Chang Myŏn government thus represented a coalition of the party politicians (at least a majority of them), intellectuals, students, and the press.[1]

1. Hahn-Been Lee characterized the Chang government as one supported "by a university-press nexus." See his *Korea: Time, Change, and Administration,* p. 117.

DISSATISFACTION OF THE ANTI-RHEE GROUPS

The record of the Chang government shows that, while it was in office, it systematically and successively alienated various political sectors—first those which could be considered "pro-revolution," and later the "anti-revolution" groups. Within a relatively short period of time it became apparent that there was little support for the Chang government from any of the major political groups, the only exceptions being the few individuals who were directly connected with it.

First to show dissatisfaction and disenchantment with the Chang government were the liberal intellectuals and university students. Specifically, they were highly critical of the government in dealing with those who had participated in the "undemocratic" actions of the Rhee government and those who had accumulated wealth during its rule by illegal means. This task was initially taken up by the interim government of Hŏ Chŏng. However, because of its "unrevolutionary" nature, as already pointed out, little progress had been made on the issue before establishment of the Chang government.

An important source of their dissatisfaction was the failure of the new government to take stern measures against the leaders of the Rhee government and the Liberal Party. Following the inauguration of the Chang government, national attention was focused upon the trials of 48 former officials of the Liberal regime who were accused of being responsible for the April 19th massacre; the Liberal Party's plot to assassinate Chang Myŏn in 1956; March 1960 election frauds; and political gangsterism under the Rhee regime.[2] While the trials were being conducted, friends and relatives of those who had been wounded during the April uprising disrupted the court proceedings when the defense attorneys requested dismissal of the charges against some of the defendants on the grounds that with the constitutional amendment of June 15, those laws concerning the presidential election of March 15 were no longer applicable and the defendants could not be prosecuted on charges of violating those laws.[3] The lawyers in turn refused to participate in the court proceedings until they could be carried out under orderly and safe conditions or until new laws concerning punishment of the defendants were passed. Since no trials could be held without the presence of defense attorneys, this constituted a critical stumbling block. It also aroused speculation that the defendants would have to be released without a trial in case the

2. *Shin-dong-a,* December 1964, p. 160.
3. *Tong-a Ilbo,* September 6, 1960, p. 1.

lawyers did not return before the end of the six-month period after their arrest.

On its part, the Chang government felt that it could not apply pressure on the courts and attempt to influence the outcome of the trials in the fashion of the Rhee government, largely because of its commitment to liberal democratic principles[4] and "due process." Chang and his close associates rejected the suggestions from many quarters to enact retroactive laws enabling the courts to impose more severe punishment on the political and economic "criminals" than was possible under the existing laws.[5] Such legislation would require an amendment to the constitution, as it specifically prohibited the enactment of retroactive laws.[6]

The situation during this period represented a deadlock between the judiciary, the administration, and the National Assembly (now consisting of two houses, the House of Representatives and the House of Councillors), none of which showed willingness to take the initiative in resolving the difficulty by taking the risk either of angering the demonstrators by defending the existing laws or violating the legalistic norms by means of retroactive legislation. The deadlock was temporarily resolved by the defense lawyers' return to the courts after they had received a promise from the government that it would make every effort to guarantee orderly and safe trials.[7]

Consequently, the defendants were tried solely on the basis of the existing laws, and the outcome of the trials proved highly unsatisfactory to those who considered themselves victims of the Rhee dictatorship and demanded heavy punishment for their past oppressors. The severe discrepancy between the penalties demanded by the prosecution and those given by the court for each of the defendants, as shown in Table VII-1, can serve as a measure of the dissatisfaction among the general public aroused by the unexpectedly light sentences.[8]

Table VII-1 shows that, of the 9 defendants for whom the prosecution demanded the death sentence, none received prison terms of over five years and 4 were released by acquittal or through suspended sen-

4. In this case the most important principle involved was the separation of powers.

5. Chang Myŏn, *Memoirs*, pp. 69–70; also, interview with Mr. Kim Yŏng-sŏn, November 4, 1968.

6. Article 23 of the Constitution stated: "No person shall be prosecuted for a criminal offense unless such act shall have constituted a crime prescribed by law at the time it was committed, nor be placed in double jeopardy." See *The Constitution of The Republic of Korea*, 1960.

7. *Kyŏnghyang Shinmun*, September 23, 1960, p. 3.

8. It should be noted that no sign of dissatisfaction was expressed from any quarters when heavy penalties were demanded by the prosecution in early August.

Table VII-1

DISCREPANCY BETWEEN PROSECUTION DEMANDS AND COURT SENTENCES IN THE TRIALS OF OCTOBER, 1960

Defendant	*Former Position*	*Charges* *	*Prosecution Demand*	*Court Sentence*
Hong Chin-gi	Minister of Internal Affairs	2, 4, 5, 6	Death	9 months (prison term)
Yu Ch'ung-yŏl	Seoul Chief of Police	1, 4	Death	Death
Kwak Yŏng-ju	Chief of Police, Presidential Residence	9, 10	Death	3 years
Im Hŭng-sun	Mayor of Seoul	3, 4, 5, 8	Death	3 years plus fine (322,360,000 hwan)
Yi Ik-hŭng	Assemblyman, Minister of Internal Affairs	3	Death	Not guilty
Kim Chong-wŏn	National Chief of Police	3, 7	Death	Not guilty
Chang Yŏng-bok	Police Officer	3, 4, 7	Death	8 months (one-year suspended sentence)
Pak Sa-il	Police Officer	3, 4, 7	Death	3 years
Oh Ch'ung-hwan	Police Officer	3, 7	Death	8 months (one year suspended sentence)

Sources: Kyŏnghyang Shinmun, October 8, 1960, evening ed., p. 1; also *Han'guk hyŏngmyŏng chaep'ansa,* I, pp. 404–415.

* Charges:
1: Manslaughter
2: Conspiracy of manslaughter
3: Attempted manslaughter
4: Violation of election laws
5: Falsification of official documents and their use
6: Conspiracy of false accusations
7: Perjury
8: Accepting bribe
9: Obstruction of official actions
10: Violation of the law concerning punishment of tax evasion

tences. Of the other 39 defendants, for whom the prosecution demanded prison terms ranging from eight months to ten years, 16 were released immediately after the trial and all of the others received far lighter sentences than those asked for by the prosecution.

As soon as the court sentences were made known to the public, protest marches and demonstrations were instigated by relatives and friends of those who had died and been wounded during the April uprising. On October 10, two days after the trials ended, an angry mob of students, including those wounded during the April demonstrations, surged into the National Assembly chamber and occupied the platform, from which they protested the National Assembly's failure to take positive action for achievement of the "revolutionary goals." Startled by the extreme course of action taken by the demonstrators, the National Assembly and the Chang government agreed to push through emergency legislation establishing a revolutionary court to try the former Liberal officials charged with brutalities and election rigging.[9] The demonstrations and protests spread throughout the major cities of the country.

Although the participants in the demonstrations were mostly students wounded in the April uprising and the relatives of those who had been killed, and were thus relatively few in number, they represented the widespread grievances of not only all the students who had participated in the uprising, but also the intellectuals and the press who encouraged such protests by providing moral justification for them. An editorial in *Tong-a Ilbo,* analyzing the contemporary situation, eloquently reflected the views of the liberal democratic intellectuals who were dissatisfied with the Chang Myŏn government's cautious manner in dealing with former officials of the Rhee regime. The editorial, entitled "The Responsibility for the Fortune of the Revolutionary Trials," is quoted below at length:

> Following the collapse of the Liberal regime with the resignation of Syngman Rhee as President on April 26, we demanded that the existing counter-revolutionary National Assembly be dissolved immediately and that the task of rewriting the Constitution be given to a newly-elected legislature. At that time, we argued that since the dictatorial regime was overthrown, not by the peaceful transfer of power, but through a revolutionary method, the Constitution of the Second Republic had to provide legal guarantees which would enable the achievement of the revolutionary goals. Instead, the existing National Assembly, which was still controlled by the Liberal members who had been elected through government manipulation, was satisfied with the adoption of a cabinet form of government. To have let the existing National

9. *New York Times,* October 12, 1960, p. 22.

Assembly assume the task of rewriting the Constitution was tantamount to leaving the task of carrying out revolutionary goals to the counter-revolutionary elements themselves. Indeed, this counter-revolutionary legislature succeeded in deceiving the nation by merely changing the institutional framework of the government. Thus, it deliberately abandoned the opportunity to make legal provisions for achieving revolutionary tasks. It is a matter of common sense that the revolutionary punishment of the counter-revolutionary pro-Rhee officials is a basic and necessary first step toward the achievement of revolutionary goals. Therefore, the fact that such a punishment was effectively blocked by the revised Constitution means that the revolutionary path was met with a serious setback at the outset. Hence, even after the establishment of the Chang Myŏn cabinet, the public was urging the government at every opportunity to enact special revolutionary laws, only to be told that the culprits could be effectively punished under the existing laws. The existing laws, however, were laws meant to serve in ordinary times, and had not been enacted in anticipation of an emergency situation like the present. Therefore, to say that the culprits should be punished under the existing laws was merely a subterfuge to ignore today's reality, namely revolution. . . . The supreme task of the Second Republic is the completion of the revolution. . . . Since all three branches of the government—the legislature, the administration, and the judiciary—have proved themselves incapable of carrying out the first objective of the revolution, their existence cannot be justified any more. For anything that has lost its *raison d'être,* the quicker its disappearance, the better.[10]

The court sentences of October 8 thus provided an opportunity for the supporters of the April uprising, led by the intellectual community, to rally together and register dissatisfaction over both the Hŏ Chŏng and Chang Myŏn administrations for their "unrevolutionary" attitude toward the pro-Rhee elements.

The court action had at least two serious consequences which had a direct bearing upon the stability of the Second Republic. In the first place, it had the effect of profoundly alienating those political sectors which were responsible for the fall of the Rhee government, and which subsequently constituted the core groups in the coalition which made the creation of the Chang government possible. Second, it forced the National Assembly to take a strong position against the pro-Rhee elements through the enactment of retroactive laws to punish them, with the result of alienating the former supporters of the Rhee regime from the Chang government.

The first consequence—the alienation of the liberal democratic elements—which was evident from the composition of the demonstrators and the general trend of editorials after the judicial "slap on the

10. *Tong-a Ilbo,* October 11, 1960, p. 1.

wrist" given to officials of the Rhee regime, continued to afflict the Democratic administration until its downfall in May 1961.[11] The intellectual sector, whose primary medium of communication with the general public consisted of the newspapers and various journals—the number of which more than doubled in 1960 after the April uprising (from 581 to 1,362)[12]—continued to criticize the Chang government in the harshest possible terms. With some truth, a member of that sector was later to state that the "intellectuals should take full responsibility for the fall of the Chang government."[13]

The second consequence—the fact that the National Assembly was forced to take a stronger position against the individuals who had been active in the Liberal regime—had an even more important impact on the Democratic government as far as its survival was concerned. The legislation for retroactive punishment of the former pro-Rhee elements, which was enacted by the National Assembly because of the pressure put upon it by the students, the intellectual-press sector, and a number of rank-and-file members of its own party, had the effect of incapacitating a large number of the police whose support the Chang government needed for its own protection. It also alienated from the Chang government many who held high-status and leadership positions in their localities, because most of those who had actively cooperated with the Rhee government were also individuals who needed a close tie with the government in order to maintain or develop some leadership position in the society.[14]

The irony was that the Chang administration had to take the blame for both the "unrevolutionary" actions of the court and the "revolu-

11. The following titles of editorials which appeared in the major newspapers in Seoul during this period reflect the disillusionment of the journalistic sector over the development of events: "Are trials for the satisfaction of the judges alone?"—*Han'guk Ilbo;* "Less-than-fair revolutionary trials"—*Tong-a Ilbo;* "Unexpected light sentences by senseless judges"—*Kyŏnghyang Shinmun;* "We urge again speedy legislation for the punishment of the culprits"—*Seoul Shinmun.* All these editorials were highly critical of the judges who passed the light sentences, but more so of the Chang government and the National Assembly for their failure to act before the embarrassing consequences of permitting trials under the "existing laws" become apparent.

12. *Haptong yŏn'gam* [Haptong Annual], 1959, p. 1004; also, *Han'guk hyŏngmyŏng chaep'ansa,* I, 258.

13. Kim Pung-gu, "The Nature and Behavior of Korean Intellectuals," p. 86.

14. This was probably one of the most important reasons for the poor showing of the Democratic candidates in the local elections of December 13. In those elections, in which local leaders had much more influence over the voters than in national elections, the Democratic Party won control of only 2 of the 10 provincial councils. The independents won 216 seats, compared to 195 for the government party and 70 for the opposition New Democratic Party. See *Taehanmin'guk sŏn'gŏsa* [History of Korean Elections], p. 963.

tionary" actions taken by the legislature. It was evident, as Chang himself made clear later,[15] that the initiative for legislation for retroactive punishment of the pro-Rhee elements was taken not by the Chang administration, but by the National Assembly. However, most of those who later became subject to prosecution under the retroactive laws regarded the Chang administration as having been primarily responsible for the enactment of those laws.[16] According to Ko Chŏng-hun, when former Liberals met Cho Chae-ch'ŏn, Chang's minister of justice, in prison following the military coup d'état, a few of them accused Cho of having initiated the retroactive laws.[17] The explanation for this paradox was that the public had been so used to the omnipotence of the executive department under the Rhee administration that they found it difficult to accept the fact that the executive department lacked the ability to control the other branches of the government under the Second Republic.

THE ENACTMENT OF SPECIAL LAWS TO PUNISH FORMER RHEE SUPPORTERS

Upon facing demonstrations and protests throughout the country following the announcement of the court decision, various branches of the government responded to the critical situation. On October 10, President Yun Po-sŏn issued a statement in which he expressed his astonishment at the light sentences conferred upon the defendants and asserted that "the only way to cope with the present crisis is to convene the National Assembly as soon as possible and pass a law which would allow the severe punishment of former government and Liberal Party officials." [18] President Yun then sent letters to the presiding officers of both houses of the National Assembly urging prompt action on the matter. In the meantime, the prosecutor's office declared that it would investigate the possibility of re-arresting those who had been freed by the court by charging them with other offenses.[19] The National Assembly, which had been in recess since October 4, reconvened on October 11 and began to revise the laws dealing with treason, so as to make possible the trial of those persons already released.

However, conspicuously absent in this flurry of activities in many branches of the government was the positive leadership and initiative

15. Chang Myŏn, *Memoirs,* p. 69.
16. Yi Chae-hak, "Memoirs," in *Sasirŭi Chŏnburŭl kisulhanda,* p. 176.
17. Ko Chŏng-hun, *Kut'o: Purŭji mot'han norae* [Songs I Could Not Sing], p. 78.
18. *Tong-a Ilbo,* October 10, 1960, evening ed., p. 1, and October 11, p. 1.
19. *Kyŏnghyang Shinmun,* October 10, 1960, evening ed., p. 3.

of Chang himself, who, apparently because of personal opposition to retroactive legislation, refused to take the lead in the move.[20] Although Chang publicly declared that "together with the legislative branch" he would try to "enact a constitutional amendment and subsequently pass extraordinary laws for the punishment of traitors to democracy and those with illegal wealth," [21] the actual initiative was taken by the old-faction members of the Democratic Party in the National Assembly rather than by the executive branch led by Chang Myŏn. Both Prime Minister Chang and his justice minister, Cho Chae-ch'ŏn, spent most of their energy criticizing the court, which had failed to accept the validity of the evidence the prosecution had presented in the cases against the former government and Liberal Party officials. Furthermore, in response to a question in the National Assembly, Justice Minister Cho failed to take a stand on the issue of retroactive legislation.[22]

In anticipation of a constitutional amendment and special legislation, the National Assembly adopted on October 12 a tentative measure which postponed all future trials of the "traitors of democracy" until enactment of the extraordinary laws; the measure also authorized the re-arrest of those defendants released following the recent trials.[23] The measure received strong support from the members of the old faction.[24] In accordance with this law, an order was issued to re-arrest 8 of those who had been freed on October 8, and all further trials for the remaining defendants, including Ch'oe In-gyu, the most condemned member of the Rhee supporters, were postponed indefinitely.

The first step toward such legislation was a constitutional revision which would nullify Article 23, prohibiting the prosecution of a person for a criminal offense by *ex post facto* laws.[25] The amendment, which passed both houses of the National Assembly without change by a two-thirds majority, made it possible for the National Assembly to enact special retroactive laws to punish those who had been responsible for the irregularities in the March 15 presidential and vice-presidential elections and for the killing and wounding of the demonstrators protesting those irregularities; to suspend the civil rights of the persons

20. Chang Myŏn, *Memoirs,* p. 69. According to Chang Myŏn, on November 11, when the Democratic caucus met to decide whether or not to support the retroactive legislation, he declared that he would consider leaving the party if the members of the party insisted on its passage.

21. *Kyŏnghyang Shinmun,* October 12, 1960, p. 1.

22. *Minŭiwŏn hoeŭirok,* 37th session, no. 28, pp. 13–15.

23. *Kyŏnghyang Shinmun,* October 14, 1960, p. 1.

24. *Minŭiwŏn hoeŭirok,* 37th session, no. 28, pp. 5–12.

25. *Constitution of the Republic of Korea.*

who had committed grave anti-democratic acts by taking advantage of special positions attained before April 26, 1960; and to undertake administrative or criminal actions against persons who had accumulated property by unlawful means during the same period.[26] Furthermore, the National Assembly was also empowered to create a special court and a special prosecuting department in order to deal with these criminal offenses.

On the surface, very few people inside or outside the National Assembly, opposed the constitutional amendment. The editorials in major newspapers all supported the proposal enthusiastically,[27] to say nothing of those who demonstrated for such legislation. The proposal passed the Lower House on November 23, *without* discussion.[28] Undoubtedly most of the representatives voted for the amendment out of necessity rather than conviction. In the voting itself, there were 191 affirmative votes compared to only 1 negative vote, 2 abstentions and 6 invalid votes. However, 33 members failed to show up for the voting, all except 9 of them without justifiable reasons. To most of them, to be absent during the voting was one way of not supporting the constitutional amendment without actively opposing it. Among the 32 representatives who either abstained or cast invalid votes were 9 former Liberal assemblymen, 2 former policemen, 12 Democrats, 2 New Democratic Party members, 1 Socialist Masses Party member, and 6 independents.[29] The fact that those who failed to show up for the crucial voting were mainly Democrats and former Liberal Party members reflected, at least in part, the lukewarm attitude of the Chang government on this particular issue.

Despite the apparent absence of formidable opposition against the constitutional amendment, there were signs of uneasiness, not only among those who would be directly affected by the retroactive laws but also among many lawyers, who feared the adverse long-term consequences of retroactive legislation. Many members of the House of Councillors also expressed reluctance to pass the amendment although, when the actual voting took place two days later, the amendment passed the House of Councillors with 44 affirmative votes against 3 negative and 3 invalid votes; 6 were absent.[30] Of the 10 councillors who

26. *Tong-a Ilbo,* January 3, 1961, p. 1.

27. See editorials in the major papers on October 17, 18, and 19, 1960.

28. *Minŭiwŏn hoeŭirok,* 37th session, no. 45, pp. 1–3; no. 48, pp. 1–3.

29. See *ibid.*, no. 48, pp. 2–3; also Chŏng Yŏng-mo, *Ibaek samshipsamin'gwa oshipp'alin* [233 Representatives and 58 Councillors] *passim.*

30. At this time, the House of Councillors was composed of 20 members of the Councillors' Friendship Club, 17 New Democratic Party members, 11 Democrats, and 8 independents; about two-thirds of the members of the Friendship Club were

failed to vote for the constitutional amendment (excluding those who were abroad), 7 were former Liberals, 1 was the former commandant of the Korean Marine Corps, and 1 a reformist. Significantly, 5 former officials of the Rhee government or party voted in favor of the amendment.

From the above discussion, it is clear that there was a considerable degree of resentment toward the proposed constitutional amendment, although those who opposed it were forced to acquiesce to the demands of the "revolutionary" forces because of "public opinion" (most conspicuous through newspaper editorial columns) and agitation favoring such legislation. An almost identical situation prevailed during the enactment of the Special Laws, on which deliberation had already begun in both houses of the National Assembly before passage of the constitutional amendment.

The special legislation, much of which was subsequently adopted by the National Assembly, could be classified into four distinctive segments: (1) laws dealing with individuals who had committed criminal offenses (according to the retroactive laws) in connection with the presidential and vice-presidential elections and were thus subject to relatively severe penalties; (2) laws dealing with the restriction of civil rights (i.e., rights to vote and to hold public offices) of those who had held relatively high positions in certain government and other public organizations such as the Liberal Party, the police department, and the Korean anti-Communist Youth Corps; (3) laws providing for the organization of a Special Court and a Special Prosecution Office to administer the Special Laws; and (4) laws dealing with those who had accumulated wealth by illegal and unjust means. All except those in the last category managed to pass both houses before the end of 1960; enactment of the laws concerning "illegal wealth" had to wait until the middle of April 1961. Table VII–2 shows the major features of the first two Special Laws in their final form.[31]

---

either former Liberals or former police officers. Voting on the constitutional amendment scheduled for November 26 had to be postponed because of the absence of 19 out of 56 councillors (including 2 who were abroad), most of whom were members of the Friendship Club. There were a number of reasons why former Liberals had a better chance of getting elected to the upper house (*ch'amŭiwŏn*) than to the lower house (*minŭiwŏn*) in the July election. The voters were not easily able to identify the candidate's political affiliation because councillors were elected from multi-member districts. And many former Liberals were in a better position in terms of campaign financing, which was particularly helpful in large electoral districts.

31. These laws were almost identical with their original bills.

Table VII-2

MAJOR FEATURES OF THE SPECIAL LAWS OF DECEMBER 31, 1960

Name of the Law	*Law Concerning Punishment of Those Involved in Election Rigging*	*Law Concerning Restriction of Civil Rights of Those Who Committed Anti-Democratic Acts*
Primary	Initiator Committee on Judiciary and Legislation, House of Representatives	Same
Purpose	To punish those who committed illegal acts in connection with the presidential and vice-presidential elections held on March 15, 1960, and those who were responsible for wounding and killing citizens protesting the election frauds. (Article 1)	To restrict the civil rights of those who performed clearly anti-democratic acts by taking advantage of special positions they occupied prior to April 26, 1960. "Anti-democratic acts" are defined as those acts which destroyed various principles of democracy by violating the constitutionally guaranteed basic rights of the citizens. (Articles 1 & 2)
Those Subject to Punishment	1. The president, cabinet members, presidential aides, directors of the Liberal Party, members of the LP election preparation Committee, and central directors of the Korean Youth Corps at the time of the March 15, 1960, elections, who participated in the conspiracy to conduct frauds in the elections	1. "Automatic Cases": Those who occupied any one of the following special positions at the time of the March 15, 1960, elections would be *considered* as having committed cleary anti-democratic acts: Liberal Party's presidential and vice-presidential candidates; chairman and vice-chairman of the LP central

Table VII-2 (Continued)

Name of the Law	*Law Concerning Punishment of Those Involved in Election Rigging*	*Law Concerning Restriction of Civil Rights of Those Who Committed Anti-Democratic Acts*
	or who played a leading role in their implementation. 2. Members of the monetary and currency committee, central directors of the banking organizations, cabinet members, and leading members of the political parties or other social organizations during the same period who supplied funds for use in the elections. 3. Those who are not included in the above categories, but who actively cooperated with the Liberal Party in carrying out fraudulent elections or supplied it with illegal funds. 4. Those who caused the death of others in connection with the elections, or those who killed the citizens protesting the election frauds, or those who ordered the acts described in the following item. 5. Those who committed assault on, wounded, threatened, confined, or arrested citizens	committee; members of the LP election preparation committee; central directors of the LP; cabinet members; presidential aides; assistants to the House speaker; chiefs of the National Police, provincial police, and local police stations, and their immediate subordinates in charge of intelligence and investigation; the mayor and vice-mayor of Seoul; governors of provinces; district chairmen of the LP; provincial chairmen and vice-chairmen of the LP; director and vice-director of the Korean Anti-Communist Youth Corps; heads of government-owned enterprises; chairman of the National Central Election Commission; and chiefs of major government agencies. (Article 4) 2. "Investigatory Cases": Those who occupied any one of the following positions at the time of the March 15, 1960, elections and who, in the judgment of the Screening Commission to be set up in accordance with the present law, committed

	protesting the fraudulent elections. (Articles 3, 4, & 5)	clearly anti-democratic acts; members of the central committee of the Liberal Party; local heads of the LP; heads of the social organizations affiliated with the LP; central and local leaders of the Korean Anti-Communist Youth Corps; the prosecutor general and his immediate staff and other prosecutors in charge of intelligence and elections; local prosecution office chiefs; Liberal Party chairmen of legislative committees and the floor leaders of the LP in the National Assembly; members of the central and provincial Election Preparation Committee of the LP; central and provincial heads and vice-heads of the General League of Korean Labor Unions; chiefs of the armed forces; commander of the Counter Intelligence Corps; floor leaders and legislative committee chairmen of the LP, the Speaker, vice-speaker, chairman of the steering committee and Secretary General of the National Assembly as of December 24, 1958. (Article 5)
Punishment	Seven-year imprisonment to death penalty for those in categories #1 and #4 of the above; 5- to 15-year imprisonment for those in #2; 1- to 10-year imprisonment for those in #3; 1- to 15-year imprisonment for those in #5. (Articles 3, 4, & 5)	A 7-year suspension of civil rights for those in automatic cases; 5-year suspension of civil rights for those in investigatory cases. "Civil rights" are defined here as rights to vote and to hold public office. (Article 12)

Table VII-2 (Continued)

Name of the Law	*Law Concerning Punishment of Those Involved in Election Rigging*	*Law Concerning Restriction of Civil Rights of Those Who Committed Anti-Democratic Acts*
Agencies Responsible for Administration of the Law	Special Court consisting of five separate divisions and a joint division under the Chief Judge, to be elected by the Lower House. Each division other than the joint division is to consist of five judges (one regular judge, one representative of the organizations representing the April revolution, one lawyer, one college professor, and one journalist) to be commissioned by the Chief Judge of the Supreme Court. The joint division will consist of the Chief Judge and all other judges of the Special Court.	A Screening Commission, to consist of the following members to be commissioned by the Chief Judge of the Special Court: one regular judge, one lawyer, one college professor, one representative of the April revolutionary organizations, three representatives of the religious, journalistic, and other communities.

A close examination of the two Special Laws indicates that there were important differences between them: one was intended to punish the leading officials of the government and the Libral Party because of the illegal *actions* they had committed; the other was intended to punish individuals for the *positions* they had held. The first law, it appeared, was a reasonable response to public demands for severe punishment of those who had been responsible for the election frauds and police brutality and a logical consequence of the constitutional amendment which made such laws possible. Consequently, there was no audible opposition to its enactment from any quarter. With regard to the second law, however, a great deal of controversy erupted both in and out of the National Assembly. A number of important political groups and individuals expressed their opposition to the bill while it was still being considered.

Those who wished to see the relaxation or removal of the law included, in addition to the individuals who were directly affected by it, a number of leading journalists,[32] a few assemblymen of various political parties, a considerable number of lawyers, and most importantly, the Chang Myŏn government itself. Although opposition to the law was made on different points and with varying degrees of intensity, its critics generally shared the notion that the bill was difficult to justify from either legal or practical points of view.

It was argued that, from the legal point of view, to *consider* that those who had held certain official positions under the Rhee regime had committed anti-democratic acts and thus to punish them (in the "automatic cases") was against the constitutional guarantee that all citizens should have the right to be tried by judges authorized by law.[33] Furthermore, it was argued that the enactment into law of such a provision was an infringement upon the powers of the judiciary by the National Assembly. For the National Assembly, by specifying the individuals to be punished, regardless of their actual actions, was in effect acting as both legislator and judge.[34]

From the practical point of view, the main consideration was that those who would be directly affected by the law would number more

32. See especially the editorials of *Chosŏn Ilbo,* a prestigious Seoul newspaper noted for its objective editorial policy. Its editorials of November 2, November 19, and November 26 were entitled, respectively, "The undemocratic nature of the bill with so-called 'automatic case' provision," "Problems concerning the bill intended to limit the civil rights of those who committed anti-democratic activities," and "The national interest should have preference over the punishment of anti-democratic elements."

33. Article 22 of the Constitution.

34. *Minŭiwŏn hoeŭirok,* 37th session, no. 49.

than 1,500 individuals in the "automatic cases" and 40,000 in the "investigatory" cases, and that it would be detrimental for the stability of the new government to seriously alienate these people, as most of them had high social, economic, or government postions. It was also argued that many of them were serving as officials of the new government, and that their removal or the threat of their removal from these public offices would seriously jeopardize the new government's effort to re-establish public order and administrative effectiveness.[35] At the same time, two of Chang's cabinet members, the ministers of finance and foreign affairs, reported after their visit to the United States that other friendly countries had misgivings about the National Assembly's attempt to enact sweeping punitive laws against the former officials of the Rhee government.

Therefore the Democratic Party proposed an amendment to the bill, abolishing the "automatic cases" and drastically reducing the categories of individuals to be included in the "investigatory cases." [36] Premier Chang explained that such an amendment was necessary if the members of the National Assembly did not wish the people to regard the legislation as a purely retaliatory measure against their political enemies and if they wished to prevent the social and political chaos resulting from anxiety and fear in numerous public servants and police personnel.[37] Meanwhile, Chang assured the former Liberal members of both houses of the National Assembly that he would do his best to protect their status as members of the National Assembly.[38]

However, those who disagreed with relaxation—i.e., those who insisted on the desirability of a strong law against the former pro-Rhee officials—argued that the revolutionary situation both justified and demanded such a measure. They asserted that suspending the civil rights of those who had actively cooperated with the Rhee regime on the local level was an important way of satisfying the grievances of the "revolutionary groups" and a necessary measure to check the growth of anti-revolutionary forces throughout the nation.[39] Although the various political parties and social groups did not speak with one voice on this issue, those who supported strong retroactive legislation in-

35. Chang Myŏn's speech in the National Assembly made on November 29, 1960. (*Ibid.*, 37th session, no. 53, pp. 6–21.)

36. For the proposal, see *Kyŏnghyang Shinmun*, November 26, 1960, evening ed., p. 1.

37. *Minŭiwŏn hoeŭirok*, 37th session, no. 53, p. 7.

38. *Kyŏnghyang Shinmun*, November 23, 1960.

39. These views were clearly reflected in the speeches of National Assembly members during the period of deliberation. See *Minŭiwŏn hoeŭirok*, 37th session, nos. 50–53.

cluded a majority of the New Democratic Party members and members of the "junior group" of the Democratic Party within the House of Representatives, and most self-styled "revolutionary organizations," numbering approximately forty.[40] A majority of newspapers also supported this strong position.[41]

The New Democratic Party took a stronger position than the Democratic Party against the former Liberal officials because, first, it feared that the lenient measures proposed by the Democratic leadership would help it win the support of local government and police officials; and second, it wished to ingratiate itself with the demonstrators and the general public by posing as strongly "pro-revolution." However, even among the New Democrats, there were many who wished to relax the bill, either by eliminating the "automatic" clause or by reducing the number of those whose civil rights were to be suspended.[42] Although the Democratic Party was more inclined than the New Democratic Party to modify the bill concerning the suspension of civil rights for former pro-Rhee officials, the younger members in both major parties were generally persistent in their opposition to change in the proposed law.

Those who advocated stronger punishment of local law enforcement officers were especially enraged when, in mid-November, former minister of internal affairs Chang Kyŏng-gŭn escaped to Japan while on bail for health reasons. Supporters of a strong bill argued that the fact that Chang, who was a faithful supporter of the Rhee regime, was able to escape to Japan despite his criminal status was indicative of and attributable to the presence of numerous anti-democratic, pro-Rhee elements at the lower levels of law enforcement.[43]

40. According to an assemblyman, only four of these groups had any type of legitimate claim to represent the "revolutionary forces." (*Minŭiwŏn hoeŭirok,* 37th session, no. 51, p. 3.)

41. In contrast with most other legislative issues, there was no unanimity of opinion among the various newspapers on this particular issue.

42. In a public hearing on this issue held on November 10, a division of opinions occurred among the various groups: Groups opposed to the "automatic clause" included the Association of Newspaper Publishers; the Democratic Party; the Republican Party (led by Kim Chun-yŏn, who had separated himself from the Democratic Party in 1956 after Chang Myŏn was nominated for the vice-presidency; and two of five "citizen representatives." Groups supporting the "automatic clause" included the Revolutionary Students Association; the University Professors' Association; the New Democratic Party; the Seoul National University Student Association; the Crippled Students' Friendship Society; and three of five "citizen representatives." (*Minŭiwŏn hoeŭirok,* 37th session, no. 51, pp. 4–5.)

43. According to Kim To-yŏn, Chang would frequently provide President Rhee with distorted arguments in cabinet meetings in order to win Rhee's favor. (*Ibid.,* pp. 1–2.) For a brief description of Chang's personal background, see Chapter Two of this book.

Despite a strong feeling against the "automatic" clause and his public stand to this effect, Premier Chang failed to rally his own party's members behind the amendment he supported. In the actual voting, the amendment proposal, which would have eliminated the "automatic cases," received only 60 votes in its favor out of 163 members present.[44] The original (automatic) clause remained in the bill by a vote of 90 affirmative votes out of 164 members present.[45] From the floor discussion itself, it is clear that not all of the 60 members who supported the Democratic Party amendment were Democrats. Among them were members of the independent group who had been closely affiliated with the Liberal regime, and of minor parties such as the Republican Party and the Socialist Mass Party, which objected to the bill as a matter of legal and political principle.[46] This indicates that those Democrats who voted for the Democratic proposal numbered less than 50, dramatizing the ineffectiveness of Chang's leadership within the Democratic Party on a very crucial issue. Other proposals, aimed at mitigating the adverse effect of the law, met similar fates.[47] Finally, when the "unrevolutionary" House of Councillors returned the bill with changes which turned the "automatic cases" into "investigatory cases," the lower house overruled it by an overwhelming vote of 161 to 6. The end product was practically the same as the bill originally proposed by the judicial and legislative committee of the lower house one and a half months earlier.

As shown in the legislative process described above, the bill concerning the suspension of the civil rights of former government and Liberal Party officials passed the National Assembly over a considerable degree of opposition and reluctance on the part of many members—especially the elderly and those who were close to the Chang government. The law (concerning the suspension of civil rights) passed the National Assembly in part because of the desire of many assemblymen to eliminate possible competitors (i.e., former Liberals) in their respective districts and to replace the former government and police officers

44. *Minŭiwŏn hoeŭirok,* 37th session, no. 54, pp. 5–7. The proposal was actually discarded because of failure to receive a majority vote after two attempts.

45. *Ibid.*

46. Yun Kil-chung, one of the three SMP assemblymen, also made it clear that he was opposed to this particular bill. See Yi Chae-hak, "Memoirs," p. 177.

47. An amendment proposed by Han Kŭn-jo, a Democrat and close associate of Chang, which attempted to strike out the "investigatory case" clause from the bill, was defeated by a vote of 10 to 9 on the floor, most of the 224 members present in the chamber not voting. (*Minŭiwŏn hoeŭirok,* 37th session, no. 58, p. 4.) A proposal by Kim Chun-yŏn, head of the Republican Party, attempting to combine the automatic and investigatory cases into a single category, also failed to pass the House of Representatives, receiving only 6 affirmative votes against 5 opposing votes out of 163 members present (*ibid.*).

with their own supporters. The desire of the New Democratic Party to support what seemed to be a popular issue at the time and to prevent the Democratic Party from strengthening its position among former officials of the Liberal regime was also an important factor in the passage of the law. However, it seems that the two most important factors were the inability of the Chang government to exert strong pressure on the Democrats to push through its own amendment, and the general passivity and lack of conviction of a majority of the assemblymen, which made it easy for the demonstrators and a few radically oriented legislators to force the National Assembly to pass a "revolutionary" law. This law, providing for the punishment of low-level officials, had the serious effect of immobilizing a number of important personnel in law enforcement agencies and of alienating them from the constitutional order of the Second Republic as well as from the Chang government itself.

DEMORALIZATION OF THE POLICE

As we noted in Chapter Four, the Hŏ Chŏng government had taken only limited and reluctant steps toward "democratizing" the national police, limiting its actions to the dismissal of a few top-ranking officers and personnel shifts between and within the various provinces.[48] Therefore, the task of a major police overhaul was left to the Democratic government of Chang Myŏn. Immediately upon assuming power, Chang Myŏn recognized the need to purge a large number of police officers at all levels who were accused of illegal or brutal actions while serving the Liberal regime, and also to restore police authority, which had been badly damaged as a result of the student uprising, as well as in anticipation of purges within the police department. Police atrocities had constituted one of the most important factors responsible for provoking the April uprising.[49]

During the first few weeks of his administration, Chang placed higher priority on the first task—that of meeting the public demand for a large-scale police purge. Within three months of taking office, the Chang Myŏn government purged a total of 4,500 police officers who had allegedly cooperated with the Liberal regime in election rigging or who were known to be the objects of public hatred. Table VII–3 shows the number of police officers at different levels who were dismissed by the Chang government during the period between September 1 and November 30, 1960.

48. See Chapter Four.
49. See Kim Sŏng-t'ae, "Psychology of the April Uprising."

Table VII-3
DISSMISSED POLICE OFFICERS BY RANK
SEPTEMBER 1–NOVEMBER 30, 1960

Rank	*Number Dismissed*	*Total number*	*Percent Dismissed*
National chiefs	18	20	90%
Superintendents	115	160	70
Inspectors	265	500	54
Lieutenants	678	4,000	18
Sergeants	1,276	6,200 *	20
Policemen	2,169	22,000 *	10
TOTAL	4,521	32,880	14%

Sources: Haptong yŏn'gam, 1961, p. 152; *Tong-a Ilbo,* May 7, 1960, p. 1.
* Estimated number.

In addition, about 80 percent of all police personnel were transferred to different positions—most of them in other localities—during the same period.[50] Among those who were dismissed, a majority consisted of the heads of provincial, county-level, and local police stations and their immediate subordinates in charge of investigative work. Although the percentage of those purged was smaller among the lower-ranking officers, the dismissal of many of the middle-level officers (inspectors, lieutenants, and sergeants) made it difficult for the police as a whole to function adequately, especially in the area of investigation. Furthermore, those police officers who had been most valuable to the Liberal Party were also those who were more experienced and capable in a professional sense, and their loss had a great impact upon the effectiveness of the police force throughout the nation.

The police and other law enforcement agencies, already undermanned in maintaining social order and public security, were further weakened with the passage of the constitutional amendment and the law concerning the suspension of civil rights for former officials of the Liberal regime. For, of the nearly 15,000 individuals affected by the law, more than 2,500, or about one-sixth, were police officers in leadership positions.[51] Of these, there were 7 inspectors, 84 lieutenants, 454 sergeants, and 1,979 policemen. Of about 600 individuals included in the "automatic" category, about 400 were former National Police offi-

50. *Haptong yŏn'gam,* 1961, p. 152.
51. *Kyŏnghyang Shinmun,* January 31, 1960, evening ed., p. 3.

cers and detectives who had allegedly intimidated voters and anti-Rhee candidates, terrorized polling places, and assisted in the burning and stuffing of ballot boxes.[52] The seriousness of the situation was such that the intelligence department of the Seoul district prosecutor's office appealed to the National Assembly and the cabinet to exempt a total of 611 police officers working for the department from civil rights suspension, stating that their expulsion from the police force would mean the loss of 74 percent of the police detectives engaged in political (anti-Communist) intelligence activities.[53]

Significantly, the ministers of both home affairs and justice testified in the National Assembly that the loss of many experienced police officers en masse would have serious consequences for the security of the nation.[54] Eventually, however, they could not stop the dismissal of the police officers. The real significance of the problem was that, although the police officers specializing in investigative work here ostensibly engaged in counterespionage missions, they also had the vital task of collecting information concerning any anti-government activities within the country. The loss of these individuals made the protection of the government from its domestic enemies virtually impossible.[55] It was also difficult to expect unreserved loyalty to and cooperation with the new government from the police officers included in the "investigatory" category.

A similar situation prevailed among the officials in other branches of the government. Chang had already dismissed about 5,000 senior officials appointed under the Rhee government in September, and another 12,000 were affected following the passage of the Special Law.[56] There was thus a sharp contrast between the way the police were treated by the Chang government in 1960 and by the American Military Government in Korea following the Japanese defeat in 1945. Under the American Military Government, those who had served in the Japanese police were effectively protected by Cho Pyŏng-ok, who headed the National Police at that time, and they subsequently played a critical role in protecting and stabilizing the occupation government and later the government of President Syngman Rhee. Now, however, under somewhat similar circumstances, many of those who had served the Liberal regime were made objects of persecution. It would seem that these police officers could easily have transferred their loyalty to

52. *New York Times,* February 1, 1961, p. 17.
53. *Kyŏnghyang Shinmun,* January 10, 1961, p. 1.
54. *Minŭiwŏn hoeŭirok,* 38th session, no. 14, pp. 19–26.
55. Interview with Kim Yŏng-sam, October 10, 1969.
56. *New York Times,* September 24, 1960, p. 3; also *Kyŏnghyang Shinmun,* January 31, 1961, evening ed., p. 3.

the new government if it had shown the willingness and capability to give them protection from those who assailed them for their past service to Rhee. Because of the Chang government's failure in this regard, the National Police not only failed to secure the absolute number of personnel necessary to carry out its task, but was also unable to restore the self-confidence among the police officers which had been lost as a result of the unsuccessful attempt to suppress the violent student uprising.

So long as no politician could provide the needed protection from their critics or justification for effective action for the government, most police officers were unwilling to risk their lives or positions in defense of the new regime. Even before the passing of the Special Law, there were many instances of police incapacitation and unwillingness in dealing with social disorder. The weakness of the police was well shown in a clash between a police-backed group and their opponents which took place in Ch'angnyŏng, Kyŏngsang Nam-do Province, immediately following the July 29 election. In that election, Shin Yŏng-ju, a former Liberal, and Pak Ki-jŏng, a Democratic candidate, competed for the National Assembly seat in this district. Both had strong kinship ties among the electorate, but Shin had the implicit backing of the Ch'angnyŏng police department as a former police officer and Liberal assemblyman. However, there were very strong feelings against his candidacy among the rival kinship groups in the district who accused Shin and his close relatives of having been responsible for the banishment of a number of villagers shortly before the end of the Korean War. It was believed that truckloads of villagers who had been branded as Communists were sent off to an island on the southwestern coast and drowned.[57]

In the midst of the ballot-counting, Shin, who had superior organization and abundant financial resources, led Pak, whose campaign workers charged Shin with election rigging. This resulted in a scuffle between the campaign workers of the two candidates, injuring some 30 people. Subsequently, the villagers and townsmen supporting Pak invaded the polling-stations and burned a number of ballot boxes. Furthermore, they kidnapped candidate Shin and gave him a "people's tribunal" which sentenced him to death. Although Shin's life was saved by visiting students, who urged restraint, a state of complete anarchy reigned during the next few days in the district as the townsmen and villagers captured the district police chief and his wife and publicly ridiculed them. The rioting, which resulted in burning and destruction of the houses of Shin's friends and relatives, as well as the

57. For detailed description, see *Kyŏnghyang Shinmun*, August 10–12, 1960; also *Han'guk hyŏngmyŏng chae-p'ansa*, I, 188–189.

lynching of government officials, ended only after an army contingent was brought in. As a result of the rioting, however, Pak, the Democratic candidate, was declared winner in the Ch'angnyŏng District by the Central Election Office.

Similar incidents took place in a number of other districts, and in all the cases of violence growing out of the election, the police found themselves completely incapable of dealing with the mobs who demanded the withdrawal of the "anti-revolutionary" candidates.

Members of the police force often refused to face a direct confrontation with the demonstrators, even when their own buildings and superiors were objects of attack by the mobs. Late in September, when some 50 students from Seoul National University stopped all automobiles without "regular" license plates (presumably because they belonged to the "privileged class"), the authorities found it necessary to mobilize a total of 1,500 policemen to free 76 automobiles from the hands of the students.[58] On October 8, when the president of Han Yang University, a former Rhee supporter, sought asylum in a major police station following student protests against his mishandling of school funds, some 500 policemen failed to prevent the students from forcibly taking the college president away from the police building. In mid-November, the home of the president and chairman of the board of directors of Yonsei University, an American, was ransacked by some 1,500 students who met with no police resistance; the students were protesting that he had failed to dismiss a number of pro-Rhee professors at the university.[59] In all these cases, the police showed themselves timid and unwilling in confronting the demonstrators.

The effectiveness of the police force was further hindered by the instability in the ministry of home affairs, which was in charge of its operation. As Table VII-4 (p. 162) shows, there were three ministers of internal affairs during the first three months of the Chang administration.

One reason for the rapid turnover among internal affairs ministers was the ineffectiveness of the National Police. However, such turnover itself contributed to the weakening of the police force. Only belatedly did the Chang government try to ameliorate the effects of its personnel policy and the Special Law passed by the National Assembly. There were three general lines of action that the government took to achieve this objective. The first was to supplement the existing police force with new recruits at various levels. Thus the new government recruited 2,000 new police officers during its administration in 1960. Of these, 430 were college graduates who, it was hoped, would provide

58. *Kyŏnghyang Shinmun*, September 23, 1960, p. 3.

59. *Tong-a Ilbo*, October 16, 1960, p. 1; also, *Kyŏnghyang Shinmun*, October 9, 1960, p. 3.

Table VII-4

TERMS OF FIRST THREE HOME MINISTERS IN THE CHANG CABINET

	Name	*Term (days in office)*	*Reason for Resignation*
1st	Hong Ik-p'yo	8/23–9/12 (20)	Major cabinet reshuffle
2nd	Yi-Sang-ch'ŏl	9/12–10/13 (31)	Invasion of the National Assembly hall by demonstrators
3rd	Hyŏn Sŏk-ho	10/13–11/20 (38)	Chang Kyŏng-gŭn's escape while on bail

needed new blood for the police department. In addition, about 120 college graduates were recruited as cadre candidates, and were later appointed as sergeants in the police force. In the major personnel reshuffle in late September, 20 new superintendents were appointed from outside the department, while 36 inspectors were promoted to that rank. In all, during the year 1960, 540 police officers were promoted to the rank of lieutenant or above as a result of intra-department reshuffling.

As Table VII-5 shows, many of the higher-ranking officers were promoted after establishment of the Chang government. Although such promotions might have served to generate their loyalty toward the new government, they instead brought about internal dissension and demoralization because of the unhappiness of those who were not

Table VII-5

NEW POSITIONS ACQUIRED BY POLICE OFFICERS AS A RESULT OF INTRA-DEPARTMENT PROMOTIONS, 1960

	Lieutenants	*Inspectors*	*Superintendents*	*Chiefs*	*Total*
Promotions	216	214	85	25	540
Total number *	4,000	500	160	30	4,690
Percent promoted	5.4%	43%	53%	83%	11%

Source: Haptong yŏn'gam, 1961, p. 152.

* The actual number might have been somewhat smaller except for the total number of chiefs. This is an estimated figure as of May 1960. As noted above, many police officers were dismissed after that date.

promoted and of those who came to occupy positions subordinate to new officers recruited from outside the department.[60]

The Chang government also tried to restore the effectiveness of the police by exhortation, and when that failed, by harassment. Police officers were constantly warned against neglect of duty and threatened with dismissal or other punitive measures. Thus, within a few weeks after the establishment of the Chang government, the Seoul police department ordered all members of the police force to work on both Saturdays and Sundays "just like any other weekday." The measure, instead of "restoring alertness" as intended, only served to demoralize and antagonize most of the police officers.[61]

Furthermore, the National Police headquarters warned in repeated declarations that those in charge of operations which failed to deal adequately with "various demonstrations and scandals" would be dismissed. Subsequently, a number of major district police chiefs were told to resign from their respective offices.[62]

Following the overthrow of the Rhee government, street demonstrations became widespread because of the extraordinary success of the April uprising and the docility of the police. Some tended to become violent, and in most cases the police were not able to cope with them.[63] In a similar manner, when the police could not capture two former top police officers who had been sought for punishment under provisions of the Special Law, the head of the Seoul police department declared that all those in charge of the investigation should resign if the former police officers were not captured before the expiration date of the arrest warrant.[64] In order to make sure that the police officers were fully cooperating with the government's effort to maintain public security, special observers were dispatched to various branches of the police.

The government action represented an attempt to rectify deficiencies in police effectiveness through internal, coercive measures. Such measures, instead of improving the effectiveness of the police, served to cause an adverse reaction from the police officers, who became more concerned with the politics of their fate than with their actual work.[65]

60. *Tong-a Ilbo,* January 15, 1961, p. 4.
61. *Kyŏnghyang Shinmun,* September 18, 1960, evening ed., p. 3.
62. *Ibid.,* March 31, 1961, p. 4.
63. According to a report made by the military government which overthrew the Chang Myŏn government, there were more than 1,800 demonstrations, involving some 950,000 participants, between May 1960 and May 1961. Half of the participants were students (*Han'guk hyŏngmyŏng chaep'ansa,* I, 246). See also Henderson, *Korea: The Politics of the Vortex,* p. 179 and pp. 431–432.
64. *Kyŏnghyang Shinmun,* February 12, 1961, p. 3.
65. *Ibid.,* April 5, 1961, p. 3.

Caught between the possibility that he might be noticed by the public in the course of suppressing demonstrations and the possibility of being dismissed for not acting vigorously enough on behalf of "law and order," most police officers chose to take an opportunistic course, acting only under obvious pressure and then only to the extent necessary to satisfy their superiors.[66]

The ineffectual and uncooperative nature of the law enforcement agencies during this period was well described in a special report of the legislative and judicial committee of the Lower House released on March 7, 1961. According to the report, the Special Prosecution Department (which had been established in order to punish the former officials of the Rhee regime) was able to bring indictments in only 31 of the 820 cases which had originally been brought to its attention, and the major reason for the unusually small number of indictments was the "uncooperative and negative attitude" of the police.[67]

It can be concluded that the Chang government's strenuous effort to restore the morale and effectiveness of the police was largely unsuccessful. The law enforcement agencies remained generally uncooperative with the new government. This situation had two serious consequences. In the first place, it became difficult for the Chang government to obtain necessary information concerning the possible activities of those conspiring against it. Secondly, it helped convince various political sectors in South Korea that a "crisis situation" the Chang government could not cope with was emerging. Rumors suggesting the possibility of a large-scale uprising, either in the cities or in the rural areas, were widespread among the population and the politicians, despite the prime minister's public denials that there was any factual basis for such rumors.[68]

Many were particularly concerned that the students would erupt again on the occasion of the first anniversary of the April uprising. A. M. Rosenthal wrote in the *New York Times,* "Many Koreans and foreigners are awaiting the anniversary of the revolution with considerable nervousness. Their fear is that the revolution created too many expectations that the Chang government, burdened by economic

66. The policeman's dilemma during this period was further dramatized when the Revolutionary Court sentenced to death a former national police officer on April 15 on charges of having killed anti-government demonstrators during the April uprising. The sentence, coming in the aftermath of the major demonstrations, served to discourage the police officers from taking vigorous steps to cope with the militant demonstrators. See *New York Times,* April 16, 1961, p. 27.

67. *Kyŏnghyang Shinmun,* March 8, 1961, p. 1.

68. *Ibid.,* February 26, 1961, p. 1.

realities, has not been able to meet. They are concerned that the student revolutionaries may go into the streets again." [69] The anxiety and nervousness of observers proved to be not without some substance, as the streets were indeed filled again with demonstrating students in late March and early April. As we will see in the next chapter, the anti-government demonstrations, organized largely by the leftist organizations (students and non-students) and reformist parties, provided a timely excuse for those in the military who were plotting to take over power from the Chang government.

THE QUESTION OF ILLEGAL WEALTH

In dealing with those who had accumulated wealth by illegal means during the Rhee regime, the Chang government followed a pattern similar to its treatment of former Liberal officials. Initially the government angered the "pro-revolutionary" elements by its failure to take strong measures against the holders of illegal wealth, but was subsequently forced to propose punitive legislation sufficiently harsh to cause a strong reaction from the business sector.

As we saw in Chapter Four, the Hŏ Chŏng government had not taken positive action concerning illegal wealth during its three-month administration. Hŏ Chŏng's interim cabinet had resolved on May 21, 1960, that the matter would be handled only "within the boundaries of existing laws." [70] From among various illegal business activities,[71] the Hŏ Chŏng government had chosen only violations of tax laws for investigation and punishment. On June 4, the ministry of finance made public a list of individuals who had at least 5 million hwan in unpaid taxes, accumulated during the five years prior to 1960. Included in this list were 71 enterprises represented by 25 individuals. In the meantime, the Hŏ government requested and received authorization from the National Assembly to establish a Consultative Committee for the Regulation of Tax Violators, which was to consist of representatives from the ministry of finance, ministry of justice and the grand prosecution office. As we noted in earlier chapters, the Con-

69. *New York Times,* March 15, 1961, p. 6.

70. *Shin-dong-a,* December 1964, p. 160.

71. See Chapter Four of this book. The illegal activities included: (1) illegal or improper purchase of government property; (2) receiving improper bank loans at rates far lower than the current ones; (3) purchase of government foreign currency (dollars) through preferential treatment; (4) tax evasion, illegal or improper tax exemption, or tax reduction; (5) illegal or improper acquisition of concessions and privileges; (6) acceptance of grafts and bribes.

sultative Committee took the rather passive step of simply asking the accused enterprises to *voluntarily report* their illegal business activities during the Rhee regime.[72]

In response to the declaration of the Consultative Committee, the 16 largest corporations in Korea, represented by the 9 wealthiest individuals, reported having evaded a total of 4.8 billion hwan (equivalent to about $7 million) in taxes. In terms of both the number of individuals admitting their guilt and the amount of delinquent taxes reported, the figures were far lower than expected by either the general public or government authorities. In recognition of this, the Committee ordered a thorough investigation of the amount of tax evasion by leading enterprises. Subsequently the Prosecution Office revealed, after a month-long investigation, that during the five years prior to 1960 more than 9 billion hwan in taxes (about $14 million) had been illegally evaded by 28 enterprises controlled by 12 individuals.[73]

One crucial factor in delaying the punishment of those guilty of large-scale tax evasion was continuing disagreement between the ministry of finance, which advocated relatively mild treatment of the delinquents, and the Prosecution Office, which demanded harsher punishment for them. For example, the ministry of finance, which had retained most of the officials who had close ties with business and who understood the adverse economic consequences of harsh treatment of the large enterprises, argued that those who were guilty of tax evasion should be required to pay only two to three times the amount evaded during the past two years as a penalty (this would be in addition to the total amount evaded during the past five years). On the other hand, the Prosecution Office wished to see them pay as a penalty four to five times the amount evaded during the past two years.[74]

Despite repeated conferences aimed at ironing out their differences, the two governmental branches could not reach agreement on this point, and the issue had to be handed over to the new government.

A still more important and basic reason for the failure of the Hŏ Chŏng government to take positive action on this matter was its reluctance to assume the responsibility of attacking the business sector too vigorously. It repeatedly postponed major decisions on the matter, until it could pass the task on to the forthcoming government. However, the Chang Myŏn government had to work on the basis of two important decisions made by the Hŏ government regarding this problem. The first was the decision to make any punishment "financial"

72. *Han'guk hyŏngmyŏng chaep'ansa*, I, 278–279.
73. *Ibid.*, pp. 279–286.
74. *Ibid.*, pp. 283–287.

rather than criminal. Hence the representatives of business enterprises were freed from the possibility of imprisonment for their unlawful business activities during the Rhee administration. Such a decision stemmed from the recognition by both the Hŏ and Chang governments that the physical punishment of businessmen might cause general panic in the economy. Secondly, owners of the enterprises were encouraged to pay whatever they were supposed to owe to the state in stocks rather than in cash, so that their enterprises would continue to operate and repayment would not have an adverse impact on the national economy.[75]

Immediately after its assumption of power, the Chang government issued notice to those guilty of tax evasion to pay back in fines the taxes evaded during the preceding five years, plus four to five times the evaded amount in fines. In addition, it announced that a second round of investigation was being launched to deal with other business enterprises. In all, notices were sent to 47 corporations represented by 25 individuals who presumably owed the government a total of 19 billion hwan (about $29.3 million). A majority of these enterprises were engaged in such crucial economic activities as manufacturing (especially cement, textile, sugar, chemical goods, and metalic goods), fuel, transportation, insurance, and foreign trade.[76]

Despite the Chang government's relatively prompt action in trying to deal with the issue of illegal wealth, dissatisfaction was voiced inside and outside the National Assembly over the facts that the Chang government was overly generous in repayment terms; that many illegal economic activities other than tax evasion were not being punished; and that tax-delinquent individuals were all treated in a uniform manner, without regard to the different ways in which the illegalities were committed. The old faction of the Democratic Party (later the New Democratic Party) was thus pushing for special legislation to correct these "shortcomings," while the Chang administration insisted that sweeping new legislation was not necessary.

One complicating matter in the resolution of this issue was the widespread belief that the Chang government's soft stand toward illegal wealth was attributable to financial contributions from its holders. The funds were allegedly used in the election campaign for new-faction members and in the later parliamentary maneuvering in the contest for the prime ministership. Shortly after the new National Assembly was convened, the old faction alleged that during the months

75. Interview with Mr. Kim Yŏng-sŏn (former minister of finance in the Chang Myŏn cabinet), November 4, 1968.

76. *Kyŏnghyang Shinmun,* September 1, 1960, p. 1.

of July and August the major banks in Seoul had provided some 2 billion hwan in loans to individuals accused of having illegally accumulated wealth, and that they suspected that much of the money went to the new faction of the Democratic Party.[77] Subsequently, a special committee created by the House of Councillors to investigate the matter revealed that during the period between July 1 and August 10, a total of 2,002,770,000 hwan had been loaned to eight major corporations, all of which were being accused of having evaded taxation, and that the final destination of the loans could not be determined.[78] There was strong suspicion that the money had indeed been used by the Democratic new faction. Chang Myŏn wrote later that his faction had indeed received a considerable amount of money from businessmen, including a group of textile industrialists who contributed some 200,000,000 hwan, "in order to forestall the rise of leftist and progressive groups." [79]

Faced with strong pressure from the students and the press, the Lower House on February 9 passed a bill aimed at punishing those who had accumulated wealth through "impure" means during the Rhee regime. The earlier constitutional amendment had called for such legislation. According to the bill, "special measures" were to be taken against certain individuals who, by taking advantage of their privileged positions, had accumulated wealth during the five years prior to April 1960. Thus the bill would have enabled the government to take administrative measures against those who had evaded taxes in excess of 50,000,000 hwan (approximately $80,000), those who had acquired wealth in excess of 30,000,000 hwan (approximately $46,000) through other "impure" practices, and government or party officials who had accumulated more than 15,000,000 hwan (approximately $25,000). "Punishment" ranged from redemption of between 100 percent to 400 percent of the illegally acquired profit.[80] The bill passed the lower house over the opposition of a considerable number of representatives who thought its provisions "too soft." [81]

However, the bill received immediate and intense reaction from the

77. *Minŭiwŏn hoeŭirok,* 37th session, no. 7, pp. 1–2.

78. *Han'guk hyŏngmyŏng chaep'ansa,* I, 203.

79. Chang Myŏn, *Memoirs,* p. 84.

80. The text of the bill passed by the Lower House can be found in *Han'guk hyŏngmyŏng chaep'ansa,* I, 644–651.

81. Most of the representatives who expressed views opposing the bill because of its "softness" were either independents or non-leadership members of the two major parties. It was suggested, although not explicitly stated, that the leadership of the two parties had close connections with the business community, so that they were anxious to pass a watered-down version of the bill. *Minŭiwŏn hoeŭirok,* 38th session, nos. 12–23.

business sector. Through a petition to the National Assembly, public announcements and paid advertisements, the leading business organizations [82] asserted that the bill would "destroy" the fabric and foundation of the free enterprise system in South Korea through the "nationalization" of private property. Their statement argued:

> If what the Kim Il-sŏng clique in the North fears most is the economic prosperity of the South, and if what it would like to see happen in the South is economic disaster, we can conclude that the present bill concerning the punishment for so-called illegal wealth that has just been passed by the House of Representatives will certainly ensure the success of its scheme. If the bill accomplishes its objectives, it would turn all businessmen into criminals, thereby bringing about economic catastrophe in South Korea. . . . Therefore, it is difficult to counter the argument that what the present bill is aiming at is a socialist revolution in South Korea. Furthermore, it is no exaggeration to say that the bill would open ways for a "Communization" of the South.[83]

Subsequently, the business groups submitted a separate proposal to both chambers of the National Assembly, which called for construction of an industrial park through mobilization of the entrepreneurial ability and industrial capital of the business enterprises accused of having committed illegal business practices under the Rhee regime.[84]

As in the case of the other laws discussed previously in this chapter, the law concerning illicit wealth was modified in the House of Councillors, limiting the number of persons liable. The final version of the bill, which passed both houses of the National Assembly on April 15, specified that only those who had accumulated substantial amounts of wealth (50 million hwan in the case of tax evasion; 30 million hwan in other activities; 15 million hwan in the case of government or party officials) through illegal means, and who also *voluntarily gave* the Liberal Party 30 million hwan or more in political contributions for the March 1960 elections, would be punished under the law.[85]

This substantially reduced the number of businessmen who were to be affected by the law. However, the Chang government was never forgiven by the business community for its presumed role in the attempt to punish illegal business activities, and they remained suspi-

82. They included the Korean Business Consultative Conference, established on January 10, 1961, with a membership of 57 leading businessmen (many of these were included in the original list of those charged with serious tax evasion); the Korean Chamber of Commerce; and the Korean Trade Association. *Kyŏnghyang Shinmun,* March 4, 1961, p. 1.

83. *Ibid.*

84. *Tong-a Ilbo,* March 3, 1961, p. 1.

85. *Han'guk hyŏngmyŏng chaep'ansa,* I, 651–659.

cious of the Democratic administration's willingness to protect the basic interests of business.[86]

"PURIFYING" THE MILITARY

Let us now turn our attention to the relationship between the military and the Chang government. During the campaign, the Democratic Party made public that it planned to reduce the size of the Korean army by some 100,000 men on assuming power.[87] The same plan was confirmed by Chang Myŏn himself, after he was elected prime minister, in a speech he made in the National Assembly on August 27, 1960.[88] In accordance with the Democratic administration's "economic development first" policy, it attempted to limit defense spending to within 20 percent of tax revenue, as compared with 30 to 40 percent under the Liberal regime.[89] The reduction in the absolute number of troops was to be compensated for by modernization of equipment and an increase in firepower capacity. The Korean plan thus envisaged a drastic reduction in the defense expenditures provided by the Korean government while maintaining or increasing the level of support from the United States, which, in the period 1954–1960, had supplied about 40 percent of South Korea's military expenses.[90]

However, the reduction plan met with serious opposition not only from high-ranking South Korean army officers, but also from American military and diplomatic officials who feared that troop reduction might bring about much uneasiness and anxiety within the Korean armed forces, basing their opposition on the grounds that the government had not yet produced a plan for the employment of the men to be released.[91] Hence, notwithstanding the government position concerning reduction in the size of the army, both South Korean military leaders and United States officials made their opposition known to the

86. Interview with Kim Yŏng-sŏn. The business community's dissatisfaction with the Chang government was also expressed in connection with the devaluation of the Korean hwan by 100 percent. See "Round Table Talks over Devaluation of the Currency."

87. For example, Kim Yŏng-sŏn, who was considered Chang Myŏn's top braintrust, expressed this view in his "Essential Elements of the Democratic Party Platform," p. 149.

88. *Minŭiwŏn hoeŭirok,* 36th session, Aug. 27, 1960, p. 4.

89. Kim Yŏng-sŏn, *op. cit.,* p. 150.

90. The South Korean side provided most of the expenses necessary for "troop maintenance," which occupied about three-quarters of the total defense budget during the same period. See Chŏn Pyŏng-wŏn, "Kukpangbi" [The Defense Budget: The Cost and the Result of Korean Security].

91. *New York Times,* August 28, 1960, p. 2.

public on numerous occasions.[92] A few weeks later, Gen. Williston B. Palmer, director of military assistance at the Pentagon, expressed his opposition to any sizable reduction in South Korea's 600,000-man army. General Palmer's statement reiterated the views expressed earlier by the Commander of the United States troops in Korea, Gen. Carter B. Magruder.[93]

Faced with opposition both within the Korean army and from United States officials, the Chang government was forced to revise its original plan. Thus on September 3, less than two weeks after assuming office, the Chang government accepted a 50,000-man reduction proposal made by a conference of top-level Korean military officers, including the chiefs of staff of the various services and the minister of defense.[94] This number was further reduced to 30,000 by the middle of October, and by early November the Chang government's minister of defense declared that, after all, South Korea would continue to maintain a 600,000-man army, although there would be some personnel cuts on a limited scale.[95]

The Chang government's eventual withdrawal of its proposal for the reduction of military size dramatically demonstrated the formidable nature of the pressures from the military and the United States, and the Chang government's inability to withstand them. Like the Hŏ Chŏng government, the Chang government was preoccupied with the fear of provoking the top-ranking officers into rebellion against the new government, and took every precaution to avoid it. At the same time, American military leaders, because of their personal ties with top Korean military officers, constantly warned the Chang government against angering the generals. By catering to the pressures from the top military officers and the American military representatives, the Chang government exposed its inability not only to carry out its own reform program in the armed forces, but also to meet the demands of the junior and more radically-minded officers within the Korean army.

The objective of cleaning up the military (*chŏnggun*), which had become an extremely popular slogan both in and out of the armed forces following the April uprising, was not achieved by the resigna-

92. For example, the newly appointed Army Chief of Staff declared that he was opposed in principle to the government's plan for troop reduction. According to him, it would seriously affect the combat capability of the South Korean Army. (*Minŭiwŏn hoeŭirok,* 37th session, no. 6, p. 23.)

93. See *New York Times,* September 21, 1960, p. 16.

94. *Kyŏnghyang Shinmun,* September 3, 1960, p. 1.

95. *Tong-a Ilbo,* October 12, 1960, evening ed., p. 1; and *Kyŏnghyang Shinmun,* November 3, 1960, p. 1.

tion of half a dozen generals, considering the extensive nature of Syngman Rhee's influence in the military and the illegal and corrupt activities of military officers during the Rhee period. The demand for a more thorough purge in the army came, predictably, from the lower-ranking officers who exhibited more ideological, nationalistic, and self-assertive characteristics than their superiors. These junior officers were critical of the senior officers who, by taking advantage of the irresponsible nature of the Syngman Rhee regime, had become involved in a series of scandalous and corrupt practices during the past years.

The junior officers, for example, demanded that many of the senior officers be held responsible for election rigging within the armed forces under the Rhee regime. In the March 1960 election, the senior commanding officers had cooperated with the Liberal candidates, and they often used the official line of command to secure support for Syngman Rhee and Yi Ki-bung. In past elections they had instructed servicemen whom to vote for, used intelligence personnel to spy on the actual voting, and fabricated election results. It was also known that a few of the relatively high-ranking officers had been transferred to less desirable posts because of their association or acquaintance with anti-Rhee politicians.

As early as May 2, 1960, on behalf of some of the junior officers, Maj. Gen. Pak Chŏng-hi reportedly asked Army Chief of Staff Song Yo-ch'an to withdraw from active service for his participation in election rigging.[96] On May 8, eight lieutenant colonels, all members of the military academy's class of 1949, were temporarily arrested when they circulated a petition for an early and thorough purge within the armed forces. Gen. Song Yo-ch'an's subsequent resignation was not sufficient to satisfy the desires of the reform-minded junior officers, who wished to see most of the senior officers depart from the army. As we pointed out earlier, Hŏ Chŏng was reluctant to carry out a major personnel change within the armed forces because of his fear of hostile reaction from the high-ranking officers. Therefore, it was the Chang government which was expected to carry out this difficult task.

During the campaign period, the Democratic Party had promised effective cleansing of the armed forces through the elimination of incompetent and corrupt military officers. Upon the Chang government's assumption of power, both of its plans—to reduce the size of the armed forces and to carry out a clean-up operation within them—faced powerful opposition within the Korean armed forces and from the military and diplomatic representatives of the United States govern-

96. *Han'guk kunsa hyŏngmyŏngŭi chŏnmo* [A Complete Picture of the Korean Military Revolution], p. 63.

ment. General Magruder was particularly concerned about the prospect of complete disorganization of the Korean armed forces resulting from a massive personnel change. He repeatedly warned the junior officers of the South Korean army to refrain from accusing their seniors of irregularities commited in the past, and counseled the Korean government to take cautious and gradual steps in pursuing reform within the armed forces.[97] The American opposition to the Chang government's plans for a military reform once resulted in an emotion-laden exchange between an American general and a Korean army chief of staff during the early days of the Chang government. When General Palmer remarked that he was gravely concerned over the fact that capable officers in the Korean armed forces were being forced to resign as a result of pressure from the lower officers, and that those who were still in office were unsettled and anxious because of such pressure, the South Korean army chief of staff publicly denounced the "American interference in South Korea's domestic affairs." Lt. Gen. Ch'oi Kyŏng-nok had been appointed to the top army post by the Chang government because of his support for the policy of eliminating officers with dishonest records, and because of the respect he received from many junior officers. Ch'oi was especially resentful of the fact that the American general had been approached by a few Korean military leaders during a recent trip to Korea. Ch'oi thus declared: "A few senseless top-ranking officers who worship the powerful have given a false impression to a foreign military leader, and such action cannot be tolerated. They must be expelled from the army." [98] The army chief of staff apparently had in mind Lt. Gen. Ch'oi Yŏng-hi, chairman of the joint chiefs of staff, who was one of the targets of the junior officers, and on whose invitation General Palmer had visited Korea.[99]

Immediately after the above exchange took place, 16 junior officers (5 colonels and 11 lieutenant colonels) visited Gen. Ch'oi Yŏng-hi [100] to demand an explanation for the Palmer statement and ask for his resignation.[101] Subsequently, Gen. Ch'oi Yŏng-hi issued an emotional statement denouncing those who treat most of the Korean generals "as if they were criminals," and condemning the junior officers who attempted to "overpower" their seniors.[102]

97. For example, see *New York Times,* May 27, 1960, p. 9; also October 15, 1960, p. 5.
98. *Kyŏnghyang Shinmun,* September 23, 1960, evening ed., p. 1.
99. *Han'guk kunsa hyŏngmyŏngŭi chŏnmo,* p. 64.
100. Ch'oi had served as army chief of staff following the resignation of Lt. Gen. Song Yo-ch'an on May 27 and until the establishment of the Chang government.
101. *Han'guk kunsa hyŏngmyŏngŭi chŏnmo,* pp. 66–67.
102. *Kyŏnghyang Shinmun,* October 5, 1960, p. 1.

The immediate result of the above incident was the resignation of Ch'oi Yŏng-hi from active service and the court-martialing of the 16 officers, who were eventually dismissed from the army.[103] In the farewell ceremony for Ch'oi, General Magruder again declared that South Korea faced a "threat of internal disruption," because of "dissension within its armed forces," and urged South Koreans to end disputes in the military forces to maintain "the confidence of her allies and of her own forces," strongly hinting that General Ch'oi was a victim of forced retirement.[104] There was, however, a far more significant consequence of this episode beyond the resignation of the chairman of the joint chiefs of staff. This was the subsequent abandonment by the Chang government of its plans to carry out a vigorous clean-up program in the armed forces.

Following the Palmer-Ch'oi exchange, the Chang government showed itself to be far more concerned with the problem of insubordination and rebelliousness within the army than with corruption among the top officers. Thus, in repeated statements, the successive ministers of defense declared that there would be no major purge within the armed forces and that the highest priority would be given to the prevention of internal dissension and the problem of insubordination.[105] The most explicit sign of the government's policy shift was shown in the appointment on December 5, of Lt. Gen. Chang To-yŏng to succeed Gen. Ch'oi Kyŏng-nok as the army chief of staff. General Chang was accused of having been rather opportunistic in his dealings with his superiors, both Koreans and Americans, and of having committed many unprincipled and irregular acts as the commander of the Second South Korean Army (support troops) prior to the April uprising.[106] General Chang had tendered his resignation to the interim government but it was returned by Prime Minister Chang Myŏn, following his election as chief executive.

When questioned in the National Assembly why General Ch'oi, who had not committed any conspicuous blunders, was prematurely ousted from the position of army chief of staff, Chang's minister of defense explained that the change was inevitable "for the strengthening of the line of command in the military and the long-term development of the Korean armed forces," and that the appointment of Chang was strictly

103. *Ibid.*, October 28, 1960, p. 3. These officers became the core members of those who engineered a military coup d'état on May 16, 1961.

104. *New York Times*, October 15, 1960, p. 5.

105. See press conferences by Minister Kwŏn Chung-don on January 19, and by Minister Hyŏn Sŏk-ho on January 31, 1961. *Kyŏnghyang Shinmun*, January 20, 1961, p. 3, and February 1, p. 3.

106. *Minŭiwŏn hoeŭirok*, 38th session, no. 30, pp. 8–9.

in accordance with the regular order of succession within the Army.[107] Although both the Chang government and the ousted General Ch'oi denied that the United States had anything to do with his resignation, major newspapers in Seoul speculated that Ch'oi's failure to serve out the normal two-year term as army chief of staff was attributable to his earlier clash with the United States generals and his outspoken advocacy of all-out reform within the Korean army.[108]

The choice of Chang To-yŏng as army chief of staff proved to be the undoing of the Chang government, partly because of his failure to command respect among the lower-ranking officers, and partly because of his less-than-absolute loyalty toward the Democratic regime. Upon assuming office, Chang ordered discontinuation of the investigation of the past illegal activities of 20 generals which had been initiated by Gen. Ch'oi Kyŏng-nok.[109] He also declared that there would be no significant personnel changes in the army, and that all future acts of insubordination and rebelliousness by junior officers would be severely punished.[110] It turned out, however, that his opportunism was responsible for the abandonment of his commitment to establish strict discipline within the army, as the plot of a military coup d'état among the junior officers unfolded.

Three months after his appointment as army chief of staff, when the military coup d'état finally materialized, Chang joined those who engineered the coup and attempted in vain to take over the military junta himself. Although he received reports concerning subversive activities among the younger officers prior to the coup, Chang failed to act to forestall the plot; instead he maintained what could be characterized as a wait-and-see attitude.[111]

In retrospect, it seems that the appointment of Chang To-yŏng, a man of questionable reliability, to the important position of army chief of staff was one in a series of crucial blunders made by the Chang

107. *Ibid.*, p. 1.

108. See February 17–20 issues of *Tong-a Ilbo* and *Kyŏnghyang Shinmun.*

109. *Ch'amŭiwŏn hoeŭirok* [House of Councillors Record], 38th session, no. 22, pp. 1–4.

110. *Kyŏnghyang Shinmun,* February 21, 1961, p. 3.

111. See for example, Chang Myŏn, *Memoirs,* pp. 86–90. Premier Chang later disclosed that he had received reports about the plot about a week before the actual coup, and that Chang To-yŏng, when asked, flatly denied any knowledge of such developments. On the morning of the coup, General Chang was again contacted by the prime minister about the reported invasion of Seoul by the rebel troops. However, the general failed to mobilize his troops to protect the Democratic government. According to a description of activities the night before the coup by the plotters of the coup themselves, General Chang had been informed about the coup before his conversation with Premier Chang on the morning of May 16th (*Han'guk kunsa hyŏngmyŏngŭi chŏnmo,* pp. 140–141.).

government in its handling of the armed forces. Furthermore, there was extremely fast turnover in the post of minister of defense—three times during the brief life of the Democratic administration. None of the three who served as defense minister had had any experience in defense matters, and they received little respect from either the senior officers or the junior officers of the armed forces.[112] The Chang government hoped in vain that the minister of defense could secure his constitutional authority over the generals and colonels as under normal and stable circumstances. Other crucial mistakes made by the Chang government in handling the military included underestimation of the *ésprit de corps* and determination of the junior-level officers to carry out their scheme to overthrow the government, and excessive dependence and reliance on the United States in maintaining control over the army and preventing possible rebellion.[113]

Our discussion in this chapter shows that the Chang government systematically alienated various political sectors during its reign without strengthening existing support or gaining new political allies. We have observed that the anti-Rhee, anti-police groups and the junior officers in the armed forces were disillusioned and disenchanted with the Chang administration because of its failure to take positive action against former supporters of the Rhee regime, whose punishment was supposedly mandated by the April uprising. At the same time, the former pro-Rhee elements, including the police, the national bureaucracy, and most local leaders, were turned against the Chang government because of the actions taken by the National Assembly against them, despite the Chang government's reluctance in the matter; they were generally understood as reflecting Chang's policies and the former Liberal officials who were affected by them blamed the Chang government for their punishment.[114] In a political culture in which people were accustomed to strong executive control—for good or bad—it was impossible for the Chang government to avoid the responsibility for this legislation, despite the limited nature of its own power and capability.

In order to meet the enormous demands made upon the Chang government from various sectors of the society during the post-uprising period, a great deal more power was required beyond that normally exerted by a government committed to liberal-democratic principles.

112. House Speaker Kwak Sang-hun complained immediately after the formation of the first Chang cabinet that Hyŏn Sŏk-ho, the minister of defense, had no experience in military affairs and that under the circumstances he doubted whether the cabinet could work smoothly. (*New York Times*, August 24, 1960, p. 3.)

113. Interview with Mr. Kim Yŏng-sŏn, November 5, 1968.

114. Ko Chŏng-hun, *Kut'o*, pp. 105–106.

This was the basic dilemma of the Chang government, and Chang proved incapable of resolving the conflicting demands through the display of decisive leadership. Consequently, he presided over the breaking up of the "coalition" which made his ascendence to power possible —the coalition of the liberal students, the intellectual-press nexus, and the conservative party politicians. At the same time, he failed to secure the support of the police, the intelligence agencies, the bureaucracy, and the armed forces. In the next chapter, we will analyze the leftist movement, which provided convenient justification for military intervention in politics, and which seemed to be having some success in strengthening itself when it was shattered by the military coup.

VIII

LEFTIST AGITATION AND RIGHTIST REACTION

When the military junta took over power from the Chang government in May 1961, it claimed that South Korea was on the verge of subversion by the Communists,[1] that only the Korean armed forces were capable of preventing Communism from taking root among the people in South Korea, and that only through their timely action was the country saved from a Communist takeover.[2]

Although it is difficult to determine the validity of this claim, it is certain that leftist agitation during the latter part of the Democratic regime provided useful justification for the military to intervene in the political process. It also led many people in and out of the government—especially many conservative politicians, government officials, and some intellectuals—to support the military coup.

The leftist movement in South Korea during the Chang government consisted of three main groups: the reformist political parties; the radical labor movement, represented by the Teachers' Labor Union; and the student movement, spearheaded by the Student League for National Unification (*Minjok T'ongil Yŏnmaeng*) in Seoul National University. In this chapter we will examine the structural and ideological characteristics of these groups and how their activities affected the survival of the Chang government itself.

As we noted in Chapter Five, the reformist parties experienced serious defeat in the National Assembly election of July 1960. Among

1. Korean Government, *Han'guk kunsa hyŏngmyŏngsa* [History of the Korean Military Revolution], I, 61–62.

2. Korean Government, *A White Paper of the Military Revolution*, p. 7.

the most important reasons for the weakness of the reformist movement were the disunity between reformist politicians of different parties and factionalism within each party. During the July election, at least four reformist parties competed against one another for voter support. In many districts several candidates from one reformist party ran for the same National Assembly seat, critically diminishing any reformist's chances of winning the seat. Factionalism within the reformist parties was also responsible for their failure to form a common front against the conservative Democratic Party. Each of the reformist parties was divided into two or more factions. As a result, no one group or individual of a party could negotiate an alliance with the other parties. Thus the Progressive faction of the Socialist Mass Party was reluctant to accept the proposal made by the non-Progressive members of the party to form a grand alliance of reformists, lest the new allies should side with the non-Progressive members in their intraparty conflict. Factionalism proved to be a serious problem for the reformist parties, particularly the SMP, during their period of growth after the July election.

REALIGNMENT OF REFORMIST PARTIES

In the post-election period, there were two major developments among the reformist parties. One was the permanent split between the Progressive and anti-Progressive factions within the SMP, the other was the overall realignment of the reformist politicians into moderate and radical groups, as a result of this split within the SMP.

Like the factional strife of many other political groupings in South Korea, including the Democratic Party, much of the antagonism between the factions in the SMP was attributable more to personality differences than to ideological differences. Kim Tal-ho, who had been vice chairman of Cho Pong-am's Progressive Party, argued that only the Progressive Party and its former members could represent the mainstream of the reformist movement in South Korea, and that all other political activists who considered themselves "reformists" were only fellow-travelers at best, and imposters at worst. Thus Kim and his followers were primarily interested in reviving the Progressive Party, which had been destroyed by the Rhee regime.

Similarly, supporters of the non-Progressive faction had a strong suspicion that the ultimate objective of the Progressive faction was a Communist-oriented socio-political revolution rather than peaceful and democratic implementation of Socialist ideas.[3] Thus, while the

3. For a discussion of the ideological and tactical differences of the two factions,

Democratic Party was undergoing a split between the new and old factions, a similar situation was developing within the SMP between the Progressive and non-Progressive factions. Each attempted to eliminate the hard-core members of the other faction, claiming that it was impossible to work with the rival faction within the same party.[4]

In recognition of the seriousness of the schism, the leaders of each faction met separately and started negotiations with non-SMP reformist politicians concerning the formation of a "grand alliance" of the reformists, each hoping to exclude the rival faction from the new alliance. The non-Progressive faction contemplated a reformist coalition under a democratic socialist banner which would place heavier emphasis on its participation in the normal political processes, while the Progressive faction worked for a separate coalition of relatively more radical reformists who were more inclined toward carrying out their objectives through extra-constitutional means.[5]

Thus on September 14, after confirming the possibility of achieving cooperation with other reformist groups such as the Korean Socialist Party led by Chŏn Chin-han and the League of Reformist Organizations, an alliance of minor reformist parties, members of the rival faction declared that they were permanently severing their political ties with the Progressive faction. With this declaration, the SMP disintegrated, only three months after its initial organization and before it was formally inaugurated. From this date until the collapse of the Second Republic in May 1961, the two reformist groups followed separate paths, weakening the strength of the reformist movement. Following the voluntary withdrawal of the non-Progressive faction from the SMP, the Kim Tal-ho faction consolidated its support among the relatively more radical members of the party and formally registered itself as a political party. On November 24, the party held an organizational meeting in Seoul which was attended by 362, or about two-thirds of the 533 party delegates from throughout South Korea.

In the meantime, the non-Progressive faction's attempt to form a right-reformist coalition resulted in the formation of the Unification Social Party (*T'ongil Sahoe-dang*) in January 1961, encompassing a wide variety of reformists. Among those who joined this new party were: Sŏ Sang-il and his supporters such as Yi Tong-hwa, Yun Kilchung, and Pak Ki-ch'ul; former Progressive Party members who were disenchanted with the hard-line attitude of the Progressive "old

---

see Kim Sŏng-yŏl, "Hyŏkshin chŏngdangŭi chŏnmo" [A Complete Picture of the Reformist Parties], pp. 96–103.

4. *Tong-a Ilbo*, September 10, 1960, p. 1.

5. *Kyŏnghyang Shinmun*, September 11, 1960, p. 1; September 12, p. 1.

Guards" headed by Kim Tal-ho; Ko Chŏng-hun, the former head of the Socialist Reform Party; and a number of elderly nationalists who had been engaged in anti-Japanese struggle in China and Japan during Japanese rule.

Shortly before the military coup on May 16, the reformist politicians were split into three broadly definable groups: the left or radical reformists, represented by the SMP and the Socialist Party; the center reformists, represented by the Unification Socialist Party; and the right reformists, represented by the National Unification Party (*Minjok T'ongil-tang*), which was formed toward the end of the Second Republic through the coalescing of certain reformists who had founded various small political parties after the fall of the Rhee government in April 1960.

What distinguished the reformist politicians most clearly from the conservatives of the Democratic Party and the New Democratic Party was their attitude toward national unification and the American presence in Korea. Most of the reformists regarded the presence of foreign powers in Korea as the main barrier to national unification, and advocated the initiation of economic and cultural exchange with the North Korean Communists as a first step toward cooperation between the North and the South. Furthermore, most of the reformists envisaged the achievement of national unification through Korea's neutrality in the conflict between the Communist and anti-Communist world powers.

For example, the SMP proposed the withdrawal of all foreign powers from the Korean peninsula; economic, cultural, and political exchange between North and South Korea; and the achievement of national unification on the basis of the principle of permanent neutrality.[6] The party proposed a national referendum to choose between the different proposals advanced by various political groups, including that of the North Korean Communist regime, which advocated a confederation of the two areas to be administered by a supreme national committee consisting of representatives of both the North and the South.[7]

Similarly, the Unification Socialist Party also advocated everlasting neutrality for a unified Korea free of the presence of foreign troops. The government of unified Korea, according to this proposal, was to be set up through an all-Korea election held on the basis of the one-man, one-vote principle, and its neutrality was to be preserved through

6. The SMP proposal concerning the unification of Korea as cited in *Han'guk hyŏngmyŏng chaep'ansa*, III, 703–704.

7. *Ibid.*

an international agreement administered by the United Nations.[8] The suggestion of the reformists for unification of Korea through neutralization was in part inspired by a proposal made on October 21 by U.S. Senator Mike Mansfield, who suggested neutralist unification of Korea along the lines of Austrian settlement in 1954.[9]

Recognizing that the unification issue would appeal especially to the young, major reformist parties helped form separate organizations solely intended to advocate the achievement of national unification. Thus the SMP organized the Consultative Committee for the Nationalist and Independent Unification of Korea (*Minjat'ong*) in mid-January 1961, and the Unification Socialist Party supported the General League for the Realization of Neutralist National Unification (*Chungnip T'ongyŏn*), to counteract the initiative taken by the SMP.

As we shall see later in this chapter, these groups actively organized demonstrations on behalf of the reformist parties, demanding that the Chang government take more positive steps toward the unification of Korea. In particular, the Consultative Committee encouraged the radical students to actively advocate and demand peaceful national unification, and it supported those students who proposed meetings with the North Korean students to be held at Panmunjŏm. The reformist party-sponsored organizations for national unification also actively opposed the unification policies of both the Democratic Party and the New Democratic Party, which insisted that Korea be unified through an all-Korea election, strictly in accordance with the South Korean constitution and under the supervision of the United Nations.[10] Such a policy, the reformists argued, was tantamount to giving up altogether the goal of reunification, as there was no chance that North Korea would come to terms with the South under those conditions.[11]

Despite the common nature of their overall goals, the two organizations differed sharply in their approaches. In fact, these organizations reflected the ideological character of their respective sponsor-parties in that, while the Consultative Committee advocated unconditional cooperation with the North Korean Communists in order to achieve "peaceful unification based upon the principle of self-determination," the General League emphasized the importance of democratic elec-

8. *Ibid.*, pp. 869–870.

9. *New York Times*, October 22, 1960, p. 1.

10. This view was officially endorsed by the National Assembly in a resolution on March 13, 1961, which received the overwhelming support of both major parties. See *Minŭiwŏn hoeŭirok*, 38th session, no. 35, pp. 10–18.

11. *Tong-a Ilbo*, March 14, 1961, p. 1; March 15, p. 1.

tions throughout Korea and a guaranteed neutrality for the reunified Korean government.[12]

The two organizations spent much of their energy in criticizing each other's unification policies and in competing for the support of the nationalist students. As a result there was little unity among the reformists, either within the party movement or among the non-party organizations promoting reformist causes. Because of their miniscule representation in the National Assembly, the reformist parties were forced to bring their case to the streets, and to try to gain support from the urban masses and the young through largely symbolic issues such as unification and nationalism.

The second important issue which the reformist organizations emphasized in their struggle against the Chang government was the economic and technical agreement between the United States and South Korea. The reformists, together with a number of nonreformist politicians, opposed a provision in the agreement which gave the United States the right to "continuous observation and review" of the way U.S. financial and technical aid was being administered by the South Koreans. Furthermore, South Korea was required under the agreement to provide "full and complete information concerning the aid programs and other relevant information which United States officials may need."[13] Opponents of the agreement charged that since U.S. funds made up more than 50 percent of the South Korean budget, the United States would be permitted to interfere in almost every aspect of Korean government. The opposition (New Democratic Party) members termed the agreement "shameful" and charged that it was intended to give the United States more power to oversee the functioning of the South Korean economy. The reformist parties and various reformist political organizations formed a united front against the aid agreement, holding rallies and carrying out street marches during most of February.[14] The coalition movement, initiated by the SMP, included student groups such as the April Revolution Corps, consisting of radical leftist students, and the National League of the Unemployed, an ad hoc organization of unemployed intellectuals.

It became evident that on this issue the reformists were again divided into two groups with fundamentally different approaches: Kim

12. *Han'guk hyŏngmyŏng chaep'ansa,* III, 855–856. Leaders of the USP asserted in court testimony that while the Consultative Committee of the SMP advocated a policy of "unification first, construction later," their own General League supported the idea of consolidating the political structures of the South before attempting to negotiate with the North Korean regime.

13. *New York Times,* February 9, 1961, p. 8.

14. *Ibid.,* February 6, 1961, p. 9; February 14, p. 5; February 16, p. 3; February 17, p. 3.

Tal-ho's SMP and a few radical leftist groups, including the Socialist Party, hoped to use the issue to bring down the Chang government and destroy the constitutional structure in Korea; the moderate reformists, including members of the Unification Socialist Party, saw great danger for the reformist movement if the Chang government was overthrown by rightist reaction, and thus offered only passive resistance to the United States-South Korean economic agreement.[15]

The immediate objective of the reformist protesters was to block approval of the agreement by the National Assembly. However, their case was considerably weakened by the anti-American connotations of the protest and the government's intimidation of the protesters through linking them with the North Korean Communists. Thus, Prime Minister Chang indicated that the North Korean regime was attempting to incite anti-American agitation in South Korea over the economic agreement, and warned that the government would take strong measures against persons found to be engaged in such Communist agitation.[16] Regardless of the actual role played by the North Korean regime in anti-government activities, the protest demonstrations failed to gain momentum and were largely ignored by most students and other citizens.

In the latter part of February, the agreement was overwhelmingly approved by the National Assembly.[17] Significantly, all but one of the 7 reformist representatives in the Lower House of the National Assembly chose to abstain from voting rather than publicly oppose the agreement. The abstention of most of the reformist legislators, who belonged to the "moderate" camp among the reformists, could be attributed to their fear of being considered anti-American—and thus pro-Communist—in voting against the agreement.

The reformists were more successful in mobilizing support by their opposition to two government-proposed security laws aimed at controlling street demonstrations and pro-Communist subversive activities. With this issue, the two reformist groups—radical and moderate—found an opportunity to cooperate for a common cause.

The Chang government, hoping to restore the authority and effec-

15. Top leaders of this group, however, were closely connected with the *Minjok Ilbo* (Nationalist Daily), which acted as the mouthpiece for all reformist groups—especially the USP—during the three-month period preceding the May 1961 military coup, and which was apparently set up with funds emanating from Communist sources in Japan. Following the military coup, its publisher received a death sentence, and many leading members of the USP, including Yun Kil-chung and Ko Chŏng-hun, received prison terms for having participated in the operation of the newspaper. See *Han'guk hyŏngmyŏng chaep'ansa,* III, pp. 831–888.

16. *New York Times,* February 16, 1961, p. 3.

17. *Kyŏnghyang Shinmun,* February 28, 1961, evening ed., p. 1; March 1, p. 1.

tiveness of the law enforcement agencies, introduced two bills to achieve this objective. The first bill would have required the organizers of public assemblies and street demonstrations to present to the police information concerning the purpose, time, place, and participants at least twenty-four hours before the scheduled event. Furthermore, the bill would have authorized the police to suspend the planned event and to use firearms at its own discretion in order to control an "unruly assembly or demonstration." [18]

The second law, aimed at suppressing the infiltration and subversive activities of the Communists, provided heavy penalties for those who willingly assisted or promoted the interests and activities of any pro-Communist groups defined as anti-state organizations. Although this anti-Communist legislation was introduced as an amendment to the existing national security law, it provided very heavy penalties for even the slightest expression of support or praise for the North Korean Communists.[19]

Both the politicians and the politically conscious groups, having become accustomed during the Liberal regime to government abuse of the national security laws, expressed strong suspicion and disapproval of the proposed laws. Virtually all newspaper editors and columnists—many of whom were university professors—criticized the proposed legislation, arguing that the law had no guarantee that one might not be charged with a serious anti-state crime by inadvertent agreement with the Communists on any matter. They also contended that the reasons for the ineffectiveness of law enforcement were to be found in the failure of government leadership rather than in the inadequacy of existing laws.[20] The second type of opposition was expressed through numerous protest meetings and demonstrations by students and labor groups. Whereas the first type of opposition was from liberal-oriented individuals who were concerned about the undemocratic nature of the proposed legislation, the second type of opposition was made by reformists and leftists whose main concern was that the legislation would make their daily political activities virtually impossible.

18. *Ibid.*, March 7, 1961, p. 1.

19. For the text of the amendment bill, see *ibid.*, March 23, 1961, p. 1. In terms of the circumstances under which the laws were proposed and the type of opposition they faced, there were close similarities between these laws and "the Police Duties Bill" proposed by the Kishi Cabinet in Japan about a year and a half earlier.

20. For example, the editorials of the March 11th issues of *Tong-a Ilbo* and *Kyŏnghyang Shinmun* were entitled, respectively, "Is Legislation a Panacea?" and "National Security and Excess Legislation." Also, an article by Yi Hang-nyŏng, a university professor, "Anti-Communism, or Making Half of the Population Communists?" *Kyŏnghyang Shinmun*, March 12, 1961, evening ed., p. 1.

Shortly after announcement of the proposals, various political groups, ostensibly representing most of the student participants in the April uprising, organized themselves into a "committee for the common struggle against the evil laws," and resolved to carry out vigorous opposition to both laws. The eight organizations which joined the committee represented only leftist political groups, with close personal and ideological ties with the reformist parties.[21]

The following chronological description of the violent confrontation between demonstrators and police during the last two weeks of March and early April gives a good picture of the seriousness of the situation.

March 18. In Taegu, some 10,000 demonstrators, mostly high school and college students, urged withdrawal of the proposed laws, chanting slogans such as "Punish the traitors of the revolution who are contemplating the enactment of evil laws," and, "Resign if you cannot save the proletarian masses." In addition, they demanded the repeal of existing national security laws, which the Chang government intended to strengthen. No one was reported seriously hurt, but ten demonstrators were arrested. The demonstration was organized by non-party social and youth groups, consisting primarily of leftist students.

March 21. In Taegu, about 15,000 demonstrators participated in a protest rally and street march organized by the reformist political parties.

March 23. In Seoul, the reformist parties organized a protest demonstration in which about 8,000 people participated. In a violent clash between the police and the demonstrators, about 60 people were seriously hurt, and 119 demonstrators were arrested by the police.

March 23. Student organizations in Pusan sponsored a protest demonstration in which about 3,000 people participated. Two students were reported badly beaten by the police.

March 24. In Taegu, about 30,000 demonstrators, most of whom were students, participated in a protest march without police resistance. Some 3,000 of the original demonstrators were involved in a

21. All the organizations claimed to be dedicated to "unification," "reformist" or "nationalist" causes by incorporating at least one of the three terms in their multi-word titles. Only two of them had the word "democratic" in their names. The words that appeared most frequently in the names of these organizations were *unification* (6), followed by *youth* (5), *nationalist* (4), *reformist* (3), *democratic* (2), and *student* (2). The names of these organizations included: Unification Youth Corps; League of Nationalist Reformist Youths; National Reform League; League of Youths for Unification and Democracy; League of Democratic Students for Unification; Youth League for National Unification; All-Nation Reformist Youth League; and National League for the Unification of the Fatherland. (*Kyŏnghyang Shinmun,* March 13, 1961, evening ed., p. 1.)

torchlight parade in the evening to dramatize their opposition to the proposed security laws.

March 25. In Masan, 3,000 students denounced the "impure elements" in the Chang government who proposed the security laws. There were protest demonstrations by students in other cities, including Pusan, Kwangju, and Chŏnju. A total of some 20,000 students participated in these demonstrations.

April 1. In Taegu, an alliance of various labor unions organized a protest meeting and march in which some 5,000 union workers (primarily in textile industries) participated. In addition, about 2,000 demonstrated against the proposed laws in Wŏnju (east central Korea) and about 7,000 in Kwangju (southwest). On the same day, about 5,000, consisting mostly of army veterans, demonstrated in Seoul, denouncing the "pro-Communist" forces who opposed the security laws.

April 2. In Taegu, about 600 activist members of the labor unions (especially the teachers' labor union), reformist parties, and student organizations clashed with 1,000 policemen, bringing about the most tense situation in the country since the beginning of the demonstrations. In the aftermath of the clash, 49 demonstrators, including a provincial legislator and the leader of the League of Labor Unions in Taegu, were arrested.[22] Violence erupted when the demonstrators defied a government ban on holding rallies in front of the railway station in Taegu.

As these demonstrations continued, the rightist organizations and the Chang Myŏn government charged the reformists with responsibility for the riots and casualties throughout the nation, particularly in Seoul and Taegu. Following the violent confrontation between demonstrators and the police in Seoul on March 22, the government actually arrested a number of leading members of the reformist parties, including Kim Tal-ho, head of the SMP; Sŏnu Chŏng, chairman of the SMP's Propaganda Committtee and Ko Chŏng-hun, chairman of the USP's Propaganda Committee. All were charged with inciting and organizing riots. It was clear from the events that there were a great many people with strong anti-leftist sentiments, many of them army veterans and police officers, whose reaction to leftist agitation compelled the Chang government to employ these repressive tactics. At the same time, effective suppression of the reformist parties by the

22. The police charged later that the leaders of the demonstration physically attacked the commanding police officer during the clash. These were later tried by the military government, following the coup d'état. For a description of the Taegu demonstration from the official viewpoint, see *Han'guk hyŏngmyŏng chae'-pansa,* III, 287–328.

government was made easy by the internal weakness of the reformists themselves, as pointed out earlier in this chapter.

The preceding discussion makes clear the weakness of the reformist parties within the National Assembly, and their vulnerability to other social forces when they tried to operate outside of it. Having failed to become a significant political force through the electoral process, the reformists attempted to mobilize their supporters in the urban areas through extra-legal and extra-parliamentary tactics. As such tactics began to gain momentum through the cooperation of radical students and other leftist forces, they were met with a strong reaction by rightist groups and by the government itself, and were effectively suppressed even before the military coup d'état of May 1961. Nevertheless, there were significant social forces which supported the reformist views and were willing to carry out a persistent struggle against the conservative forces of the society, including the government and the two major parties. In the following section, we will examine the structure and strength of two such groups—the teachers' labor union and the radical student organization.

ORGANIZATION OF TEACHERS' UNIONS

As we observed in Chapter Five, labor organizations could not function effectively as independent interest groups under the Syngman Rhee regime; rather, they existed as a political arm of the ruling Liberal Party and the Rhee administration. These organizations were completely dominated by a leadership sponsored by the Liberal Party, and they provided unconditional support for the regime. Chŏn Chin-han, a non-Communist labor leader, was forced out of the General League of Korean Labor Unions (*Taehan Noch'ong*), a unified body of labor organizations, because of his uncooperative attitude toward Syngman Rhee and his party. The primary function of the leadership of the League had been to mobilize support for the regime rather than to represent the interests of the workers.

With the fall of the Rhee government, a totally new situation came into being on the labor front. The General League turned into a nominal body, having been denounced by the membership and neglected by the government. New labor organizations sprang up, especially among white-collar workers such as bank employees and school teachers, and a new movement was initiated to coordinate and combine scattered labor groups into a unified body. As Table VIII-1 (p. 189) indicates, labor organizations increased rapidly in number and membership size after the April uprising. In less than six months, the number of labor unions increased by almost one-third, from 621 to

Table VIII-1

NUMBER AND MEMBERSHIP SIZE OF LABOR UNIONS, BY YEAR

Year	*No. of Unions*	*Membership*
1957	534	246,486
1958	654	246,049
1959	587	285,461
1960 (prior to April 19)	621	307,415
1960 (Sept. 1)	821	333,735

Source: Haptong yŏn'gam, 1961, p. 280.

821, and membership increased by more than 25,000. Accordingly, the number of labor disputes also increased drastically. As Table VIII-2 shows, there were at least 80 percent more disputes reported during the eight-month period in 1960 following the April uprising than the total number of disputes in 1959.

Table VIII-2

NUMBER OF LABOR DISPUTES, BY YEAR AND CAUSES

Year	*Wage Increase*	*Working Conditions*	*Job Security*	*Delinquent Wage Payment*	*Right of Collective Bargaining*	*Total*
1957	39	5	3	1	10	58
1958	23	5	17	–	5	50
1959	79	4	7	–	19	109
1960 (prior)	7	1	2	5	14	29
1960 (after)	51	25	24	22	67	189

Source: Haptong yŏn'gam, 1961, p. 282.

One of the most notable and politically significant developments in the labor movement, however, was the formation of the National School Teachers' Labor Union (*Kyowŏn Nojo*), because of its radical ideology and the controversy over its legality. As in many other areas of Korea's public life, the educational system under the First Republic was highly centralized and bureaucratic: almost all public funds for all levels of education were provided by the central government. The administration of educational personnel also faithfully reflected this centralization. All public school teachers, including the principals, were considered government employees and assigned to their positions by the provincial governor through the superintendents of the school districts at various levels. The provincial governors, in turn, were appointed by the home minister and received dual direction from the home minister and the education minister in Seoul. The boards of education on provincial, city, and district levels were intended to be autonomous bodies with the responsibility of making recommendations to the executive officials, including the president, the education minister, city mayors, and superintendents. But they were largely nominal bodies and shared little in the actual exercise of administrative power.

Under such tightly and centrally organized administration, it was virtually impossible for the school teachers to organize, despite serious dissatisfaction among them concerning personnel policy, wages, teaching environment, and political pressure on them from the ruling party. The only national organization of teachers, the Association of Korean Educators (*Taehan Kyoryŏn*), established in 1947 with the ostensible purpose of promoting welfare, unity, and friendship among the teachers in the nation, only served to keep the teachers at the lower levels under the tight control of the high educational officials. The Association, whose organizational structure largely coincided with the educational administrative structure itself—for example, the principal was usually the head of the school branch of the Association—was more an apparatus for controlling the school teachers than an organization which could represent their interests.[23]

Some of the most serious sources of dissatisfaction among school teachers under the Rhee regime were:

1. *The political use of schools by the government and the ruling party.* In most schools, teachers were forced to join the Liberal Party through pressure by either the principal or the assistant pincipal. Afternoon classes were often canceled so that teachers could make visits to pupils' homes to campaign for Liberal candidates. Teachers were also forced to participate in the formation of three-man and five-man teams to facilitate group voting, to investigate the political orientation of pupils' parents, and to engage in many other illegal political practices. It was impossible for most teachers to refuse to carry out the illegal activities demanded of them, because of the arbitrary power held by the state to dismiss them or transfer them to remote locations.

2. *Profiteering in the schools.* Teachers were asked to sell supplementary texts and other teaching-aid materials which were supplied

23. For an official description of the activities of the Association of Korean Educators, see the Association's *Kyoryŏn ishimnyŏnsa.*

by the Association of Korean Educators at high prices. Furthermore, teachers were forced to extract various types of contributions from the pupils' parents in order to make payoffs to their superiors.

3. *Lack of job security.* Teachers had no job security at all. Honest suggestions and criticisms were ignored, and those who expressed frank opinions were either dismissed or transferred to undesirable positions; only those who were obsequious and sycophantic could maintain their positions or be promoted. The regular exchange of personnel between rural and urban schools could not be carried out. Teachers were in constant fear of being removed from their positions.[24]

The grievances of the school teachers, which had accumulated throughout the Syngman Rhee period, finally came to the surface following the April uprising. Many radical-minded school teachers at the elementary and secondary levels got together to form an autonomous and self-assertive national organization for the protection of the interests of low-ranking teachers and the establishment of minimum standards for teaching conditions at their respective schools.

Like many other radical movements in Korea, the teachers' union movement originated in Taegu, through the initiative of a number of young school teachers. Thus on April 29, 1960, about 60 representatives from various secondary schools in Taegu formed the Secondary School Teachers' Labor Union in Taegu. Subsequently, an organizational meeting was held on May 7, which formally elected the union's officers and adopted a declaration demanding an end to government interference with educators, the enactment of a law concerning teachers' unions which would guarantee and improve the economic and social security of teachers, and the purging of teachers who had accumulated wealth or acquired high positions through close ties with government officials and superiors.

The organization of the Secondary School Teachers' Labor Union was received with great enthusiasm by teachers at other educational levels, who immediately formed their own unions. On May 7, some 1,200 elementary school teachers attended a convention held in Taegu for the formation of their own union. Like the union of secondary school teachers, it demanded social, economic, and political freedom for the teachers. Subsequently, the National League of Teachers' Labor Unions (NLTLU) was organized in Seoul on May 22, at a convention attended by 200 representatives of school teachers throughout the nation. The newly organized League demanded the dissolution of the Association of Korean Educators and official government recognition of the League as the only national organization of teachers.

24. *Han'guk hyŏngmyŏng chaep'ansa,* III, 1078.

The creation of teachers' unions in major areas of Korea, and of the National League, alarmed the conservative Hŏ Chŏng government, which suspected that the organizers of the teachers' unions were as much interested in broader leftist ideological goals as in the immediate betterment of the teachers' socioeconomic conditions. In particular, government officials observed certain similarities between the Teachers' League in Korea and the General League of the Japanese Teachers' Unions (*Nikkyoso*) which had acted as an action arm of the Japanese Communist Party.[25] Similarly, the Association of Korean Educators, the rival organization of the League of Teachers' Labor Unions, said in its declaration: "In view of the record of the Japanese Teachers' Labor Unions, we demand the destruction of any scheme by any group which attempts to turn us over to the Communist camp through the Communization of the schools." [26] The Hŏ Chŏng government was also concerned by the rapid growth in membership (to nearly 20,000 teachers) of the League, as shown in Table VIII-3.[27]

Table VIII-3

ELEMENTARY AND SECONDARY SCHOOL TEACHERS WHO JOINED THE TEACHERS' UNION

	LTLU members (A)	*Total teachers (B)*	*Percentage*
Seoul	218	8,187	2.66%
Kyŏnggi	463	8,395	5.52
Ch'ungbuk	0	5,143	0
Ch'ungnam	910	8,020	11.09
Chŏnbuk	371	8,470	4.38
Chŏnnam	230	10,957	2.10
Kyŏngbuk	8,142	12,896	63.14
Kyŏngnam	8,087	14,083	57.38
Kangwŏn	0	6,148	0
Cheju	178	1,191	14.95
Student Teachers	79	383	20.63
TOTAL	18,678	83,873	22.27%

Source: Kyoyuk yŏn'gam [Education Annual], 1961, p. 214.

25. In fact, the leaders of the Korean Teachers' unions were also well informed about the nature and activities of the Japanese *Nikkyoso* and were very much impressed by them. (Interview with former school teachers, November 1968.)

26. *Kyoyuk yŏn'gam* [Education Annual], 1961, p. 198.

27. The leadership of the unions claimed that shortly before the May military coup, they had almost 40,000 members (*Han'guk hyŏngmyŏng chaep'ansa,* III, 1101.)

Furthermore, a few of the union leaders were known to have participated in leftist activities after Korean Liberation in 1945.[28] For example, Kim Mun-sim, chairman of the Kyŏngsang Puk-to Union, the strongest in the nation, had served as the chairman of a *kun* people's committee in his native P'yŏngan Puk-to under the Communist regime, before he came to South Korea during the Korean War.[29]

Alarmed by the rapid growth of a potentially radical body of school teachers with nationwide organization, the ministry of education declared that the League has no legal basis, arguing that the law pertaining to government officials (Article 27) prohibited all public officials, including school teachers, from participating in any political activities or joining in collective action except when carrying out public duties. A declaration by Education Minister Yi Pyŏng-do, a venerable professor of history and president of the National Academy of Arts and Sciences, demonstrated the government's failure to understand the sources of the teachers' grievances and inability or unwillingness to cope with problems involving the social, economic, and political security of teachers. In a statement made on June 22, Minister Yi declared that, notwithstanding the provisions in the law concerning labor unions (which guaranteed the right of citizens to join labor unions), the teachers as government employees could not involve themselves in any collective action. The minister then ordered the teachers to refrain from organizing new labor unions and to disband all unions already organized.[30] In a press conference held the next day, Minister Yi stated that all those teachers who disobeyed his directives concerning the disbanding of labor unions would be dismissed. At the same time, the ministry of health and social affairs, which was in charge of labor unions, returned the application of the teachers' unions for official recognition on the ground that the ministry of justice had ruled the formation of labor unions among school teachers to be illegal.[31]

The unions' response to the government's pronouncement concerning their illegality was immediate and emphatic. They declared that the formation of unions was clearly sanctioned by the constitution, which guaranteed all citizens freedom of speech, press, assembly, and association. Furthermore, they claimed, other laws (especially the laws concerning labor unions) also provided for the right of all citizens, including public servants (with the exception only of military per-

28. *Sasanggye,* September 1960, p. 229.
29. *Han'guk hyŏngmyŏng chaep'ansa,* III, 297.
30. *Kyoyuk yŏn'gam,* 1961, p. 211.
31. *Han'guk hyŏngmyŏng chaep'ansa,* I, 154.

sonnel, police officers, firemen, and prison wardens), to organize themselves for the protection of their interests. The labor unions further declared that an authoritative interpretation of various conflicting laws could be made only by a court ruling, and the executive department was not entitled to determine the legality of a social organization like theirs. They denounced the minister of education's threatening statement and his preferential treatment of the discredited Association of Korean Educators and demanded his resignation. The teachers' unions were joined in their fight for survival by other labor unions, including those of the railroad workers and workers in state-owned enterprises.

Although the dispute between the teachers' unions and the Hŏ Chŏng government centered around the interpretation of conflicting legal provisions, it was clear to both sides of the dispute that it was primarily an ideological and political issue rather than a matter of law. The teachers' unions therefore attempted to settle the dispute through strikes, mass rallies, and street demonstrations rather than through orderly legal processes.

The issue of the legality of the teachers' labor unions had not been settled by the time Chang Myŏn took over the government from Hŏ Chŏng in late August, and the new government was unable to take a clearcut position toward the teachers' labor unions. Instead, the Chang Myŏn government decided to determine the legality of the teachers' unions after an extensive hearing of the views of lawyers, scholars, educators, and students' parents.[32] Subsequently, Minister of Education O Ch'ŏn-sŏk stated in the National Assembly that although the law was not clear, the government was prepared to recognize the teachers' unions, but only as a social organization of teachers, and not as an instrument of collective bargaining. Minister O stated that the duties of the teachers were too sacred for them to act like ordinary workers. However, the Chang Myŏn government's fence-straddling on the issue only resulted in arousing critical reactions from both the teachers' unions and members of the National Assembly.

The teachers' unions held an emergency meeting of representatives on September 11, and three days later filed a suit against the ministry of health and social affairs, claiming that its failure to grant formal recognition of the teachers' unions infringed upon the right of citizens to join associations as guaranteed by the constitution. On the other hand, in the National Assembly many conservative members of both major parties moved to make the teachers' unions illegal through a revision of the existing law concerning labor unions. These assembly-

32. *Ibid.*

men argued that the labor unions were controlled by "impure elements" made up of former Communist sympathizers, and that the organization was analogous to the Communist-controlled All-Korea Council of Labor Unions (*Chŏnp'yŏng*) of the immediate post-Liberation period. The assemblymen pointed out that, in Japan, teachers' unions had been responsible for recent anti-American demonstrations which had prevented President Eisenhower's visit to that country, and that it was evident that the Korean teachers' unions, like their Japanese counterpart, would soon become strongly leftist.[33] The National Assembly then voted to form a special committee to consider legislation prohibiting teachers' labor activities.[34]

In the National Assembly debate, only 2 assemblymen out of 10 who spoke on the issue on the floor expressed a sympathetic attitude toward the labor union movement, while 8 members were strongly hostile to it. Such a move in the National Assembly brought about strong opposition from teachers throughout the nation. Protest rallies were held in front of the National Assembly and in other major cities, including Taegu and Pusan. In those two cities, about 2,500 members of the teachers' unions went on a hunger strike, some of them collapsing in the classroom. In the meantime, a national conference of the unions' representatives was held in Seoul on September 28, and demanded immediate recognition of the legality of the unions; immediate withdrawal of the bill to revise the labor union law; and neutrality of the National Assembly and the government in the struggle between the National League of Teachers' Unions and the conservative Association of Korean Educators. Of those who had attended the conference, 400 representatives marched to the ministry of education, where they obtained the assurance of the vice-minister of education that the government would work to table the bill in the National Assembly.

In the Taegu area, some 200 more school teachers collapsed in their classrooms as a result of their hunger strike, and more than 10,000 students carried out a sympathy demonstration for their teachers. The situation deteriorated further when almost all the secondary school students in Taegu started a hunger strike of their own, and certain conservative groups such as the veterans' association strongly denounced the "radical" elements in the teachers' union, and the Chang government which could not control them. The National Assembly subsequently capitulated to the pressure of the teachers' unions and their student supporters, tabling the bill to amend the labor union

33. *Minŭiwŏn heoŭirok*, 37th session, nos. 5–17.
34. *Ibid.*, no. 17.

laws.[35] The government—both the cabinet and the National Assembly—showed itself to be incapable of withstanding the militant pressure of the teachers' unions, which had won their immediate objective through the use of extra-legal and often violent methods.

The politically radical nature of the teachers' unions was most dramatically demonstrated by their participation in the nationwide protest of the progressives against the government-sponsored legislation intended to regulate demonstrations and pro-Communist subversive activities. Following the government's announcement about the proposed laws, leaders of the teachers' unions declared their strong opposition to it. Kang Ki-ch'ŏl, acting president of the National League of Teachers' Unions, declared that because of the anti-labor provisions of the proposed laws, the teachers' unions would carry out a militant national struggle to prevent their passage in the National Assembly.[36] The Central Action Committee of the League warned the government that if it insisted on the enactment of laws intended to suppress labor movements, the teachers' unions would fight the government to the end "in the name of their own survival." [37] Subsequently, members of the teachers' unions in Taegu led protest meetings and marches which resulted in a violent clash with the police on April 2.[38]

In view of the fact that the government had already deleted provisions strictly regulating labor activities from the proposed laws, the militancy of the union leadership against the legislative measures can be understood by reference to its radical ideological orientation. The teachers' unions thus showed themselves to be an organization with "political" objectives going beyond the immediate professional grievances of school teachers. It was consistent with this *political* nature of the teachers' unions that they strongly supported the radical students in their attempt to hold a North-South student conference at Panmunjŏm to discuss ways of achieving national unification. On May 6, the propaganda chairman of the NLTLU declared:

We have to clearly understand the present international situation (i.e., rising demand for peaceful unification of South Korea), as it makes Korean unification inevitable. Our students have proposed a North-South student conference, and it has been warmly welcomed by North Korea. Therefore, we cannot be satisfied with simply communicating dead knowledge to our students

35. *Kyoyuk yŏn'gam,* 1961, p. 213.
36. *Minjok Ilbo,* March 15, 1961, p. 1.
37. *Han'guk hyŏngmyŏng chaep'ansa,* III, 1053.
38. For detailed descriptions of the April 2nd confrontation by both sides of the clash, see *ibid.,* pp. 297–328.

in schools. Instead, we have to actively enlighten and educate everybody in the nation through our students and their parents.[39]

Despite their heavy involvement in the progressive political movement, the leaders of the teachers' unions carefully refrained from publicly supporting the existing reformist parties. One important reason for their failure to join the political parties was that, as public servants, they were legally barred from participating in party politics. It was obvious to the union leaders, however, that because of their internal division and external isolation, the reformist parties were too weak to be of any help to their cause in the foreseeable future.[40]

It should be noted also that although the teachers' unions throughout the nation claimed a membership of over 20,000, only a small minority of them actually participated in the ideological struggle of the unions. In fact, a number of provincial committees of the League, including that in Kyŏngsang Nam-do Province, resolved to refrain from actively opposing the anti-riot, anti-Communist legislation.[41]

These limitations on the potential power of the unions notwithstanding, they showed considerable strength in Taegu in connection with the major issues discussed above, and it was difficult for the government officials and rightist groups to ignore the formidable nature of the anti-government activities of the teachers' unions.

In fact, one significant development during the latter part of the Second Republic was the rise, apparently without government sponsorship, of rightist groups which initiated rallies denouncing anti-government demonstrations, including those of the teachers' unions. This reaction from the rightists was especially strong against the leftist students who, like the teachers' unions, advocated radical social change in South Korea and national unification through accommodation with the North Korean Communists. Let us now turn to a discussion of these "radical" students.

STUDENT INVOLVEMENT IN POLITICS

During the First Republic, under the Syngman Rhee government, students at all levels of education showed little inclination to partici-

39. Quoted in *ibid.*, p. 1054.

40. This was clearly seen in the debate in the National Assembly over the legislation concerning labor unions. Because of the weakness of the reformist side, the teachers' unions received little support or protection from any of the existing political parties.

41. *Han'guk hyŏngmyŏng chaep'ansa,* III, 1055.

pate in the political process, especially for an anti-government or leftist cause. Needless to say, this was not because of the absence of radical sentiments among them, but rather because it was impossible to engage in any organizational activities without government sponsorship. The great potential for student activism in Korea was well demonstrated during the post-Liberation period in the violent struggle between leftist and rightist student groups. In the course of the Korean War, however, most college and high school students, like their elders, were forced to make a choice between ideological extremes. Consequently, it became impossible for them to engage in any progressive anti-government activities in South Korea without being branded as pro-Communist or subversive.

From the time of its establishment, the Rhee government made a special effort to enlist student support through the Korean Student Corps for National Defense (*Hakto Hokuk-tae*). An Ho-sang, first minister of education under the Rhee government and a loyal supporter of Yi Pŏm-sŏk's National Youth Corps, was instrumental in its initial organization and acted as "supreme commander" of the Corps. Under the system, every college and high school student was compelled to join the Student Corps and receive military training and anti-Communist indoctrination. During the Korean War, thousands of students joined the Student Volunteers' Corps, which was organized by the leadership of the original Student Corps. After the war, the Student Corps survived and continued to function as an "autonomous" student body in the colleges and high schools. Although branches of the student corps were supposed to be independent of the school authorities and run by the students themselves, they were directly linked to the government through the ministry of education and provincial educational bureaus, which fully controlled these organizations. Furthermore, beginning in the war period, a regular army officer was dispatched to each of the schools to supervise the indoctrination and military training given to the students. Representatives of the ministry of national defense also made inspection tours at regular intervals to examine the quality of this military training.

Thus, because of the wartime atmosphere and as a result of the acute ideological conflict between North and South Korea following the armistice, the student movement could not develop in South Korea except as an auxilliary of the government. "Radical" activity at this time was limited to a few "study groups" with very limited membership. One such semi-clandestine student organization was the New Progressive Club (*Shinjin-hoe*), consisting primarily of students in political science at Seoul National University. The Shinjin-hoe was a small, closed group; invitation to a prospective member to join the group was made only after a thorough examination of his family background, school record, and ideological orientation, and upon the unanimous consent of existing members. At any given time during its existence under the Rhee regime (1956–1960), active student membership did not exceed 15. Literature forbidden by the Rhee government, such as *Communist Manifesto,* Marx's *Capital,* and Lenin's *State and Revolution,* was circulated and discussed among the members.

However, the club was watched closely by the police after 1957, when one of its members was arrested on charges of having written a subversive article in the college newspaper. In the article, entitled "Toward the creation of a society for the dispossessed masses," Yu Kŭn-il, whose father was known to be teaching at the Kim Il-sŏng University in Pyŏngyang, called for the unity of the dispossessed class in order to achieve national unification and an egalitarian society in Korea. Although Yu was subsequently acquitted by the district court,[42] Shinjin-hoe's limited activities became even more hampered, and it was forced to go even further underground after this incident.

Although Shinjin-hoe remained a "study group," and most of its members were committed to national unification and democratic socialism in Korea, it had the potential of becoming a militant revolutionary group under favorable circumstances. Most of its members came from families that had produced nationalists and socialists who had fought against the Japanese before Korean Liberation in 1945, and were deeply dissatisfied with the Rhee regime, which they considered reactionary and America-controlled.

Upon graduation from Seoul National University, many of its members became reporters for major newspapers and continued to support and participate in the group's activities in advisory capacities. The group, however, carefully avoided affiliating itself with any of the existing political parties, such as the Progressive Party or the Democratic Reformist Party. When government surveillance became oppressive and continued activities of the group unfeasible, some members, including Yu Kŭn-il, joined the South Korean Army in order to temporarily protect themselves from the scrutiny of the police. By the end of the Rhee regime, very little remained of the organized radical

42. Yu was tried again in 1961, by the military revolutionary tribunal, and was sentenced to a two-year prison term for the same offense. In addition, he received a 15-year sentence from the same court for having proposed a North-South student conference during the Chang government.

student movement at Seoul National University, to say nothing of other college campuses.

Although the radical students did not play a central role in the April student uprising itself,[43] the relatively free atmosphere following the collapse of the police-supported Rhee regime provided ready ground for an active progressive student movement. During the interim period, many radical students went to local districts to campaign for reformist candidates in the July 29 general election. The almost complete defeat of the reformist candidates deeply disappointed the students, who went back to their respective campuses and organized various associations and clubs which later became the basis of the Student League for National Unification (*Minjok T'ong'il Yŏnmaeng*).

The Student Unification League, which was started by the progressive students of Seoul National University, was a unified organization of students dedicated to the idea of achieving national unification and the removal of foreign influence in both North and South Korea.

The League was conceived and first organized by members of the Shinjin-hoe, and attracted many moderately progressive students in the Liberal Arts and Sciences College and the Law College of Seoul National University. Similar organizations were subsequently created in major universities throughout the country by students who shared the unification objectives of their Seoul colleagues. The Student Unification League of Seoul National University, which was joined by about 300 students during the first few months after its organization in early November, operated under the leadership of a 20-member central committee chosen by a meeting of student "delegates," most of whom were self-appointed. Many of the Central Committee members (about 50 in all) were students who had been affiliated with Shinjin-hoe prior to the April uprising and who worked together on a personal and informal basis. The former Shinjin-hoe members also occupied many key position in the League, such as chairman of the central committee, president of the delegates' conference, and chairmen of the propaganda committee and the research committee for the unification problem.

As we suggested earlier, the League was primarily preoccupied with the unification issue. The members of the League attributed many of the difficulties in South Korea—poverty, political oppression, social demoralization, etc.—to the division of the country, for which they in turn blamed self-seeking foreign powers, particularly the United States

43. Shortly before the April uprising, Shinjin-hoe had decided to adopt a "wait-and-see" attitude instead of taking the major risk of exposing itself by leading the anti-Rhee demonstrations.

and the Soviet Union. They advocated achievement of peaceful national unification through the removal of foreign influence from both parts of Korea and the initiation of cultural, economic, and political exchange between the two areas.

The inaugural convention of the Student Unification League, held on November 1, adopted the following declaration directed to the Chang government and to society at large:

1. The old generation must recognize their moral responsibility for the division of our country and must admit that it has no right to ignore or suppress the righteous views of the younger generation concerning national unification.

2. All political parties and social organizations in South Korea must prepare themselves for an all-Korea general election in which they must compete with the Communist Party.

3. The Government must adopt a positive attitude based on hard reality concerning the unification issue. To demonstrate such a positive policy, Prime Minister Chang must make special visits to the United States and the Soviet Union and confer with their leaders.

4. Freedom of communication as guaranteed by the Universal Declaration of Human Rights must be realized as soon as possible throughout North and South Korea.[44]

The students' open and active advocacy of national unification through reconciliation with North Korea and withdrawal of the foreign powers represented a radical departure from their passive attitude under the Rhee government, which had insisted on a policy of achieving national unification through a U.N.-supervised, all-Korea election in accordance with the procedures provided by the South Korean constitution.[45] In this respect, the students shared the views of the reformist politicians who, as we saw earlier in this chapter, also demanded reappraisal of the South Korean position on the unification issue.

While the Chang government predictably rejected the students' proposal, the North Korean government welcomed it with enthusiasm. On November 24, the North Korean Supreme People's Assembly made the following proposal to the South Korean National Assembly:

44. Quoted in *Han'guk hyŏngmyŏng chaep'ansa*, I, 216.

45. For a summary of the South Korean position concerning unification, see U. S. Department of State, *The Record on Korean Unification, 1943–1960, passim.*

1. South Korea should not continue to insist on an all-Korea general election under U.N. supervision. If the South Korean government cannot accept a free election in Korea under the supervision of neutralist countries, it should at least agree to the establishment of normal relations between the North and the South.

2. Both North and South Korea will maintain their respective systems of government and their independent existence for the time being, but federal organs would be set up to coordinate and promote the common economic and cultural activities of the North and South.

3. If the South Korean government cannot accept the "federal proposal," an economic commission of North and South Korean businessmen should be set up to achieve economic cooperation and exchange.

4. South Korea will carry out a land reform through the confiscation of land from the landlords, distributing it to the farmers free of charge.

5. Free travel, exchange of letters, and the exchange of reporters will be permitted. Facilities will be opened for land and water transportation of goods and passengers. Telephone and telegraph lines will be restored.

6. Both sides will reduce their troop strength to 100,000 men or less.

7. A North-South Conference will be held immediately in Panmunjŏm, P'yŏngyang, or Seoul.[46]

Although these proposals were immediately rejected by the Chang government as "cunning" and unworkable, they caused considerable optimism among the students and reformists who had initially proposed negotiations with the North. Even a number of junior members of the conservative New Democratic Party criticized the Chang government for its failure to adopt a more positive and conciliatory attitude toward North Korean proposal.

In order to promote their nationalist cause, the Student Unification League actively organized and participated in anti-government demonstrations, especially in connection with the U.S.–Korean economic agreement in February and the security legislation in March. In the course of these confrontations with the government, the leaders of the League demonstrated their radicalism and militancy. Their declarations concerning these two major issues reflected strong anti-American and leftist sentiments of the leading members of the League. Concerning the U.S.–Korean economic agreement, the League declared

46. Quoted in *Han'guk hyŏngmyŏng chaep'ansa*, I, 218.

that the United States, taking advantage of Korea's weak economic position, was forcing Korea to accept an unequal agreement which was comparable to the "treaties of aggression of the past century." The agreement represented a "national humiliation," because it enabled the United States to intervene in Korea's internal affairs, gave the United States wide administrative power in Korea, and opened up Korea as an American market.[47] The leaders of the League claimed that the anti-Communist, anti-riot legislation proposed by the Chang government would make it impossible to achieve national unification, and that they would become instruments of oppression to be used by the "traitors to Korea," who were identified as "the reactionary politicians, foreigner-controlled businessmen, and bureaucrats." [48]

The radical nature of the ideology of the Student Unification League's leadership was also expressed by militant actions. They mobilized students and other citizens to participate in protest rallies and street demonstrations against the U.S.–Korea economic agreement and the anti-Communist legislation. Although small in number—usually ranging between 200 and 300—the demonstrators showed a firm commitment to their nationalist cause and relatively strong internal solidarity in their confrontations with the police. With the radicalization of the Student League, however, many moderately progressive students ceased participation in its activities. It thus became increasingly clear that the League had again become dominated by the radical-oriented former members of the Shinjin-hoe and other extremists as a result of its active participation in militant anti-Government activities.

The League then adopted a resolution, in early May, which proposed a North-South student conference in the immediate future. In a statement entitled, "To our School Friends," the League also praised the scientific and economic achievements of the socialist countries, and warmly supported the "struggle for national liberation" in Cuba.[49] The proposal for a North-South student conference received enthusiastic support from North Korea; in South Korea, the SMP-supported Unification Consultative Committee (*Minjat'ong*) held a supporting rally in Seoul on May 13, only three days before the military coup d'état.

The most significant reaction to the radical students came from the rightist forces, who held their own rallies and demonstrations denouncing the "pro-Communist" activities of the reformists and the radical students. Usually sponsored by rightist youth organizations and veterans' groups, these rallies were held throughout the country, causing fear on the part of the government and the press that a vio-

47. *Ibid.*, III, 959. 48. *Ibid.*, p. 961. 49. *Ibid.*, p. 962.

lent confrontation was imminent. New organizations of rightist persuasion sprang up overnight, claiming that the leftists and pro-Communist elements were about to take over South Korea.

On March 23, a rightist organization which called itself the "Preparatory Committee for the Mobilization of Rightist Organizations Against the Pro-Communist Elements" called for the unity of all anti-Communist forces in South Korea. Among the 61 organizations which ostensibly joined in this effort were veterans' groups, religious groups, associations of North Korean refugees, associations of the survivors of deceased police and military personnel, athletic groups, commercial groups, and other socio-cultural groups. Interestingly, among the groups which joined the rightist alliance were those which had most actively supported the Liberal Party and the Syngman Rhee regime prior to their collapse in April 1960. In a paid newspaper advertisement, these groups declared: "The time has come for the anti-Communist camp to rise up. Whose land is this in which Communist elements cavort? This is a critical moment. Let us unite and destroy the Communists. Let us smash the pro-Communist elements disguised as reformists." [50]

After the announcement by the radical student group of its plans to march to Panmunjŏm for a North-South student conference, a Unified Committee of Anti-Communist Organizations, consisting of a few youth groups which had sprung up suddenly, made the following declaration:

> Does the so-called Student League of National Unification (in Seoul National University) indeed wish to open ways for a unification of Korea under Communism? . . . We warn again that should the League force its way to Panmunjŏm to meet the North Korean students, it constitutes an act which defiles those millions who have died in anti-Communist struggle and insults our one million men who are now guarding the country against the Communists.[51]

These declarations by rightist elements clearly contained the threat that, should the leftist activities go unchecked, a major anti-leftist reaction would follow. This tense state of affairs reflected the sharp ideological division of South Korean society, in which it was impossible for the two opposing ideological groups to co-exist in a democratic environment. No such confrontation between leftists and rightists took place under the Rhee regime, because of its use of suppressive techniques. The Chang government proved to be both incapable and un-

50. *Kyŏnghyang Shinmun,* March 23, 1961, p. 1.
51. *Tong-a Ilbo,* May 6, 1961, p. 1.

willing to employ overwhelming force against one or the other of these ideologically polarized groups.

Interestingly, however, following the major confrontation in Taegu on April 2, which resulted in mass arrests and heightened anxiety among politicians and newspaper commentators alike, the demonstrations tapered off, to the considerable relief of government officials. Although there is little doubt that the Chang government's show of force contributed to the reduction of leftist activities,[52] the major reason for the relative calm following the April 2 demonstration in Taegu seems to have been the self-imposed restraint of the leftists themselves. Through various channels, such as family ties and government sources, the leftist students and reformist parties learned about the movement within the armed forces to use the chaotic situation as a pretext to topple the Chang government. The reformists were consequently determined not to provide such an opportunity to the plotters in the military.[53]

The military junta that took over the government following the May 16 coup claimed that the restraint on the part of the radical activists could be attributed to the fact that the Chang government had bought off the radical and activist students with bribes,[54] and the North Korean regime, having realized that further agitation in the South would cause the emergence of a stronger anti-Communist government, had directed its agents not to destroy the Chang regime.[55] Although it is possible that the Chang government offered certain privileges or money to some of the activist students, and that the North Korean regime preferred the continued existence of the Chang government to the rise of a strong anti-Communist regime, it does not appear plausible that such factors could have been sufficient to keep the mass of demonstrators off the streets. It is much more reasonable to believe that the reformist politicians and the radical students themselves realized that their continued militancy would bring about a strong reaction from the conservative sectors of the society, such as the military and the police.[56]

Our discussion of the three major groups of the progressive movement during the Second Republic—the reformist parties, the teachers'

52. Chang Myŏn, *Hanarŭi miri chukchi ankonŭn,* pp. 76–77. For a description of the military mobilization plans of the Chang government, see *O-il-yuk hyŏngmyŏngŭi chŏnmo,* [A Complete Picture of the May 16th Revolution] pp. 90–91. Gregory Henderson also expresses the opinion that the street demonstrations were tapering off during the final weeks of the Second Republic. (Henderson, *op. cit.,* p. 179 and p. 432n.)

53. Interviews with former student activists, November 1968.

54. *O-il-yuk hyŏngmyŏngŭi chŏnmo,* p. 91.

55. *Han'guk hyŏngmyŏng chaep'ansa,* III, 920.

56. Interviews with former student activists, November 1968.

union, and the student activists—indicates that, despite the apparent ability of the progressive forces to engage in social agitation and propaganda activities, they were basically weak in terms of broader social support, internal solidarity, and organizational effectiveness. Such weaknesses forced them to resort to militant and often violent methods in presenting their demands and opposing government policy. The militancy of the progressive forces, in turn, created a sense of crisis on the part of many citizens and rightist groups, to whom the threat of a Communist takeover or subversion appeared to be real and imminent. The uneasiness which prevailed among the population during the latter days of the Chang government was attributable to the extreme bipolarization of ideological orientations between important sectors of the society—such as the police, military, and conservative politicians, on one hand, and the activist students, intellectuals, and reformist politicians, on the other. This situation provided a convenient setting for a rightist organization like the military to step in.

The Chang government, operating in a setting of acute ideological polarization, was subjected to attack from both the leftists and the rightists. Having already lost much of its support from the moderate "liberal" sectors of the society, as we saw in the preceding chapter, the Chang government found it difficult to defend itself from the secret and determined scheme in the armed forces to replace it with a government which would be able to bring about "social order" and restore government supremacy through destruction of the leftist forces.

IX

CONCLUSIONS: *The Collapse of the Chang Myŏn Government*

In this study we have attempted to explain the failure of a liberal democratic government to survive and take root in South Korea during the 1960–1961 period. One obvious reason for the fall of the Chang Myŏn government was its inability to detect and destroy a coup d'état plot within the army. In this book, however, we have emphasized the importance of the ideological and social cleavages between various opposing groups and sectors in South Korea. The Chang government was unable to deal with such cleavages effectively, and consequently lost much of the support with which it came to power and gained little new support or loyalty for the regime.

Before we offer our conclusions concerning the relationship between social polarization and the failure of liberal democracy in South Korea, let us briefly consider the question whether economic difficulties of the country had a direct bearing upon the fall of the Chang government. Clearly, it is difficult if not impossible to discover a one-to-one relationship between the Chang government's performance in the economic area and its support level among the masses. For one thing, the Chang government did not stay around long enough to see the long-term effect of its own policies. Furthermore, there exists no firm basis on which to judge the degree of support or nonsupport for the Chang regime among the general population during the period.[1] Although

1. Some isolated surveys do exist, however. According to a government-sponsored survey of 3,000 college students conducted in December 1960, less than 4 percent indicated strong support of the Chang government. A majority of them would wait and see. (Oh, *Korea: Democracy on Trial,* p. 82.)

the fact that there was no conspicuous reaction against the May 16th military coup can be considered an indication of the low degree of support for the Democratic regime, it is doubtful that a mass uprising would have taken place against such a coup even if the Chang government had been very popular among the people. What we know for sure is that the Chang government was not forced out of office by a mass uprising. Therefore, we can only judge the political significance of the economic situation on the basis of the immediate and short-term social effects of the policies of the Chang administration as seen through the official data and other available economic indicators.[2]

Chang Myŏn and his administration inherited a very weak and unstable economy. Among the major factors contributing to the weakness of the Korean economy were massive destruction during the Korean War, meager resources (especially in energy output), corruption and poor administration, and the necessity to support a large military force (600,000 men), which took up nearly half the budget. Annual per capita income was well below $100; even with massive foreign economic aid, which amounted to some $250 million each year since the end of the Korean War, or about half the national budget, the economy grew at an annual rate of slightly over 5 percent, or about 2.5 percent over the rate of population growth. Furthermore, Korea was importing about 15 times as much as she exported annually.[3] The rates of inflation and unemployment were quite high, averaging respectively about 10 percent and more than 20 percent each year.[4]

Since many of the economic difficulties prior to the April uprising were attributed to the dictatorial rule and mal-administration of the Rhee regime, the new government which succeeded it was expected to improve the economic situation through honesty and efficient administration. Such expectations, however, were not to be met satisfactorily by the new government within the short time available to it. The Chang government was faced with new problems in addition to the old ones that hampered economic development under the Rhee regime. Most of the largest businessmen in the country were reluctant to make new investments, because of uncertainty and fear concerning the possibility of punishment for their "illegal wealth" accumulated during the Rhee regime. Private savings in the major banks decreased considerably (from 66.1 billion hwan to 55 billion hwan) during the

2. W. D. Reeve asserts that "various measures the government either adopted or attempted to adopt made [the Chang government] increasingly unpopular." See his *The Republic of Korea: A Political and Economic Study*, p. 145.

3. In 1959, the import-export balance was $19,162,000 to $291,709,000. See *Korea Statistical Yearbook*, 1962, p. 253.

4. Reeve, pp. 126, 136.

three-month period between June and September 1960, because of the "sense of economic crisis" felt by many savings account holders.[5] In addition, United States economic assistance for the fiscal year 1960–1961 was set at $180 million, an all-time low since the end of the Korean War. At the same time, the government came under strong pressure from the United States to devaluate Korean currency to make the dollar-hwan exchange rate more realistic.

Until the fall of the Rhee regime in April 1960, the Korean government had been adamant on this demand of the United States and some Korean sectors to change the rate in order to make possible more effective use of the aid funds and the improvement of Korea's meager export business. Eventually the exchange rate between the U.S. dollar and Korean hwan was revised from 500 hwan per dollar to 1,000 to one in January 1961, and 1,300 to one in February 1961, pushing up the price of commodities using imported materials. Furthermore, most of the "urgent" social and welfare measures that the new government was expected to take required large sums of money, the benefits of which were not forthcoming soon enough to generate new support for it.[6]

Thus it is not surprising that available economic indicators do show that the Korean economy deteriorated somewhat after the fall of the Rhee regime and through May 1961. During this period, the overall economy experienced a shortage of capital and a rise in the price of major commodities, especially grains. As Table IX-1 shows, there was little or no increase in the amount of currency in circulation and in the index of industrial production during the one-year period since April 1960, while the wholesale price index rose by almost 10 percent.

Business stagnation and rise in prices made the chronic problem of unemployment even more serious, especially that of high school and college graduates. The government attempted to solve this problem by initiating a "New Deal" type of public works program under which millions of the unemployed, especially the educated unemployed, would find jobs and purpose in the newly created National Construction Service. Initially announced in December 1960, and its detailed plans known in February 1961, the project was to have used a total of 45 million man-days of labor at a cost of 40 billion hwan (about $30 million at the revised rate) for works in irrigation, forestation, road-

5. *Haptong yŏn'gam*, 1961, p. 182.

6. An opinion poll conducted in November 1960 identified the following most "urgent requests" to the government: relief measures for the unemployed; price stabilization; adjust prices of farm products; liquidate usurious loans to farmers and fishermen; crime control and maintenance of order; equitable taxation; support of medium and small business; and solution of housing problems. Cited in Oh, *Korea: Democracy on Trial*, p. 83.

Table IX-1

PRINCIPAL ECONOMIC INDICATORS, *1958–1961*

	Money Supply (in billion hwan)	Currency in Circulation (in billion hwan)	Gold and Foreign Exchange Holdings (in $ million)	Export (in $ million)	Import (in $ million)	Index Number of Industrial Production	Wholesale Price Index
1958 (Dec.)	192.6	111.1	146.5	16.5	67.2 (annual)	100.0	143.3 (1955-100)
1959 (Dec.)	209.9	123.6	147.3	19.2	81.0 (annual)	114.7	146.7
1960						119.5	158.7
Mar.	211.1	111.7	141.1	1.4	8.9 (monthly)		
June	206.9	117.9	139.1	3.2	8.0	122.7	164.5
Sept.	199.3	123.6	149.4	3.7	6.1	133.5	168.5
Dec.	219.1	139.3	157.0	4.9	9.8	125.9	164.4
1961							
Jan.	217.6	128.4	157.2	2.5	7.1	124.5	179.2
Feb.	222.5	132.0	155.0	2.2	8.2	115.0	190.8
Mar.	215.1	115.4	169.7	2.8	9.3	124.5	190.6
Apr.	219.6	118.9	172.7	2.8	7.2	127.6	193.3
Dec.	312.2	166.6	207.0	4.7	14.9	146.0	192.9

Source: Bank of Korea, *Economic Statistics Yearbook,* 1962, pp. 2–3.

building, city construction, and dam-building.[7] The project, for which the United States promised assistance in the form of surplus agricultural products, had scarcely been started when the military coup d'état took place in May, making it impossible for us to guess what its contribution to social and economic stability would have been. Similarly, a five-year economic plan drafted by the Economic Development Council early in 1961 could not be implemented because of the Chang government's fall, but it was to become the foundation of the new military government's five-year plan, started in 1962, which proved to be highly successful in alleviating Korea's economic difficulties.

One could observe, however, that many of the measures taken by the Chang government concerning economic development failed to enhance the popular confidence and support the Chang government hoped to receive. The decision to devalue Korean currency was taken as a sign of weakness on the part of the Chang government (in contrast to, many people thought, the courageous and persistent stand taken by Syngman Rhee); the National Construction Service, whose start could not be made in time to relieve the "spring hunger" common in the Korean countryside, seemed to underscore the poor planning and general inefficiency of the Chang administration.

Yet it would be an exaggeration to suggest that there was anything near an economic disaster in Korea at the time of the military coup d'état. In fact, contrary to most predictions, the unemployment rate was decreasing during the first four months of 1961.[8] Other hopeful indications included the gradual recovery of the money supply (see Table IX-1); a nearly 20 percent increase in tax revenue receipts by the government in 1960 over the year 1959 (from 193.2 billion hwan in 1959 to 235.2 billion hwan in 1960);[9] the growing amount of gold and foreign exchange holdings; promises from the United States for increased assistance, especially in connection with the National Construction Project; and the prospect of economic cooperation between Japan and Korea resulting from the Chang government's more flexible attitude toward the normalization of relationship between the two countries, which had been suspended in the past largely because of Syngman Rhee's persistent anti-Japanese attitude.

Therefore, it cannot be argued that economic difficulties and the

7. *Han'guk yŏn'gam,* 1962, p. 250.

8. According to the *Korea Statistical Yearbook* published by the Economic Planning Board, the respective numbers of the "totally unemployed" and "employed" were 347,000 and 8,768,000 in 1959; 434,000 and 8,521,000 in 1960; 212,000 and 8,476,000 in February 1961; and 126,000 and 9,774,000 in April 1961. For the year 1961 as a whole, the respective numbers were 226,000 and 9,787,000 (p. 220).

9. *Haptong yŏn'gam,* 1961, p. 196.

government's failure to cope with them were primarily responsible for the collapse of the Chang regime. Economic difficulties did exist; but they were not any more serious than they had been before the Chang administration came to power; they were certainly not getting worse. One can only assert with fairness that those policies that the Chang government had adopted, and measures taken in economic areas, failed to arouse the enthusiasm of the masses and increase the popular support of the new government.

This brings us back to our main concern, the impact on the survival of the Second Republic of the social and ideological polarization between the conservative and radical political groups and that between the pro- and anti-Syngman Rhee groups. Concerning these two sets of conflicts, the following conclusions seem warranted: first, the Chang Myŏn government, with its indecisiveness and inconsistency regarding punishment of former leaders of the Rhee regime, alienated itself from both the supporters and opponents of the Rhee regime; second, given the acuteness of the conflict between the anti-Communists and the radical groups within the country, any government committed to political toleration ultimately would have fallen victim to one of these conflicting groups. In this sense, it was difficult to achieve liberal democracy in its true sense. A regime would have survived only by means of alliance with one of these groups and suppression of the other.

CONFLICT BETWEEN THE ANTI-RHEE AND PRO-RHEE SECTORS

Concerning the division between supporters and opponents of the Rhee regime, we can state that the first group consisted of Syngman Rhee's immediate subordinates in the Liberal Party, police and bureaucratic personnel, military officers (especially the top-ranking ones) and businessmen, while their opponents included the opposition politicians of the Democratic Party, the intellectuals in the "university-press nexus," and the students. Thus the April "revolution" can be understood as a successful challenge to and overthrow of the rule of the first group by the second.

However, because of the absence of organized leadership among the anti-Rhee forces which had brought about "the revolution," and because of the internal split within the Democratic Party, the Rhee government was immediately succeeded by a "non-revolutionary" cabinet led by Hŏ Chŏng, who was committed to the preservation of the existing basic socio-political structure. During Hŏ Chŏng's "interim period," characterized by the slogan "Revolution with a nonrevolutionary method," a number of "revolutionary tasks," such as the punishment of former Liberal officials and individuals with illegally accumulated wealth, were neglected, leaving for its successor regime the task of completing the "democratic revolution." At the same time, despite its unfriendly relationship with the leadership of the South Korean military, the Hŏ Chŏng government succeeded in preventing their political intervention by minimizing personnel changes and other disruptions in the armed forces. The presence of the military nevertheless enabled the Hŏ Chŏng government to effectively suppress the radical movement of the reformist parties and other leftist student and labor groups.

The Chang Myŏn government, which owed its creation to a loose coalition of intellectuals, newspaper editors, liberal students, and party politicians, was expected to satisfy the immediate aspirations of the anti-Rhee forces—namely, the "revolutionary" punishment of former pro-Rhee officials. The Chang government's commitment to due process and liberal democracy was largely responsible for its initial failure to fulfill this task. This failure, however, alienated many of its coalition partners from the Democratic regime. Subsequent punitive legislation of the National Assembly against former Rhee supporters in turn served to alienate from the Chang government those conservative groups which supported the Rhee regime and which could conceivably have been wooed to the side of the Democratic regime by offering them protection and other favors. As a result, the Chang government not only lost the support of its electoral and intellectual constituencies, but also succeeded in neutralizing the effectiveness of its administrative and law enforcement apparatus.

THE CONSERVATIVE—RADICAL CONFLICT

The dilemma of liberal democracy in South Korea was especially acute because of the presence of powerful groups strongly committed to oppose any form of leftist radicalism. The division of the country between the Communist-controlled North and non-Communist South was primarily responsible for the intolerant anti-Communist attitude among key groups in South Korea such as the armed forces, the police, the bureaucracy, and most party politicians. Communist agitation in South Korea during the immediate post-liberation period, "red" and "white" terror during the Korean War, and the threat of North Korean subversion and attack accounted for the development of such a rigid anti-Communist attitude in South Korea.

Under the First Republic, Syngman Rhee and his regime dealt with the ideological conflict by ruthlessly suppressing any leftist movement as "Communist-controlled" or "Communist-inspired" conspiracies. Such a policy proved to be quite effective because of the support it received from the powerful anti-Communist sectors, which feared the prospect of a real social revolution in the South in the event of a leftist takeover. The short-lived Progressive Party movement under Cho Pong-am's leadership, and its tragic end, testify to the impossible position of leftist movements during this period.

The relatively liberal political atmosphere following the collapse of the Rhee regime in April 1960 provided leftist politicians and other political groups with an opportunity to organize and advocate their "radical" views without the same type of pressure they had felt in the past. The radical movement after the collapse of the Rhee government was supported not only by former leftist politicians but also by many college students and school teachers who felt the need to correct what they considered to be socioeconomic injustice at home, and to achieve national unification, which they believed was being hindered by the presence of foreign powers on Korean territory. However, the July legislative election brought about a near-complete defeat of the reformist candidates, revealing that a significant gap existed between them and a great majority of the voters. The ideologically conservative nature of the urban voters and the culturally traditional nature of the rural voters made the electoral success of the reformist candidates quite difficult. As a result of its failure in the electoral process, the leftist movement turned its emphasis from parliamentary to nonparliamentary politics.

The leftists, consisting primarily of individuals with strong nationalistic, anti-American, and egalitarian beliefs, thus confronted the liberal-democratic, yet conservative, government of Chang Myŏn on a series of issues, including the United States–Korea economic assistance agreement, national unification, and the government-proposed anti-riot, anti-Communist legislation. Because of the weakness of the leftists in the National Assembly, the confrontation took place mainly on the streets. Leftist agitation in turn helped to mobilize the anti-Communist elements in the society, who discredited the Chang government because of its failure to firmly suppress the leftists. Furthermore, when the choice was between a radical leftism and a radical anti-Communism, most supporters of liberal democracy, such as the leading members of the opposition New Democratic Party, chose the latter, as shown by their attitude toward the military coup d'état.[10] For, in a society directly threatened by Communist subversion and invasion, the real choice appeared to many to be one between a Communist dictatorship and an anti-Communist dictatorship, instead of one between liberal democracy and dictatorship.

Throughout the Second Republic, the military continued to be a key factor in Korean politics. Despite the pervasive factionalism among the top-ranking officers and the division between them and the lower-ranking officers, the military constituted the only nationally effective organization with the capacity to exercise powerful coercive force during the post-Rhee period. The military was thus capable of preventing a radical change in the status quo, and suppressing the rise of any significant leftist or other revolutionary groups if necessary. When the conservative politicians (i. e., the Chang Myŏn cabinet) appeared unable to carry out that task, most of the military officers refused to commit themselves to defending them against their enemies, making it easier for organizers of the May coup d'état to accomplish their goal.

In our introduction, we noted various "explanations" for the "failure" of the liberal democratic government of Chang Myŏn to survive and to provide a foundation for democracy in South Korea. These explanations emphasized South Korea's socio-economic "immaturity," its undemocratic authority patterns, the inadequacy of its constitutional forms, and the shrewdness and skill of the plotters of the military coup d'état. Without denying the relevance of these explanations, we have approached the problem from a different angle, focusing on the social and ideological cleavages in South Korea. This study has been an attempt to show the critical impact of such cleavages on Korean politics. During the Second Republic, these social and ideological cleavages were more visible than at any other period following establishment of the Korean republic in 1948, because of its liberal character. This visibility of the cleavages, however, became one of the most important reasons for the government's downfall.

Given the acute nature of the social conflict, the government faced the necessity of allying itself with one of the antagonists and suppressing the other. This, however, would have been diametrically opposed to what a liberal democracy should stand for, and the Chang government was both unable and unwilling to abandon its commitment to liberal institutions to insure its own survival. Such was the tragedy of liberal democracy in South Korea.

10. President Yun Po-sŏn, who was a leading member of the NDP, reportedly declared after learning about the coup: "The inevitable has come!" See his *Kugugŭi kasibatkil,* p. 110.

BIBLIOGRAPHY

(*In English*)

BOOKS AND MONOGRAPHS

Adelman, Irma (ed.). *Practical Approaches to Development Planning: Korea's Second Five-Year Plan.* Baltimore: Johns Hopkins Press, 1969.

Allen, Richard C. *Korea's Syngman Rhee: An Unauthorized Portrait.* Rutland, Vt., and Tokyo: Charles E. Tuttle, 1960.

Almond, Gabriel A., and James S. Coleman (eds.). *The Politics of the Developing Areas.* Princeton: Princeton Univ. Press, 1960.

Almond, Gabriel A., and Bingham G. Powell, Jr. *Comparative Politics: A Developmental Approach.* Boston: Little, Brown, 1966.

Almond, Gabriel A., and Sidney Verba. *The Civic Culture: Political Attitudes and Democracy in Five Nations.* Princeton: Princeton Univ. Press, 1963.

Apter, David E. *Ghana in Transition.* Princeton: Princeton Univ. Press, 1963.

——— (ed.). *Ideology and Discontent.* New York: Free Press, 1964.

———. *The Politics of Modernization.* Chicago: Univ. of Chicago Press, 1965.

Arendt, Hannah. *On Revolution.* New York: Viking, 1963.

Beer, Samuel H., and Adam Ulam (eds.). *Patterns of Government,* 2nd ed. New York: Random House, 1962.

Bendix, Reinhard. *Nation-Building and Citizenship.* New York: Wiley, 1964.

Berger, Carl. *The Korea Knot, A Military-Political History,* rev. ed. Philadelphia: Univ. of Pennsylvania Press, 1965.

Brinton, Crane. *The Anatomy of Revolution,* rev. ed. New York: Vintage, 1965.

Bryce, James B. *Modern Democracies.* New York: Macmillan, 1921.

Brzezinski, Zbigniew, and S. P. Huntington. *Political Power: USA/USSR.* New York: Viking, 1963.

Chung, Kyung Cho. *New Korea: New Land of the Morning Calm.* New York: Macmillan, 1962.

Cnudde, Charles F., and Dean E. Neubauer. *Empirical Democratic Theory.* Chicago: Markham, 1969.

Cole, David C., and Princeton N. Lyman. *Korean Development: The Interplay of Politics and Economics.* Cambridge: Harvard Univ. Press, 1971.

Coleman, James, and Carl Rosberg (eds.). *Political Parties and National Integration in Tropical Africa.* Berkeley and Los Angeles; Univ. of California Press, 1964.

Crozier, Michel. *The Bureaucratic Phenomenon.* Chicago: Univ. of Chicago Press, 1964.

Dahl, Robert A. *A Preface to Democratic Theory.* Chicago: Univ. of Chicago Press, 1956.

——— (ed.). *Political Oppositions in Western Democracies.* New Haven: Yale Univ. Press, 1966.

———. *Who Governs? Democracy and Power in an American City.* New Haven: Yale Univ. Press, 1961.

Dahrendorf, Ralf. *Class and Class Conflict in Industrial Society.* Stanford: Stanford Univ. Press, 1959.

Deutsch, Karl W. *Nationalism and Social Communication,* 2nd ed. Cambridge: M.I.T. Press, 1966.

Downs, Anthony. *An Economic Theory of Democracy.* New York: Harper, 1957.

Duverger, Maurice. *Political Parties: Their Organization and Activity in the Modern State,* trans. Barbara and Robert North. London: Methuen, 1959.

Easton, David. *The Political System.* New York: Knopf, 1953.

———. *A Systems Analysis of Political Life.* New York: Wiley, 1965.

Eckstein, Harry. *Division and Cohesion in Democracy: A Study of Norway.* Princeton: Princeton Univ. Press, 1966.

——— (ed.). *Internal War: Problems and Approaches.* New York: Free Press, 1964.

———. *A Theory of Stable Democracy.* Princeton: Princeton Univ. Press, 1959.

Eisenstadt, S. N. *Modernization: Protest and Change.* Englewood Cliffs, N. J.: Prentice-Hall, 1966.

Feith, Herbert. *The Decline of Constitutional Democracy in Indonesia.* Ithaca, N.Y.: Cornell Univ. Press, 1962.

Finer, Herman. *The Theory and Practice of Modern Government,* rev. ed. New York: Holt, 1949.

Finer, S. E. *The Man on Horseback.* New York: Praeger, 1962.

Frey, Frederick W. *The Turkish Political Elite.* Cambridge: M.I.T. Press, 1965.

Friedrich, Carl J. *Constitutional Government and Democracy: Theory and Practice in Europe and America,* rev. ed. Waltham, Mass: Blaisdell, 1950.

Geertz, Clifford (ed.). *Old Societies and New States.* New York: Free Press, 1963.

Gerth, H. H., and C. Wright Mills (ed. and trans.). *From Max Weber: Essays in Sociology*. New York: Oxford Univ. Press, 1946.

Hartz, Louis. *The Liberal Tradition in America.* New York: Harcourt, Brace, 1955.

Henderson, Gregory. *Korea: The Politics of the Vortex.* Cambridge: Harvard Univ. Press, 1968.

Ilchman, Warren F., and Norman T. Uphoff. *The Political Economy of Change.* Berkeley and Los Angeles: Univ. of California Press, 1969.

Janowitz, Morris. *The Military in the Political Development of New Nations: An Essay in Comparative Analysis.* Chicago: Univ. of Chicago Press, 1964.

Johnson, Chalmers A. *Revolutionary Change.* Boston: Little, Brown, 1966.

Johnson, John J. (ed.). *The Role of the Military in Developing Countries.* Princeton: Princeton Univ. Press, 1962.

Kautsky, John H. (ed.). *Political Change in Underdeveloped Countries: Nationalism and Communism.* New York: Wiley, 1962.

Kim, C. I. Eugene (ed.). *A Pattern of Political Development: Korea.* Kalamazoo, Mich.: Korean Research and Publication, 1964.

Kim, Se-jin. *The Korean Military Government.* Chapel Hill: Univ. of North Carolina Press, 1971.

Kornhauser, William. *The Politics of Mass Society.* New York: Free Press, 1959.

LaPalombara, Joseph (ed.). *Bureaucracy and Political Development.* Princeton: Princeton Univ. Press, 1963.

———, and Myron Weiner (eds.). *Political Parties and Political Development.* Princeton: Princeton Univ. Press, 1966.

Lasswell, Harold D., and Daniel Lerner (eds.). *World Revolutionary Elites: Studies in Coercive Ideological Movements.* Cambridge: M.I.T. Press, 1965.

Lee, Chong-sik. *The Politics of Korean Nationalism.* Berkeley and Los Angeles: Univ. of California Press, 1963.

Lee, Hahn-Been. *Korea: Time, Change, and Administration.* Honolulu: East-West Center Press, 1968.

Lee, Yong-ho, "Democratic Political Culture in Korea," unpub. Ph.D. diss., Yale Univ., 1968.

Lenski, Gerhard. *Power and Privilege: A Theory of Social Stratification.* New York: McGraw-Hill, 1966.

Lerner, Daniel. *The Passing of Traditional Society.* New York: Free Press, 1958.

Lipset, Seymour Martin. *The First New Nation.* New York: Basic Books, 1963.

———. *Political Man.* New York: Doubleday, 1960.

McCune, George M. *Korea Today.* Cambridge: Harvard Univ. Press, 1950.

MacFarland, Andrew S. *Power and Leadership in Pluralist Systems.* Stanford, Calif.: Stanford Univ. Press, 1969.

Maruyama, Masao. *Thought and Behavior in Modern Japanese Politics.* London: Oxford Univ. Press, 1963.

Meade, E. Grant. *American Military Government in Korea*. New York: Columbia Univ. Press, 1951.

Neumann, Sigmund (ed.). *Modern Political Parties: Approaches to Comparative Politics*. Chicago: Univ. of Chicago Press, 1956.

Oh, John Kie-Chang. *Korea: Democracy on Trial*. Ithaca: Cornell Univ. Press, 1968.

Pettee, George S. *The Process of Revolution*. New York: Harper, 1938.

Pye, Lucian. *Aspects of Political Development*. Boston: Little, Brown, 1966.

———, and Sidney Verba. *Political Culture and Political Development*. Princeton: Princeton Univ. Press, 1965.

Reeve, W. D. *The Republic of Korea: A Political and Economic Study*. New York: Oxford Univ. Press, 1963.

Sawyer, Robert K. *Military Advisors in Korea: KMAG in Peace and War*, ed. Walter G. Hermes. Washington, D.C.: U.S. Govt., 1962.

Scalapino, Robert A. (ed.). *The Communist Revolution in Asia*. Englewood Cliffs, N.J.: Prentice-Hall, 1965.

———. *Democracy and the Party Movement in Prewar Japan: The Failure of the First Attempt*. Berkeley and Los Angeles: Univ. of California Press, 1953.

———. *The Japanese Communist Movement, 1920–1966*. Berkeley and Los Angeles: Univ. of California Press, 1968.

———, Ki-shik Han, and Sungjoo Han. *The Political Attitudes of Korean Students and Academicians in the United States—1967*. Berkeley and Los Angeles: Univ. of California Press, forthcoming.

Scalapino, R. A., and Junnosuke Masumi. *Parties and Politics in Contemporary Japan*. Berkeley and Los Angeles: Univ. of California Press, 1962.

Schumpeter, Joseph A. *Capitalism, Socialism, and Democracy*, 2nd ed. New York: Harper, 1947.

Schurmann, Franz. *Ideology and Organization in Communist China*. Berkeley and Los Angeles: Univ. of California Press, 1966.

Seligman, Lester G. *Leadership in a New Nation: Political Development in Israel*. New York: Atherton Press, 1964.

Truman, David B. *The Governmental Process: Political Interests and Public Opinion*. New York: Knopf, 1951.

UNESCO Korean Survey. Compiled by the Korean National Commission for UNESCO. Seoul: Dong-a Publishing Co., 1960.

Ward, Robert E., and Dankwart A. Rustow (eds.). *Political Modernization in Japan and Turkey*. Princeton: Princeton Univ. Press, 1964.

Weiner, Myron. *The Politics of Scarcity: Public Pressure and Political Response in India*. Chicago: Univ. of Chicago Press, 1962.

Wildavsky, Aaron. *Leadership in a Small Town*. Totawa, N.J.: Bedminster Press, 1964.

Wittfogel, Karl A. *Oriental Despotism*. New Haven: Yale Univ. Press, 1957.

GOVERNMENT PUBLICATIONS

Korean Government. *A White Paper of the Military Revolution*. Seoul, 1961.

———. *Constitution of the Republic of Korea*, Seoul, 1960.

Korean National Assembly. *The National Assembly of the Republic of Korea*. Seoul, 1961.

U.S. Department of State. *The Korean Problem at the Geneva Conference, April 26–June 15, 1954*. Washington D.C., 1954.

U.S. Department of State. *The Record on Korean Unification, 1943–1960*. Department of State Publication 7048, 1960.

ARTICLES

Ake, Claude. "Charismatic Legitimation and Political Integration," *Comparative Studies in Society and History*, 9 (October 1966), 1–13.

Allen, Richard C. "South Korea: The New Regime," *Pacific Affairs*, 34 (1961).

Almond, Gabriel A. "A Developmental Approach to Political Systems," *World Politics* (January 1965).

———. "Comparative Political Systems," *Journal of Politics*, 18:3 (August 1956).

Apter, David E. "Some Reflections on the Role of the Political Opposition in New Nations," *Comparative Studies in Society and History* (January 1961).

Barr, John M. "The Second Republic of Korea," *Far Eastern Survey*, 29 (September 1960).

———. "South Korea in the Wake of an Election." *World Today*, 16 (June 1960), 242–249.

Bendix, Reinhard. "Reflections on Charismatic Leadership," *Asian Survey*, 7:6 (June 1967), 341–352.

Cutright, Phillips. "National Political Development: Measurement and Analysis," *American Sociological Review*, 28 (April 1963).

Deutsch, Karl W. "Social Mobilization and Political Development," *American Political Science Review*, 55 (1961).

Douglas, William A. "Korean Students and Politics," *Asian Survey*, 3 (December 1963).

———. "The Role of Political Parties in the Modernization Process," *Korea Journal*, 3 (September 1963).

———. "South Korea's Search for Leadership," *Pacific Affairs*, 37 (Spring 1964).

Dupeux, Georges. "Citizen Participation in Social Life in France," *International Social Science Journal* (1960).

Earl, David M. "Korea: The Meaning of the Second Republic," *Far Eastern Survey*, 29 (November 1960), 169–175.

Eckstein, Harry. "Constitutional Engineering and the Problem of Viable Representative Government," in H. Eckstein and D. E. Apter (eds.), *Comparative Politics: A Reader*. New York: Free Press, 1963.

Edinger, Lewis J., and Donald D. Searing. "Social Background in Elite Analysis: A Methodological Inquiry," *American Political Science Review,* 61:2 (June 1967).

Hahn, Bae-ho, and Kyu-taik Kim. "Korean Political Leaders (1952–1962): Their Social Origins and Skills," *Asian Survey,* 3 (July 1963).

Han, Tai Yun. "Constitutional Development in Korea," *Koreana Quarterly,* 5:1 (Spring 1963), 45–55.

Hodge, John R. "With the U.S. Army in Korea," *National Geographic,* 91 (June 1947).

Huitt, Ralph K. "Democratic Leadership in the Senate," *American Political Science Review,* 55 (June 1961).

Huntington, Samuel P. "Political Development and Political Decay," *World Politics,* 17 (April 1965), 386–430.

Kim, C. I. Eugene, and Ke-soo Kim. "The April 1960 Korean Student Movement," *Western Political Quarterly,* 17 (March 1964).

Kim, K. W. "Ideology and Political Development in South Korea," *Pacific Affairs,* 38 (Summer 1965).

Kim, Kyu-taik. "The Behavior Patterns of the Rulers and Ruled in Korean Politics," *Korean Affairs,* 1 (1962).

Ko, Yong-bok. "Leading Class and Leadership in Korean Nationalism," *Korea Journal,* 6:12 (December 1966).

Lee, Ick-whan. "Motivations of the Student Movement in Korea," *East-West Center Review,* 2:3 (February 1966).

Lee, Joung-sik. "Some Characteristics of Korean Political Culture: A Study on Korean Political Leaders' Statements (1948–1960)," *Koreana Quarterly,* 8:3 (Autumn 1966).

Lee, Man-gab. "Korean Village Politics and Leadership," trans. Glenn D. Paige. *Korean Affairs,* 1 (1962).

Lee, Yong-hee. "Problems of Korean Nationalism," *Korean Journal,* 6:12 (December 1966).

Lipset, Seymour Martin. "Some Social Requisites of Democracy: Economic Development and Political Legitimacy," *American Political Science Review,* 53 (March 1959), 69–105.

McCloskey, Herbert. "Consensus and Ideology in American Politics," *American Political Science Review,* 58 (June 1964), 361–382.

McCune, Shannon. "The United States and Korea," in American Assembly, ed., *The United States and the Far East,* 2nd ed. Englewood Cliffs, N.J.: Prentice-Hall, 1962, pp. 74–97.

Minn, Byong-tae. "Political Development in Korea: 1945–1965," *Korea Journal,* 5:9 (September 1965), 25, 28–33.

Neubauer, D. E. "Some Conditions of Democracy," *American Political Science Review* (December 1967).

Park, Chung Hee. "Korean Political Philosophy: Administrative Democracy," *Korean Affairs,* I (1962), 111–121.

Park, Il-kyung. "Review of 14-Year History of Korean Constitutional Government," *Koreana Quarterly,* 4:2 (Winter 1962), 22–34.

Pye, Lucian W. "The Non-Western Political Process," *Journal of Politics,* 20:3 (August 1958).

———. "Administrators, Agitators, and Brokers," *Public Opinion Quarterly,* 22 (Fall 1958).

Scalapino, Robert A. "Which Route for Korea?" *Asian Survey,* 2:7 (September 1962).

Shils, Edward. "Concentration and Dispersion of Charisma," *World Politics,* 11 (October 1958), 1–19.

———. "Political Development in the New States," *Comparative Studies in Society and History,* 2:3, 4 (April and July 1960).

Yu, Chin O. "Korean Democracy Under Overlapping Attack," *Koreana Quarterly,* 3:1 (Summer 1961), 7–10.

(*In Korean*)

BOOKS, MONOGRAPHS, AND PAMPHLETS

Chang Myŏn. *Hanarŭi miri chukchi ankonŭn* [Except a Grain of Wheat Fall into the Ground and Die: Memoirs of Dr. Chang Myŏn]. Seoul, 1967.

Cho Hwa-yŏng (ed.). *Sawŏl hyŏngmyŏng t'ujaengsa* [A History of the Struggle in the April Revolution]. Seoul, 1960.

Cho Pong-am. *Uriŭi tangmyŏn kwaŏp* [Our Tasks Today]. Seoul, 1954.

———. *Urinŭn wae kaehŏnŭl pandae haenna* [Why Did We Oppose the Constitutional Amendment?]. Seoul, 1950.

Cho Pyŏng-ok. *Minjujuŭiwa na* [Democracy and I]. Seoul, 1959.

———. *Naŭi hoekorok* [My Memoirs]. Seoul, 1959.

Ch'oi Hŭng-jo. *Minju Kungmindangŭi naemak: haebang p'alnyŏn chŏnggye pisa* [A Secret History of the Democratic Nationalist Party]. Seoul, 1957.

Chŏng Hae-yŏng (ed.). *Minŭiwŏn ŭiwŏn saenghwal* [Life of an Assemblyman]. Seoul, 1958.

Chŏnggye yahwa [Behind-the-Scenes Stories of Korean Politics], 2 vols. Seoul, 1966.

Han T'ae-su. *Han'guk chŏngdangsa* [A History of Korean Political Parties]. Seoul, 1961.

Han'guk kunsa hyŏngmyŏngŭi chŏnmo [A Complete Picture of the Korean Military Revolution]. Seoul, 1963.

Han'guk kyŏngch'al chedosa [A History of the Korean Police]. Seoul, 1955.

Hong Sŭng-jik. *Han'guginŭi kach'igwan yŏn'gu* [A Study of the Value Orientations of Koreans]. Seoul, 1969.

Hong Sŭng-myŏn, et al. *Haebang ishimnyŏn* [Twenty Years After the Liberation]. Seoul, 1965.

Hŭngmak: apchŏng shibinyŏne chitpalp'in minjuyŏksa [Smokescreen: A History of Despotism for Twelve Years in Korea]. Seoul, 1960.

Kim Chun-yŏn. *Han'guk Minjudang sosa* [A Brief History of the Korean Democratic Party]. Seoul, 1948.

Kim Sŏk-yŏng (ed.). *Kyŏngmudaeŭi pimil: p'okchŏng shibinyŏn* [Secrets of the Presidential Mansion: Despotism for Twelve Years]. Seoul, 1960.

Kim To-yŏn. *Naŭi insaeng paeksŏ* [A White Paper of My Life]. Seoul, 1967.

Kim Tu-hwan. *P'iro muldŭrin kŏnguk chŏnya: Kim Tu-hwan hoegogi* Bloodstained Eve of Independence: Memoirs of Kim Tu-hwan]. Seoul, 1963.

Ko Chŏng-hun. *Pirok: kun* [The Military: An Unofficial Record]. Seoul, 1967.

———. *Kut'o: purŭji mothan norae* [Songs I Could Not Sing]. Seoul, 1966.

Kyoryŏn ishimnyŏnsa [Twenty-Year-History of the Association of Korean Educators]. Seoul, 1967.

Ma Han. *Han'guk chŏngch'iŭi ch'ongbip'an* [A Critique of Korean Politics]. Seoul, 1959.

Min Kwan-shik. *Nakchesaeng: naŭi yadangsaenghwal shimnyŏn'gwa chŏnggye imyŏn* [The Flunkout: Ten Years in Opposition and Inside of the Political World]. Seoul, 1962.

Mun Ch'ang-ju. *Han'guk chŏngch'iron* [A Study of Korean Politics]. Seoul, 1965.

Myŏngin okchunggi [Celebrities Write About Their Life in Prison]. Seoul, 1968.

O-il-yuk hyŏngmyŏngŭi chŏnmo [A Complete Picture of the May 16th Revolution]. Seoul, 1962.

Ŏm Sang-sŏp. *Kwŏllyŏkkwa chayu* [Powder and Freedom]. Seoul, 1957.

Paek Nam-hun. *Naŭi ilsaeng* [My Life]. Seoul, 1968.

Paek Nam-ju. *Han'guk chŏnggye ch'irinjŏn* [Biographies of Seven Prominent Men in Korean Politics]. Seoul, 1962.

———. *Ŭihoksogŭi ishimnyŏn* [Twenty Years in Darkness]. Seoul, 1965.

Pak Mun-ok. *Han'guk chŏngburon* [A Study of the Korean Government]. Seoul, 1963.

Pak Yong-man. *Kyŏngmudae pihwa* [Untold Stories of the Presidential Mansion]. Seoul, 1965.

Sasirŭi chŏnburŭl kisulhanda [Collected Memoirs of Nine Political Leaders]. Seoul, 1968.

Sŏ Min-ho. *Naŭi Okchunggi* [My Life in Prison]. Seoul, 1962.

Sŏ Pyŏng-jo. *Chukwŏnjaŭi chŭngŏn* [The Testimony of a Sovereign People]. Seoul, 1963.

Sŏnu Chong-wŏn. *Mangmyŏngŭi kyejŏl* [Season of Exile]. Seoul, 1965.

Yi Chong-hang. *Han'guk chŏngch'isa* [A Political History of Korea]. Seoul, 1963.

Yi Hae-nam. *Han'guk hyŏndae chŏngch'i munhwasa* [A History of Modern Korean Politics]. Seoul, 1963.

Yi Kang-hyŏn. *Minju hyŏngmyŏngui paljach'wi* [The Path of the Democratic Revolution]. Seoul, 1960.

Yi Ki-ha. *Han'guk chŏngdang paltalsa* [A History of Political Parties in Korea]. Seoul, 1961.

Yi Pyŏng-do, *et al. Haebang ishimnyŏn* [Twenty Years After the Liberation]. Seoul, 1965.

Yŏ Un-hong. *Mongyang Yŏ Un-hyŏng* [A Biography of Yŏ Un-hyŏng]. Seoul, 1967.

Yun Ch'ŏn-ju. *Han'guk chŏngch'i ch'egye* [The Korean Political System]. Seoul, 1961.

Yun Ki-jŏng. *Han'guk kongsanjŭi undong pip'an* [A Critical Study of the Korean Communist Movement]. Seoul, 1959.

Yun Po-sŏn. *Kugugŭi kasibatkil* [Thorny Road Toward National Salvation]. Seoul, 1967.

GOVERNMENT PUBLICATIONS AND REFERENCES

Chŏng Yŏng-mo. *Ibaek samshipsamin'gwa oshipp'arin* [Two Hundred Thirty-Three Representatives and Fifty-Eight Councillors]. Seoul, 1960.

Han'guk chŏmyŏng insa ch'ongnam [A Complete List of Prominent Individuals in Korea]. Seoul, 1964.

Han'guk yŏn'gam [Korea Annual]. Seoul, 1961, 1962.

Haptong yŏn'gam [Haptong Annual]. Seoul, 1959–1965.

Hyŏndae han'guk inmyŏng sajŏn [A Biographical Dictonary of Modern Korea]. Seoul, 1967.

Kim Chong-bŏm. *Che-i-dae minŭiwŏn ŏpchŏkkwa inmulgo* [A Review of the Achievements and Personalities of the Second National Assembly]. Seoul, 1954.

Korean Government. Bank of Korea, *Economic Statistics Yearbook*. Seoul, 1962. (In Korean and English.)

———. Chungang sŏngŏ kwalli wiwŏnhoe [Central Election Management Commission], *Taehanmin'guk sŏn'gŏsa* [History of Elections in Korea]. Seoul, 1964.

———. Economic Planning Board, *Korea Statistical Yearbook*. Seoul, 1962. (In Korean and English.)

———. *Han'guk hyŏngmyŏng chaep'ansa* [History of the Korean Revolutionary Trials], 5 vols. Seoul, 1962.

———. *Han'guk kunsa hyŏngmyŏngsa* [History of the Korean Military Revolution], Seoul, 1963.

———. *Minjuhan'guk hyŏngmyŏng ch'ongsa* [The Revolutionary History of Democratic Korea]. Seoul, 1963.

———. National Assembly, *Ch'amŭiwŏn hoeŭirok* [House of Councillors Record], 37th and 38th Sessions. Seoul, 1960–1961.

———. National Assembly, *Ch'amŭiwŏnbo* [Bulletin of the House of Councillors]. Seoul, 1961.

———. National Assembly, *Kukhoe kyosŏptanch'eŭi pyŏnch'ongwa kak chuyo chŏngdang sahoe tanch'eŭi chŏnggang chŏngch'aek tanghŏn* [History, Platforms, Policies, and Constitutions of the Parliamentary Groups and Political Parties in the National Assembly]. Seoul, 1957.

———. National Assembly, *Kukhoe shimnyŏnji* [One Decade of the National Assembly]. Seoul, 1958.

———. National Assembly, *Minŭiwŏn hoeŭirok* [House of Representatives Record], 35th through 38th Sessions. Seoul, 1959–1961.
———. *Taehanmin'guk chibang haengjŏng kuyŏk pyŏnnam* [Handbook of Local Administrative Districts in Korea]. Seoul, 1963.
Kyoyuk yŏn'gam [Education Annual].

ARTICLES

Chang Myŏn. "My Four Years as Vice President," *Sasanggye,* 8 (June 1960), 240–246.
Ch'oe Ki-il. "Todays Leader," *Sasanggye,* 8 (September 1960), 127–233.
Ch'oe Mun-hwan. "Revolution von Seiten," *Segye,* 2 (June 1960), 88–90.
———. "Socio-historical Nature of the April Revolution," *Sasanggye,* 8 (July 1960), 218–224.
Chŏn Pyŏng-wŏn. "The Defense Budget," *Shin-dong-a,* 4 (April 1968), 93–113.
Chŏng Pyŏng-jo. "A Report on Student Enlightenment Activities in the Countryside," *Sasanggye,* 8 (October 1960), 138–143.
Chu Yo-han. "Citizen Revolution of April 19th: Its Significance," *Saebyok,* 8 (June 1960), 37–43.
"Former Politicians Speak Out," *Sasanggye,* 9 (August 1961), 142–159.
Han Ki-shik. "The Dilemma of Korean Democracy," *Kukhoe P'yŏngnon,* 1 (December 1960), 37–39.
Han T'ae-yŏn. "The Family Tree of the Conservatives," *Sasanggye,* 8 (August 1960), 60–67.
Im Hong-bin. "The Death of Cho Pong-am," *Shin-dong-a,* 1 (August 1965), 368–382.
———. "The Death of Cho Pong-am and the Judicial Power," *Shin-dong-a,* 2 (December 1965), 169–176.
"An Interview with Kim Chong-p'il," *Shin-dong-a,* 2 (March 1966), 220–229.
Kim Ch'ŏl. "Let the Reformist Parties Speak," *Segye,* 2 (July 1960), 104–111.
Kim Mum-yŏng. "Chang Myŏn Cabinet's Immediate Tasks," *Koshigye,* 5 (September 1960), 183–188.
Kim Pung-gu. "The Nature and Behavior of Korean Intellectuals," *Sasanggye,* 9 (September 1961), 86–97.
Kim Sang-hyŏp. "New Conservatism in Korea," *Sasanggye,* 8 (June 1960), 121–127.
Kim Sŏng-jong. "Gen. Yi Chong-ch'an's Refusal to Dispatch Troops to Pusan," *Hŭngmak,* 1 (June 1960), 154–157.
Kim Sŏng-shik. "Students and the Civil Rights Movement," *Sasanggye,* 8 (June 1960), 64–72.
Kim Sŏng-t'ae. "Psychology of the April Uprising," *Sasanggye,* 9 (April 1961), 80–81.
Kim Sŏng-yŏl. "A Complete Picture of the Reformist Parties," *Saebyŏk,* 7 (November 1960), 96–103.
Kim Yŏng-sŏn. "Essential Elements of the Democratic Party Platform," *Sasanggye,* 8 (June 1960), 144–155.

Ko Chŏng-hun. "Is the Political Opposition Dead?" *Saebyŏk,* 7 (February 1960), 78–85.

Oh Byŏng-hŏn. "An Analysis of the July 29th General Election," *Journal of Asiatic Studies,* 3:2 (December 1960), 29–70.

Pak Chun-gyu. "How to Rebuild Responsible Party Politics," *Sasanggye,* 10 (January 1962), 78–89.

"Problems of Handling the Illegal Wealth," *Sasanggye,* 8 (August 1960), 88–91.

Pu Wan-hyŏk. "Return of the Illegal Wealth and Its Effective Use," *Sasanggye,* 8 (September 1960), 106–111.

"Round Table Talks on Devaluation of the Currency," *Sasanggye,* 9 (March 1961), 220–243.

Shin Pŏm-shik. "The Future of the Korean Socialist Forces," *Segye,* 2 (July 1960), 88–95.

Shin Sang-ch'o. "Fifteen Years of Socialist Movement in South Korea," *Sasanggye,* 3 (August and September 1960), 179–183.

———. "An Experiment Named Election," *Saebyŏk,* 7 (September 1960), 124–126.

———. "Pressure Groups in Korea," *Sasanggye,* 7 (April 1959), 138–143.

———. "The Creation and Toppling of a Slave Regime," *Sasanggye,* 8 (October 1960), 46–51.

Song Kŏn-ho. "A Psychological Analysis of the Democratic Revolution," *Sekye,* 2 (June 1960), 79–87.

T'ae Ryun-gi. "Dangers of the Reformist Forces," *Segye,* 2 (July 1960), 112–117.

T'ak Hi-jun and Yi Chŏng-jae. "An Analysis of Taegu Society," *Sasanggye,* 9 (May 1961), 150–176.

Yi Hŭi-sŭng. "The Korean Language Association Incident," *Sasanggye,* 7 (August–December 1959) and 8 (January–May 1960).

Yi Ku. "The Agony of the Korean Reformists," *Chaejŏng,* 10 (January 1961), 128–131.

Yi Sang-ŭn. "Students and Election Campaigns," *Sasanggye,* 8 (August 1960), 92–99.

Yi Tong-hwa. "The Path of Socialism in Korea," *Sasanggye,* 9 (January 1961), 135–143.

Yi Tong-uk. "The Secret Flow of Political Funds," *Sasanggye,* 8 (March 1960), 68–79.

Yi Ung-hŭi and Kim Chin-hyŏn. "Political Funds: The Cost of Korean Democracy," *Shin-dong-a,* 1 (September 1964), 108–133.

Yu Chin-san. "A Complete Picture of the Kyŏngmutae Conference," *Chinsang* (October 1960).

Yu Pyŏng-muk. "The Socialist Mass Party's Plans for the Nationalization of Major Industries." *Sasanggye,* 8 (October 1960), 179–186.

Yun Ch'ŏn-ju. "Illusions of a Cabinet System," *Sasanggye,* 9 (March 1961), 110–122.

———. "Trust or Too Many Seats? The July 29th Election and the Democratic Party," *Sasanggye,* 8 (September 1960), 203–209.

KOREAN NEWSPAPERS AND PERIODICALS

Chaejŏng [Fiscal Policy]
Chinsang [True Picture]
Han'guk Ilbo [Han'guk Daily]
Hŭngmak [Smokescreen]
Kyŏnghyang Shinmun [Kyonghyang Daily]
Koshigye [World of Higher Civil Service Examination]
Kukhoe P'yŏngnon [National Assembly Commentary]
Sasanggye [World of Ideas]
Saebyŏk [Dawn]
Segye [World]
Shin-dong-a [New East Asia]
Tong-a Ilbo [Tong-a Daily]

INDEX

Northern M
3 1854 0
EZNO
JQ1723 1948 H
The failure of demo